Old and Middle English Poetry

Blackwell Essential Literature

Old and Middle English Poetry

Edited by Duncan Wu

based on
*Old and Middle English:
An Anthology*

edited by Elaine Treharne

Blackwell
Publishing

Editorial matter, selection and arrangement copyright © Duncan Wu
and Elaine Treharne 2002

Editorial Offices:
108 Cowley Road, Oxford OX4 1JF, UK
Tel: +44 (0)1865 791100
350 Main Street, Malden, MA 02148-5018, USA
Tel: +1 781 388 8250

First published 2002 by Blackwell Publishers Ltd.

Library of Congress Cataloging-in-Publication Data

Old and Middle English poetry / edited by Duncan Wu.
p. cm. (Blackwell essential literature)
"Based on Old and Middle English : an anthology, edited by Elaine Treharne."
Includes bibliographical references and index.
ISBN 0-631-23073-4 (alk. paper)—ISBN 0-631-23074-2 (pbk. : alk. paper)
1. English poetry—Old English, ca. 450-1100. 2. English poetry—Middle English, 1100-1500.
I. Wu, Duncan. II. Old and Middle English. III. Series.
PR1203 .O43 2002   829′.108—dc21   2002020868

A catalogue record for this title is available from the British Library

Set in 8/10pt Galliard
by Kolam Information Services Pvt. Ltd, Pondicherry, India
Printed and bound at T. J. International Ltd, Padstow, Cornwall

For further information on
Blackwell Publishers, visit our website:
www.blackwellpublishers.com

Contents

Series Editor's Preface

The Blackwell Essential Literature series offers readers the chance to possess authoritative texts of key poems (and in one case drama) across the standard periods and movements. Based on correspondent volumes in the Blackwell Anthologies series, these volumes run to no more than 200 pages. The acknowledged virtues of the Blackwell Anthologies are range and variety; those of the Essential Literature series are authoritative selection, compactness and ease of use. They will be particularly helpful to students hard-pressed for time, who need a digest of the poetry of each historical period.

In selecting the contents of each volume particular attention has been given to major writers whose works are widely taught at most schools and universities. Each volume contains a general introduction designed to introduce the reader to those central works.

Together, these volumes comprise a crucial resource for anyone who reads or studies poetry.

Duncan Wu
St Catherine's College, Oxford

Introduction

Elaine Treharne

This selection of literary texts ranges from the earliest writings in the vernacular up to the time of Chaucer. The time-span of almost seven centuries is greater than that from Chaucer to the present day, and encapsulates the foundation and consolidation of literature written in English. This volume aims to demonstrate the continuities and changes in this literature and to give sufficient explanatory annotation and bibliographical information for readers to begin study of particular works. There has been no attempt to divide the volume between the periods traditionally known as Old English and Middle English, though more is included from the later centuries by virtue of the fact that more survives from them. It is hoped that this anthology will allow the student to view the earlier medieval period as a whole, perceiving connections between genres and themes that span the centuries.

Works included here are those considered essential for anyone with a serious interest in English medieval literature. They are arranged broadly by date of manuscript. In the case of the Old English material in particular, it is impossible to offer a hard and fast date of composition as many poems may have existed in oral form long before they were committed to manuscript; manuscripts, however, can usually be dated to within a couple of decades of date of origin, because of the script in which they are written. Most works are presented in their entirety; where complete inclusion is precluded, extracts usually comprise episodes or whole sections. In all such cases, the context is provided.

General Historical and Literary Background

In *c.*410 Rome was under threat of invasion from Northern tribes such as the Goths. Legions posted in the many provinces of the Roman Empire were recalled to defend the capital and its environs. In parts of Britain where the Romans had maintained authority for four centuries, the Celts, Picts and Irish were left to fight among themselves for political power. As Bede relates in his *Ecclesiastical History*, Book I chapter xv, in the late 440s Vortigern, king of the Celts, invited Anglo-Saxon mercenaries to assist him in his wars, and chief among the warriors who arrived were two brothers, Hengest and Horsa. This was the legendary beginning of the Anglo-Saxon settlement of the area that has become modern-day England.

The 'Anglo-Saxons' is a convenient label for a number of different tribes from the Low Countries, Jutland in Denmark, and parts of Germany. The Angles, Saxons and Jutes are mentioned by Bede, but it is likely that settlers came from other tribes such as the Frisians. The Anglo-Saxons pushed the Celts back to the Western fringes of the country – to Wales, Cumbria, Cornwall, and across the Channel to Britanny – and took control of England. These Anglo-Saxon tribes settled in various parts of England where they created their own kingdoms; for example, Sussex, Essex, Middlesex and Wessex were settled by the Saxons; East Anglia, Northumbria and parts of the Midlands by the Angles. In this early period, and for some centuries to come, there was no single kingdom of England; rather, the different kings controlled their own regions, and each sought to obtain political hegemony. In the eighth century, Northumbria and Mercia were dominant; by the late ninth century, Wessex was the most powerful.

The Anglo-Saxons who arrived in the fifth and sixth centuries were pagan, sharing the same religion as related Germanic tribes on the Continent. However, the country they conquered had been Christian since the fourth century when Constantine declared that the Roman Empire was to adopt Christianity, although Bede relates that Christianity had fallen into decline and that defeat of the Celts at the hands of the Anglo-Saxons was a result of their sins against God. It was not until 597, and the arrival in Kent of Augustine, that the long process of converting the Anglo-Saxons began in the South of the country. Augustine, sent by Pope Gregory, converted King Ethelberht of Kent, and throughout the seventh century the Christianizing of Anglo-Saxon England continued. In the North Christianity was spread by Celtic missionaries from Ireland and Scotland. In 664, at the Synod of Whitby, the Roman and Celtic Christians came together to decide upon the course of Christianity in England: the Roman advocates won the day, and from that time onwards, Roman methods of organizing the church prevailed.

The arrival of Christianity had implications for the production and survival of literature in Latin and, later, Old English. Christianity, by virtue of the fact that it is dependent on the Word of God, required the production of preaching and teaching materials. In the period up to the ninth century these materials were written in Latin, though this does not mean that composition in Old English did not occur; on the contrary, English was spoken by the ordinary population and used for the oral recitation of poetry, but it was not yet considered suitable for writing. The earliest piece of Old English to survive in a contemporary manuscript is Cædmon's *Hymn*, transcribed into two manuscripts of Bede's Latin *Ecclesiastical History* in the 730s. Although used by Cædmon to impart a Christian message, it employs the form of alliterative poetry used by Germanic tribes to relate their legends of heroes and battles.

While Latin works and manuscripts were written and produced throughout the eighth and ninth centuries, the major task of the English kings in the ninth century was to fend off Viking incursions that had begun in 793 with the sacking of Lindisfarne in Northumbria. The Vikings, who, like the Anglo-Saxons, were Germanic peoples, eventually settled in Northumbria, East Anglia and parts of Mercia (in the Midlands).[1] It was during the reign of King Alfred of Wessex (871–99) that this division of the country was recognized by the creation of the Danelaw ruled by the Vikings.[2] It was

---

[1]   In 869, for example, Edmund, King of East Anglia, was killed by the Vikings who thus took control of his kingdom. See Ælfric's *Life of St Edmund*.
[2]   In the Treaty of Wedmore, 878, between Guthrum, the Danish king and Alfred. Guthrum had to convert to Christianity to obtain this treaty.

during his reign that Old English became authorized as a language for written texts. In his later years, distraught at the decline of learning in England, he initiated the Alfredian programme of education in the vernacular.[3] To achieve this, he sought assistance from abroad and from neighbouring kingdoms (Wales and Mercia, for example) to determine the books most necessary for people to read, and for help in translating them into English. Those at the top of his agenda were: St Augustine's *Soliloquies*; Gregory's *Cura Pastoralis* and *Dialogues*; Bede's *Ecclesiastical History*, Orosius's *Historiae adversum paganos*; and Boethius's *Consolation of Philosophy*. Each was considered throughout the medieval period to be fundamental to the acquisition of Christian knowledge and to a wider knowledge of the world and its history. It was also during Alfred's reign that the *Anglo-Saxon Chronicle* recording the history of the English was started; the earliest manuscript, *The Parker Chronicle*, written in Winchester, dates from the last decade of the ninth century.

The first half of the tenth century saw far less activity in the continuation of the *Chronicle* and in the production of English prose in general. By the middle of the century, however, a significant religious reform was under way in Wessex and Southern England, deriving its impetus in part from the Carolingian reforms on the Continent. The Benedictine reform movement, supported by King Edgar (959–75), was crucial in reviving learning and the production of manuscripts in the second half of the tenth century. Its major figures were Dunstan, Archbishop of Canterbury (959–88), Oswald, Bishop of Worcester (961–92) and Archbishop of York (971–92), and Æthelwold, Bishop of Winchester (963–84). While in exile abroad, Dunstan had seen at first hand the results of Benedictine reforms, and on his return to England he was instrumental in putting the practices of the reform into place. New monasteries such as Ramsey were established during this period, and existing monasteries were improved. The *Regularis Concordia*, an adaptation of the Benedictine Rule for English religious houses, became the principal reform document.

Benedictine reform fostered education within the monastic system. The four major poetic codices, the Exeter Book, the Vercelli Book, the *Beowulf* or Nowell codex, and the Junius manuscript were compiled during this period, and can be dated variously from the second half of the tenth century to the second quarter of the eleventh. Together with other surviving fragments and texts (*The Battle of Maldon*, for example), this corpus represents the largest and most significant body of poetry in any vernacular from this period.[4] A substantial amount of the surviving Old English poetry (and some prose) copied during these decades concerns the adaptation and versification of biblical stories.

This religious poetry often concerns the presentation of the heroic code in action through the Christian protagonist. Alongside this is the depiction of the heroic code portrayed through the battles of English or Germanic heroes, material that in many

---

[3] See Alfred's Preface to Gregory's *Pastoral Care* for the motives and methods behind this programme.

[4] A major point to bear in mind is that although the majority of poetry copied into the four main poetic codices can be dated to *c*.970–1025, that dating represents the period in which the texts were committed to writing. It is extremely difficult to determine the date of actual, original composition of many of these poetic texts and this aspect of Old English literature has occupied critics for generations. Many linguistic features, presumably contained within the original text, will have been eradicated in the process of copying – especially so since copying took place in the literary standard West Saxon dialect.

ways reflects the Germanic origins of the Anglo-Saxons themselves. The major themes of this heroic poetry concern the *comitatus* (the lord and his loyal band of warriors), the loyalty of kinship and kingship (often contradictory, as in *Beowulf*), the feasting and glory of the beerhall, the dedication to a lord in battle, the boasting of bravery in battle and living up to that boast in a public display of valour, fighting to the death and urging other comrades to do the same, the giving and receiving of treasure as a reward, and the desire to achieve immortal glory and praise.

During the eleventh century Old English prose and poetry continued to be copied into manuscripts, the *Anglo-Saxon Chronicle* continued, and some additional translations were made, such as *Apollonius of Tyre*. Norman influence was felt during the reign of Edward the Confessor (1042–66), who had been brought up in Normandy by his mother, Emma, and it was his promise of the English throne to William, Duke of Normandy, that precipitated the events of 14 October 1066.[5] Following the death of Edward on 5 January 1066, Harold Godwineson, ruler of East Anglia and Wessex, laid claim to the throne of England and was crowned king on 6 January 1066. Harold had allegedly pledged his support some years earlier to William in his claim on the throne, and thus William attacked, in order to regain his crown.

In 1066, 5,000 Normans invaded, and between 1066 and 1100 20,000 more settled in England. If, as suggested by the *Doomsday Book* (compiled in 1087 by William as a stock-take on his English lands), the population of England was some 1.5 million, the Norman settlers represented only 1.3 per cent of the population. The crucial aspect of the Norman conquest of England, though, was that the Conqueror placed his men in the positions of power – in the church,[6] in central and local government, in the court, and as local magnates.

The consequence for the production of literature in the period was that English ceased to be the language of the monarchy and its related administrative bodies. Latin continued, as always, in its role as the main language of learning and religious writings; French was used for administration, law and the production of literature for aristocrats, the aspiring gentleperson and the educated. English continued to be copied throughout the period; numerous manuscripts survive from the second half of the eleventh century into the late twelfth and beyond. The majority of those copied between *c.*1070 and *c.*1170 tend to be adaptations and copies of earlier Old English religious prose texts, but there was some new composition and translation in English. *The Peterborough Chronicle*, one of the *Anglo-Saxon Chronicle* manuscripts, continued to record events in some detail until 1154, the end of Stephen's reign; the Lives of St Nicholas and St Giles were translated in the half-century after the Conquest, and it is to this period that numerous homilies and didactic writings can be assigned.

During the twelfth century education and many aspects of intellectual culture throughout Europe underwent a renaissance. Universities were created in Paris, Bologna and Oxford, complementing and eventually overtaking the education given in the monastic and cathedral schools. The age gave rise to scholars who produced works that had a lasting effect on the development of literature, religion and philosophy. Key figures include Anselm, Archbishop of Canterbury, Peter Abelard, Bernard of Clairvaux, John

---

[5]   Emma was the great-aunt of William the Conqueror, providing him with another reason to make a claim on the throne after Edward died.

[6]   The longest surviving Anglo-Saxon bishop was Wulfstan of Worcester who died in 1095.

of Salisbury and Geoffrey of Monmouth. Through his Latin *Historia Regum Britanniae* Geoffrey of Monmouth began the dissemination of the legend of Arthur that spawned Romances and histories in many vernaculars. The focus on Arthur as the greatest of heroes in terms of 'Matter of Britain' Romances was part of the new trend of Romance and the Lyric, both of which came from France. Henry II's marriage to Eleanor of Aquitaine in the middle of the twelfth century had important implications for the emergence of these new trends in England. For example, the Anglo-Norman *Brut* of Wace written in *c.*1155, a verse history of England derived from Geoffrey of Monmouth, was presented to Eleanor, and it formed one of the sources for Laʒamon's English *Brut* some fifty years later. The Arthurian Romances of Chrétien de Troyes in the second half of the twelfth century were to influence numerous successors, including the fourteenth-century *Ywain and Gawain*; the love poetry of the French troubadours and trouveres influenced English lyric poetry; and the Breton Lays of Marie de France, composed in the second half of the twelfth century, provided the generic impetus for later English Breton Lays such as *Sir Orfeo*.

The influence of Romance and texts dedicated to chivalry and the exploits of great heroes rapidly made itself felt. French lyrical forms such as the *pastourelle*, the *reverie* and the *chanson d'aventure* are employed in English Lyrics of the thirteenth century. In many works there is a distinct movement away from Germanic motifs of the lord and his *comitatus*, the public duty of the hero to his subjects, towards those of Romance and the personal quest of the individual, his self-development and deeds of bravery for his own, as well as his king's and, occasionally, lady's glory.

Later medieval attitudes to the world and the afterlife were represented in traditions already established in the Anglo-Saxon period. The '*Ubi Sunt?*' motif, seen in such poems as *The Wanderer*, was prevalent in the later period, not only in penitential lyrics but also in Romances such as *Sir Orfeo*. The hero of such Anglo-Saxon poems as *The Battle of Maldon* or *Beowulf* was transformed into the knight of *King Horn* and other romances of the later Middle Ages.

The period as a whole saw transitions in the vernacular that reflected major social events and concerns. Much of the religious literature commented explicitly or implicitly on the corruptions of society and the need to reform. Secular Romance literature provides examples of the heroes whose behaviour represented the epitome of the courtly and the chivalric – a behaviour to be emulated by the aristocratic and aspiring middle classes. From this literature the anxieties, concerns and mores of the English can be deduced, and the thoughts, aspirations and lives of many understood more fully.

Manuscript Culture

Works in this volume survive only in manuscript. Printing in England did not begin until the end of the fifteenth century, and there was no comparable mass-production of written materials prior to that. Literacy in the Anglo-Saxon period was confined to relatively few: those of the aristocratic stratum of society, and those who chose to enter a monastic or regular religious life. In the post-Conquest period literacy became more widespread and the demand for literature in the three languages of French, Latin and English grew. By the thirteenth and fourteenth centuries considerably more manuscripts were produced than in previous centuries as a result of the increase in literacy and greater accessibility of education.[7] However, manuscripts were costly in terms of labour and resources to produce, and only relatively wealthy individuals and institutions, or educated people, owned or had access to them.

What survives from the medieval period probably represents only a small proportion of what existed: much has perished, either as a result of its unintelligibility and subsequent destruction, or by accident – such as the fires that broke out in Canterbury Cathedral in the late eleventh century, and in 1731 in the library housing the medieval manuscripts of Sir Robert Cotton. Texts from these centuries survive in manuscript, copied by scribes on vellum or parchment and incorporated into a unified codex, or a composite text containing disparate material. Many works survive in only one copy; for example, most of the poems in the Exeter Book, *Beowulf* and *Judith*. Very few manuscripts are written by the authors themselves. The issue of authorial control is important: scribes not only copied material, but also acted as editors. Ælfric asked for the integrity of his work to be maintained, but his texts were nonetheless copied into manuscripts alongside the anonymous homilies that he appears to have despised. Because scribes, or the compilers of manuscripts, often acted in an editorial capacity, we cannot be sure that what we are reading is what the author actually intended. What we can be sure of is that editions of texts such as those in this volume represent one step further from authorial composition of the work.

Where texts survive in more than one copy variant readings can provide a fuller understanding of the text. However, irregularity of spelling and lexis can complicate this reconstruction. *The Owl and the Nightingale*, for example, exists in two manuscripts, both of which can be dated to the last quarter of the thirteenth century. Neither is a copy of the other and they contain differences in spelling and vocabulary that complicate construction of the original.

In addition, the anonymity of the greater proportion of works in the medieval period imposes an immediate distance between reader and text. If little or nothing is known about the author, we may be unsure of when the work was written, the author's agenda and methods, his or her intended audience, and thus its interpretation. This is true of much Old English poetry.

Forms of Poetry

Many Anglo-Saxon poems may first have existed in oral form. They operate through alliteration and regular metre, reflecting the patterns of natural speech and thus being wholly appropriate to performance. This alliterative verse is common to all the Germanic tribes, though few texts survive in vernaculars other than English. The first recorded example is Cædmon's *Hymn*, which appropriates the Germanic heroic form for a Christian work, praising God the creator.

> Nu **we** sculen **herigean**   **heofonrices Weard**,
> **Meotodes meahte**   ond his **modgeþanc**,

---

[7]   See especially M. T. Clanchy, *From Memory to Written Record: England 1066–1307*, 2nd edn (Oxford, 1993).

> weorc **Wuldorfæder**,   swa he **wundra** gehwæs,
> **ece** Drihten,   **or** onstealde.
> He **ærest** sceop   **eorðan** bearnum
> **heofon** to **hrofe**,   **halig** Scyppend;
> þa **middangeard**   **moncynnes** Weard,
> **ece** Drihten,   **æfter** teode
> **firum foldan**,   **Frea** ælmihtig.

In this work alliteration occurs on stressed syllables; that is, on the important and emphatic words in the verse-line. The poetry can be described as two half-lines (a and b), each linked by the alliteration which runs across the verse-line. In the first line, alliteration falls on the 'w' of 'we' and 'Weard', and on the 'h' of 'herigean' and 'heofonrices'. the caesura in the middle represents the break between the two half-lines: the natural pause for added emphasis. For this kind of poetry the poet needs a stock of vocabulary; here, Cædmon required a variety of epithets for the Deity. In other poems such as *Beowulf* the poet needs an alliterating stock of words for 'warrior', 'hero', 'battle', 'sword' and so on. In *The Dream of the Rood* there are a number of different words for wood or tree or cross: 'treow', 'sigebeam', 'beacen', 'gealga', 'tacen', 'rod'. Each word highlights a particular aspect of the cross's metamorphic appearance and signification.

This alliterative poetry continues, albeit in a less regular metrical and alliterative form, into the fourteenth century, particularly in the West Midlands region with works such as Laʒamon's *Brut* and *Wynnere and Wastoure*. In addition to this native tradition, the thirteenth century saw the use of patterns of prosody associated with French Romance. The octosyllabic rhyming couplet, for example, is used in *The Owl and the Nightingale*, *The Fox and the Wolf* and *Sir Orfeo*; in *King Horn* a short rhyming couplet of two or three stresses is used; while later, in the fourteenth century, the tail rhyme stanzas of *Athelston* represent a form common to East Anglian texts. Other varied types of metre are illustrated particularly by the Digby, Trinity and Harley Lyrics.

Editorial and Translation Policies

Works selected here are essential teaching texts, representative texts or are simply enjoyable and instructive. Many appear elsewhere: there will always be a core of canonical works that cannot be ignored. Some are not usually included in anthologies, and others are personal favourites that will be useful on courses of Medieval Literature.

This book is aimed primarily at students and does not contain much language information. Instead of providing a glossary (of enormous proportions), I have chosen to translate and gloss. This will not be to everyone's taste, but it does make these texts accessible to those who are not language specialists. Excellent translations are available but they do not usually provide the original text. Readers should be able to study renderings alongside the original as a starting-point in their study of early literature.

I have adopted what I believe to be a sensible mixed translation policy, providing full translations for all the Old and earlier Middle English material,[8] and only marginal glosses for the later texts. I have endeavoured to translate texts accurately using Clark Hall and Meritt, *A Concise Anglo-Saxon Dictionary* for the Old English, and *The Middle English Dictionary,* ed. Kurath and Kuhn et al., for the Middle English. I have also used the glossaries supplied by editors of anthologies and individual texts. This book builds on the scholarship of many excellent medievalists for which I have been very grateful.

As the translations adhere closely to the original wherever possible, this has some-times resulted in a syntactically stilted Modern English version with the inevitable loss of the poetic poise of the Old or earlier Middle English. In addition, translating an individual, often polysemic, medieval word into a Modern English 'equivalent' results in a single interpretation that may not be to everyone's satisfaction.[9] However, a close, semi-literal translation means that those engaged in a reading of the original text should be able to follow it with ease. With the additional assistance of a dictionary and grammar, readers ought to be able to interpret the text for themselves, as I hope they might wish to do.

Students should be aware that the edited text is one remove from the original. There can be no substitute for returning to the manuscript and putting trust in the scribe rather than in the editor's mediation. For much of the Old English material, in particular, I have had recourse to printed editions and editorial emendations, and for many texts the work of previous scholars has proved invaluable. My principle is always to provide the manuscript reading rather than to emend; emendation occurs only when the scribe's form makes no sense or is illegible.

Within the editions in this volume I have provided no standardization of the host of orthographic variations in this period of literature. I have not normalized 'þ' or 'ð', 'æ' or 'ʒ' to 'th', 'a/e' or 'y/gh', as I believe this misleads the student and makes the subsequent study of Old and Middle English more difficult. I have, however, provided modern punctuation, capitalizing the first-person personal pronoun, the names of the Deity and personal pronouns. I have normalized the letters 'u/v' and 'i/j' throughout as I believe them to represent graphic rather than phonetic convention; following that principle, I have not emended 'u' for 'w' as in 'suete', for example, as this use of 'u' is clearly phonetic. I have expanded all abbreviations silently, and set verse into its now conventional format for both the Old and Middle English texts.

The edition necessarily becomes my interpretation of the text. This, together with the provision of selective translations and glosses, imposes a subjective reading on the Old and Middle English that can be no substitute for the student's reading of the original.

---

[8]   In two instances, on pp. 16 and 70, it has been necessary to introduce a line space in the Old English text, as the modern translation is substantially longer than the original.

[9]   See E. G. Stanley's exemplary discussion of the difficulties of interpreting the semantic range of individual Old English words in 'Some Problematic Sense-Divisions in Old English: "glory" and "victory"; "noble", "glorious", and "learned"' in *Heroic Poetry in the Anglo-Saxon Period: Studies in Honor of Jess B. Bessinger, Jr.*, ed. H. Damico and J. Leyerle, Studies in Medieval Culture 32 (Kalamazoo, MI, 1993), pp. 171–226.

Further Reading

Burrow, J. A. and Turville-Petre, Thorlac (1996) *A Book of Middle English* (Oxford: Blackwell).

Clanchy, Michael (1993) *From Memory to Written Record* (Oxford: Blackwell).

Little, Lester K. and Rosenwein, Barbara H. (ed.) (1998) *Debating the Middle Ages: Issues and Readings* (Oxford: Blackwell).

Mitchell, Bruce (1994) *An Invitation to Old English and Anglo-Saxon England* (Oxford: Blackwell).

Mitchell, Bruce and Robinson, Fred (2001) *A Guide to Old English* (Oxford: Blackwell).

Pulsiano, Philip and Treharne, Elaine (ed.) (2001) *The Blackwell Companion to Anglo-Saxon Literature* (Oxford: Blackwell).

Treharne, Elaine (ed.) (2000) *Old and Middle English: An Anthology* (Oxford: Blackwell).

Acknowledgement

The editors wish to thank Dr. Jeremy Dimmick for assistance with the proof-reading of this volume.

From the Exeter Book

Deor

Welund him be wurman   wræces cunnade,
anhydig eorl,   eorfoþa dreag;
hæfde him to gesiþþe   sorge ond longaþ,
wintercealde wræce,   wean oft onfond,
siþþan hine Niðhad on   nede legde,   5
swoncre seonobende   on syllan monn.
Þæs ofereode,   þisses swa mæg.

Beadohilde ne wæs   hyre broþra deaþ
on sefan swa sar   swa hyre sylfre þing:
þæt heo gearolice   ongieten hæfde   10
þæt heo eacen wæs;   æfre ne meahte
þriste geþencan   hu ymb þæt sceolde.
Þæs ofereode,   þisses swa mæg.

We þæt Mæðhilde   monge gefrugnon:
wurdon grundlease   Geates frige,   15
þæt him seo sorglufu   slæp ealle binom.
Þæs ofereode,   þisses swa mæg.

Ðeodric ahte   þritig wintra
Mæringa burg.   Þæt wæs monegum cuþ.
Þæs ofereode,   þisses swa mæg.   20

We geascodan   Eormanrices
wylfenne geþoht;   ahte wide folc
Gotena rices.   Þæt wæs grim cyning!
Sæt secg monig   sorgum gebunden,
wean on wenan,   wyscte geneahhe   25
þæt þæs cynerices   ofercumen wære.
Þæs ofereode,   þisses swa mæg.

Siteð sorgcearig   sælum bidæled,
on sefan sweorceð;   sylfum þinceð
þæt sy endeleas   earfoða deal.   30
Mæg þonne geþencan   þæt geond þas woruld

Deor

Weland knew the torment of the serpents upon him,
resolute man, he had suffered hardships;
he had sorrow and longing for his companions,
the pain of winter-cold, he often encountered misfortune
since Niðhad had laid constraints upon him,   5
supple sinew-bonds upon the better man.
As that passed over, so will this.

Beadohild was not so pained in spirit
about her brothers' death as about her own situation:
that she had perceived clearly   10
that she was pregnant; she could not ever consider
without fear what she should do about that.
As that passed over, so will this.

Many of us have heard about that business of Mæðhilde:
the passion of Geat was bottomless,   15
so that this sorrowful love deprived her of all sleep.
As that passed over, so will this.

Theodric possessed the city of the Mærings
for thirty winters. That was known to many.
As that passed over, so will this.   20

We have discovered the wolfish thought
of Eormanric; he widely ruled the people
of the kingdom of the Goths. That was a cruel king!
Many men sat bound by sorrows,
in expectation of misfortune, would often wish   25
that his kingly power would be overcome.
As that passed over, so will this.

Filled with anxiety and care, he sits, deprived of happy times,
grows dark in spirit; it seems to him that
his share of hardships is endless.   30
Then he is able to consider that throughout this world

witig Dryhten   wendeþ geneahhe:
eorle monegum   are gesceawað,
wislicne blæd;   sumum weana dæl.
Þæt Ic bi me sylfum   secgan wille,   35
þæt Ic hwile wæs   Heodeninga scop,
dryhtne dyre;   me wæs Deor noma.
Ahte Ic fela wintra   folgað tilne,
holdne hlaford,   oþþæt Heorrenda nu,
leoðcræftig monn,   londryht geþah   40
þæt me eorla hleo   ær gesealde.
Þæs ofereode,   þisses swa mæg.

The Wanderer

Oft him anhaga   are gebideð,
Metudes miltse,   þeah þe he modcearig
geond lagulade   longe sceolde
hreran mid hondum   hrimcealde sæ,
wadan wræclastas.   Wyrd bið ful aræd.   5
   Swa cwæð eardstapa,   earfeþa gemyndig,
wraþra wælsleahta,   winemæga hryre:
   'Oft Ic sceolde ana   uhtna gehwylce
mine ceare cwiþan.   Nis nu cwicra nan
þe Ic him modsefan   minne durre   10
sweotule asecgan.   Ic to soþe wat
þæt biþ in eorle   indryhten þeaw
þæt he his ferðlocan   fæste binde,
healde his hordcofan,   hycge swa he wille.
Ne mæg werig mod   wyrde wiðstondan,   15
ne se hreo hyge   helpe gefremman.
Forðon domgeorne   dreorigne oft
in hyra breostcofan   bindað fæste.
Swa Ic modsefan   minne sceolde,
oft earmcearig,   eðle bidæled,   20
freomægum feor   feterum sælan,
siþþan geara iu   goldwine minne
hrusan heolstre biwrah   ond Ic hean þonan
wod wintercearig   ofer waþema gebind,
sohte seledreorig   sinces bryttan,   25
hwær Ic feor oþþe neah   findan meahte
þone þe in meoduhealle   mine wisse,
oþþe mec freondleasne   frefran wolde,
wenian mid wynnum.   Wat se þe cunnað
hu sliþen bið   sorg to geferan   30
þam þe him lyt hafað   leofra geholena;
warað hine wræclast,   nales wunden gold,
ferðloca freorig,   nalæs foldan blæd.

the wise Lord often causes change:
he shows favour to many men,
certain prosperity; to some a portion of misfortune.
I want to reveal about myself   35
that I was the scop of the Heodenings for a while,
dear to my lord; my name was Deor.
I had a good position in service for many winters,
a loyal lord, until now Heorrenda,
a man skilled in poetic craft, has received the land-rights   40
that my protector of men formerly gave to me.
As that passed over, so will this.

The Wanderer

Often the solitary man himself experiences favour,
the mercy of the Lord, although sorrowful in heart he
must long throughout the waterways
stir with his hands the ice-cold sea,
travel the paths of an exile. Fate is very inflexible.   5
    So spoke the earth-stepper, mindful of miseries,
of the cruel battles, the deaths of kinsmen:
    'Often, at every dawn, alone I must
lament my sorrows. There is now no one living
to whom I might dare to reveal clearly   10
my heart. I know too truly
that it is a noble custom that a man
should bind fast his breast,
should hold fast his thoughts, think as he will.
Nor can the weary mind withstand fate,   15
nor the turbulent mind find help.
Therefore those eager for glory must often
bind a heavy heart fast.
Thus I have had to bind my heart with fetters,
often wretched and sad, deprived of my homeland,   20
far from noble kinsmen,
since years ago my generous lord
I covered in the earth's hiding-place, and wretched I
went from there winter-sorrowing over the binding waves,
sad at the loss of the hall, sought a giver of treasure,   25
where I might find near or far
he who might show me affection in the meadhall,
or would comfort me, friendless,
entertain me with joys. He knows, he who is able to know,
how cruel sorrow is as a companion   30
to him who has few beloved confidants;
the paths of an exile occupy his mind, not wound gold at all,
a frozen heart, not the riches of the earth at all.

Gemon he selesecgas   ond sincþege,
hu hine on geoguðe   his goldwine   35
wenede to wiste.   Wyn eal gedreas.
    Forþon wat se þe sceal   his winedryhtnes
leofes larcwidum   longe forþolian,
ðonne sorg ond slæp   somod ætgædre
earmne anhogan   oft gebindað,   40
þinceð him on mode   þæt he his mondryhten
clyppe ond cysse,   ond on cneo lecge
honda ond heafod,   swa he hwilum ær
in geardagum   giefstolas breac.
Ðonne onwæcneð eft,   wineleas guma,   45
gesihð him biforan   fealwe wegas,
baþian brimfuglas,   brædan feþra;
hreosan hrim ond snaw   hagle gemenged.
Þonne beoð þy hefigran   heortan benne,
sare æfter swæsne.   Sorg bið geniwad   50
þonne maga gemynd   mod geondhweorfeð;
greteð gliwstafum;   georne geondsceawað
secga geseldan;   swimmað oft on weg.
Fleotendra ferð   no þær fela bringeð
cuðra cwidegiedda.   Cearo bið geniwad   55
þam þe sendan sceal   swiþe geneahhe
ofer waþema gebind   werigne sefan.
    Forþon Ic geþencan ne mæg   geond þas woruld
for hwan modsefa   min ne gesweorce
þonne Ic eorla lif   eal geondþence,   60
hu hi færlice   flet ofgeafon,
modge maguþegnas.   Swa þes middangeard
ealra dogra gehwam   dreoseð ond fealleþ.
Forþon ne mæg wearþan wis   wer ær he age
wintra dæl in woruldrice.   Wita sceal geþyldig: 65
ne sceal no to hatheort,   ne to hrædwyrde,
ne to wac wiga,   ne to wanhydig,
ne to forht, ne to fægen,   ne to feohgifre,
ne næfre gielpes to georn,   ær he geare cunne.
Beorn sceal gebidan   þonne he beot spriceð,   70
oþþæt collenferð   cunne gearwe
hwider hreþra gehygd   hweorfan wille.
Ongietan sceal gleaw hæle   hu gæstlic bið
þonne eall þisse worulde wela   weste stondeð,
swa nu missenlice   geond þisne middangeard   75
winde biwaune   weallas stondaþ,
hrime bihrorene,   hryðge þa ederas.
Woriað þa winsalo.   Waldend licgað
dreame bidrorene;   duguþ eal gecrong
wlonc bi wealle.   Sume wig fornom,   80
ferede in forðwege;   sumne fugel oþbær

He remembers retainers and the receiving of treasure,
how in his youth his gold-giving lord   35
accustomed him to feasting. Joy has entirely gone.
   Therefore he knows, who must long forgo
his beloved lord's counsel,
when sorrow and sleep both together
often bind the wretched solitary man,   40
it seems to him in his mind that he embraces and kisses
his lord, and on his knee might lay
hands and head, as before he sometimes
enjoyed the gift-stool in days of old.
Then he awakes again, the friendless man,   45
sees before him fallow waves,
bathing seabirds, with spread feathers;
falling frost and snow are mixed with hail.
Then the wounds of the heart are the more heavy,
sorrowful for the beloved. Sorrow is renewed   50
when the memory of kinsmen pervades the mind;
he greets them joyfully; eagerly surveys
the companions of men; they often swim away again.
The spirits of seabirds do not bring many
familiar utterances there. Sorrow is renewed   55
to those who must send a weary heart
frequently over the binding waves.
   Therefore I cannot think throughout this world
why my mind should not grow dark
when I meditate on the lives of earls,   60
how they quickly left the floor of the hall,
brave young warriors. So this middle-earth
each and every day declines and falls.
Therefore no man may become wise, before he has had
his share of winters in the worldly kingdom. A wise man shall be patient: 65
he shall not be too hot-hearted, not too hasty of speech,
nor too weak a warrior, not too reckless,
nor too timorous nor too eager, nor too greedy for riches
nor ever too desirous of boasting, before he clearly may have knowledge.
A warrior shall wait when he speaks a boast,   70
until, stout-hearted, he knows clearly
where the thoughts of his heart might tend.
The wise warrior is able to perceive how terrifying it will be
when all this world's wealth stands waste,
just as now in various places throughout this middle-earth   75
walls stand blown by wind,
covered with frost, the buildings snow-swept.
The wine-halls topple. The rulers lie
deprived of joys; mature men all perished
proud by the wall. Battle destroyed some,   80
carried them off on the way; a bird carried one away

ofer heanne holm;   sumne se hara wulf
deaðe gedælde;   sumne dreorighleor
in eorðscræfe   eorl gehydde.
Yþde swa þisne eardgeard   ælda Scyppend   85
oþþæt burgwara   breahtma lease,
eald enta geweorc   idlu stodon.
   Se þonne þisne wealsteal   wise geþohte
ond þis deorce lif   deope geondþenceð,
frod in ferðe,   feor oft gemon   90
wælsleahta worn,   ond þas word acwið:
"Hwær cwom mearg? Hwær cwom mago?   Hwær cwom maþþumgyfa?

Hwær cwom symbla gesetu?   Hwær sindon seledreamas?
Eala beorht bune!   Eala byrnwiga!
Eala þeodnes þrym!   Hu seo þrag gewat,   95
genap under nihthelm   swa heo no wære.
Stondeð nu on laste   leofre duguþe
weal wundrum heah,   wyrmlicum fah.
Eorlas fornoman   asca þryþe,
wæpen wælgifru,   wyrd seo mære,   100
ond þas stanhleoþu   stormas cnyssað,
hrið hreosende   hrusan bindeð
wintres woma,   þonne won cymeð,
nipeð nihtscua,   norþan onsendeð
hreo hæglfare   hæleþum on andan.   105
Eall is earfoðlic   eorþan rice;
onwendeð wyrda gesceaft   weoruld under heofonum.
Her bið feoh læne;   her bið freond læne;
her bið mon læne;   her bið mæg læne.
Eal þis eorþan gesteal   idel weorþeð."'   110
   Swa cwæð snottor on mode,   gesæt him sundor æt rune.
Til biþ se þe his treowe gehealdeþ: ne sceal næfre his torn to rycene
beorn of his breostum acyþan,   nemþe he ær þa bote cunne,
eorl mid elne gefremman.   Wel bið þam þe him are seceð,
frofre to Fæder on heofonum,   þær us eal seo fæstnung stondeð.   115

The Seafarer

Mæg Ic be me sylfum   soðgied wrecan,
siþas secgan,   hu Ic geswincdagum
earfoðhwile   oft þrowade.
Bitre breostceare   gebiden hæbbe,
gecunnad in ceole   cearselda fela,   5
atol yþa gewealc,   þær mec oft bigeat
nearo nihtwaco   æt nacan stefnan
þonne he be clifum cnossað.   Calde geþrungen
wæron mine fet,   forste gebunden
caldum clommum,   þær þa ceare seofedun   10

over the high sea; a hoary wolf
shared one in death; one a sad-faced warrior
concealed in an earth-cave.
The Creator of men thus laid waste this earth   85
until deprived of the joy of its inhabitants,
the ancient work of giants stood empty.
   Then he who wisely reflects upon this foundation
and deeply meditates on this dark life,
wise in mind, far off remembers   90
a large number of slaughters, and utters these words:
"Where has the horse gone? Where has the man gone? Where have the
      treasure-givers gone?
Where has the place of banquets gone? Where are the joys of the hall?
Alas the gleaming cup! Alas the armoured warrior!
Alas the prince's glory! How the time has passed away,   95
grown dark under the helm of the night, as if it never were.
There stands now in the track of the dear retainer
a wall, wondrously high, adorned with serpent-patterns.
The might of ash-spears snatched away noble men,
weapons greedy for carnage, notorious fate,   100
and storms beat the stone-heaps,
hailstorms falling binds the earth,
winter's chaos, then the darkness comes,
night-shadows spread gloom, sending from the north
fierce hailstorms to the terror of men.   105
All is hardship in the earthly kingdom;
the operation of fate changes the world under the heavens.
Here, wealth is transitory; here a friend is transitory;
here a man is transitory; here a kinsman is transitory.
All this earth's foundation will become empty."'   110
   So spoke the wise man in his mind, he sat apart in secret meditation.
It is good for him who retains his faith: never shall a man express too quickly
the grief from his heart, unless beforehand he might know how to bring about
the cure, an earl with courage. It will be well for him who seeks mercy,
consolation from the Father in heaven, where for us all security stands.   115

The Seafarer

I can narrate a true story about myself,
speak of the journey, how, in days of toil, I
often suffered a time of hardship.
Grievous heartfelt anxiety I have experienced,
explored in a boat many places of sorrow,   5
dreadful tossing of waves, where the anxious night-watch
often held me at the prow of the boat
when it crashes beside the cliffs. Afflicted by cold
were my feet, frost bound
by cold fetters, where the sorrows surged   10

hat ymb heortan.   Hungor innan slat
merewerges mod.   Þæt se mon ne wat
þe him on foldan   fægrost limpeð:
hu Ic, earmcearig,   iscealdne sæ
winter wunade   wræccan lastum,   15
winemægum bidroren,
bihongen hrimgicelum;   hægl scurum fleag.
Þær Ic ne gehyrde   butan hlimman sæ,
iscaldne wæg.   Hwilum ylfete song
dyde Ic me to gomene,   ganetes hleoþor,   20
ond huilpan sweg   fore hleahtor wera;
mæw singende   fore medodrince.
Stormas þær stanclifu beotan,   þær him stearn oncwæð
isigfeþera;   ful oft þæt earn bigeal,
urigfeþra.   Ne ænig hleomæga   25
feasceaftig ferð   frefran meahte.
    Forþon him gelyfeð lyt,   se þe ah lifes wyn,
gebiden in burgum,   bealosiþa hwon,
wlonc ond wingal,   hu Ic werig oft
in brimlade   bidan sceolde.   30
Nap nihtscua,   norþan sniwde,
hrim hrusan bond,   hægl feol on eorþan,
corna caldast.   Forþon cnyssað nu
heortan geþohtas   þæt Ic hean streamas,
sealtyþa gelac   sylf cunnige;   35
monað modes lust   mæla gehwylce
ferð to feran,   þæt Ic feor heonan
elþeodigra   eard gesece.
Forþon nis þæs modwlonc   mon ofer eorþan,
ne his gifena þæs god,   ne in geoguþe to þæs hwæt,   40
ne in his dædum to þæs deor,   ne him his dryhten to þæs hold,
þæt he a his sæfore   sorge næbbe
to hwon hine Dryhten   gedon wille.
Ne biþ him to hearpan hyge   ne to hringþege,
ne to wife wyn   ne to worulde hyht,   45
ne ymbe owiht elles   nefne ymb yða gewealc;
ac a hafað longunge   se þe on lagu fundað.
    Bearwas blostmum nimað,   byrig fægriað,
wongas wlitigiað,   woruld onetteð;
ealle þa gemoniað   modes fusne   50
sefan to siþe,   þam þe swa þenceð
on flodwegas   feor gewitan.
Swylce geac monað   geomran reorde,
singeð sumeres weard,   sorge beodeð
bitter in breosthord.   Þæt se beorn ne wat,   55
esteadig secg,   hwæt þa sume dreogað,
þe þa wræclastas   widost lecgað.
    Forþon nu min hyge hweorfeð   ofer hreþerlocan,

hot about the heart. Hunger within tore
the spirit of the sea-weary. The man who lives most happily
on land does not know this:
how I, wretched and sad, dwelt a winter
on the ice-cold sea on the paths of the exile,   15
deprived of dear kinsmen,
hung round with icicles; hail flew in storms.
There I heard nothing but the roar of the sea,
the ice-cold wave. Sometimes, the song of the swan
I had as my entertainment, the cry of the gannet,   20
and the curlew's sound instead of the laughter of men;
the seagull singing in the place of mead-drinking.
Storms beat the rocky cliffs there, where the tern calls out to them
icy-feathered; very often that sea-eagle cries in response,
wet-feathered. No protective kinsman   25
might comfort the desolate spirit.
    Thus he little believes, he who possesses life's joy,
lives in the city, free from dangerous journeys,
proud and merry with wine, how, weary, I had often
to survive in the sea-path.   30
The shadow of night grew dark, it snowed from the north,
frost gripped the earth, hail fell on the ground,
the coldest of grains. Therefore now the thoughts of my heart
are troubled whether I should try out for myself
the deep seas, the tossing of salty waves;   35
the mind's desire at all times prompts
the spirit to travel so that I, far from here,
might seek the home of those living in a foreign land.
Therefore there is no man so proud-hearted on the earth,
so generous of his gifts, so keen in youthfulness,   40
in his deeds so brave, nor his lord so gracious to him,
that he will never be anxious in his sea voyage
about what the Lord will bring to him.
Nor is his thought on the harp nor on the receiving of rings,
nor on pleasure in a woman nor the joy of worldly things,   45
nor about anything else except the tossing of the waves;
but he always has a longing who sets out on the sea.
    The groves assume blossoms, they adorn the cities,
the meadows grow beautiful, the world quickens;
all of this urges those eager of spirit,   50
the spirit to the journey, to him who is so inclined
to venture far on the paths of the sea.
Likewise the cuckoo urges him with a melancholy voice,
the watchman of summer sings, announces sorrow
bitter in his heart. This the warrior does not know,   55
the man blessed with luxury, what some endure,
those who travel furthest on the paths of exile.
    And yet now my spirit roams beyond the enclosure of the heart,

min modsefa   mid mereflode
ofer hwæles eþel   hweorfeð wide,   60
eorþan sceatas;   cymeð eft to me
gifre ond grædig;   gielleð anfloga,
hweteð on wælweg   hreþer unwearnum,
ofer holma gelagu.   Forþon me hatran sind
Dryhtnes dreamas   þonne þis deade lif,   65
læne on londe.   Ic gelyfe no
þæt him eorðwelan   ece stondeð.
Simle þreora sum   þinga gehwylce,
ær his tidege,   to tweon weorþeð:
adl oþþe yldo   oþþe ecghete   70
fægum fromweardum   feorh oðþringeð.
Forþon bið eorla gehwam   æftercweþendra
lof lifgendra   lastworda betst
þæt he gewyrce   ær he on weg scyle,
fremman on foldan   wið feonda niþ,   75
deorum dædum   deofle togeanes
þæt hine ælda bearn   æfter hergen,
ond his lof siþþan   lifge mid englum,
awa to ealdre   ecan lifes blæd,
dream mid dugeþum.   Dagas sind gewitene   80
ealle onmedlan   eorþan rices;
næron nu cyningas   ne caseras
ne goldgiefan   swylce iu wæron,
þonne hi mæst mid him   mærþa gefremedon
ond on dryhtlicestum   dome lifdon.   85
Gedroren is þeos duguð eal;   dreamas sind gewitene.
Wuniað þa wacran   ond þas woruld healdaþ,
brucað þurh bisgo.   Blæd is gehnæged.
Eorþan indryhto   ealdað ond searað,
swa nu monna gehwylc   geond middangeard: 90
yldo him on fareð,   onsyn blacað,
gomelfeax gnornað;   wat his iuwine,
æþelinga bearn,   eorþan forgiefene.
Ne mæg him þonne se flæschoma,   þonne him þæt feorg losað,
ne swete forswelgan   ne sar gefelan,   95
ne hond onhreran,   ne mid hyge þencan.
Þeah þe græf wille   golde stregan
broþor his geborenum,   byrgan be deadum
maþmum mislicum   þæt hine mid wille,
ne mæg þære sawle   þe biþ synna ful   100
gold to geoce   for Godes egsan,
þonne he hit ær hydeð   þenden he her leofað.
    Micel biþ se Meotudes egsa,   forþon hi seo molde oncyrreð;
se gestaþelade   stiþe grundas,
eorþan sceatas   ond uprodor.   105
Dol biþ se þe him his Dryhten ne ondrædeþ: cymeð him se deað unþinged.

my thought of mind, along with the sea-flood,
travels widely over the whale's haunt,   60
over the world's expanse; it comes again to me
eager and greedy; the solitary flier yells,
incites the spirit irresistibly on the whale's path
over the sea's expanse. Thus the joys of the Lord are
warmer to me than this dead life,   65
transitory on land. I do not believe
that earthly happiness will endure eternally.
Always, in all conditions, one of three things
hangs in the balance before his final day:
disease or old age or attack by the sword   70
will wrest life from those doomed to die, on their way hence.
Therefore for every man, praise from those who speak of him afterwards,
from the living, is the best memorial
that he might earn before he must depart,
achievements on earth against the wickedness of enemies,   75
opposing the devil with brave deeds
so that the children of men might praise him afterwards,
and his glory will live then among the angels,
always forever in the glory of eternal life,
joy among the host. The days are gone   80
of all the pomp of the kingdoms of earth;
there are now no kings or emperors
or gold-givers such as there formerly were,
when they most performed glorious deeds among themselves,
and lived in magnificent renown.   85
The whole of this noble band has fallen; joys are departed.
Inferior ones live and possess the world,
they enjoy it by way of toil. Glory is brought low.
The earth's nobility grows old and withers,
as does each man now throughout the earth: 90
old age overtakes him, his face grows pale,
a grey-haired one laments; he knows that his friends of old,
the children of princes, have been consigned to the earth.
Nor when his life is lost will his body
taste sweetness or feel pain,   95
or move a hand, or think with the mind.
Though a brother might wish to scatter the grave
with gold for his sibling, to bury with the dead
various treasures that he would like to have with him,
the gold that he hid before while he lived here   100
cannot be a help to the soul which is full of sins
when it comes into the presence of the terrible power of God.
    Great is the terrible power of the Ordainer before which the earth will quake;
he established the firm ground,
the expanse of the earth and the heavens above.   105
Foolish is he that does not fear his Lord: death will come to him unexpectedly.

Eadig bið se þe eaþmod leofaþ: cymeð him seo ar of heofonum.
Meotod him þæt mod gestaþelað   forþon he in his meahte gelyfeð.
Stieran mon sceal strongum mode,   ond þæt on staþelum healdan,
ond gewis werum,   wisum clæne.   110
Scyle monna gehwylc   mid gemete healdan
wiþ leofne   ond wið laþne bealo,
þeah þe he hine wille fyres   fulne
oþþe on bæle   forbærnedne
his geworhtne wine.   Wyrd biþ swiþre,   115
Meotud meahtigra   þonne ænges monnes gehygd.
   Uton we hycgan   hwær we ham agen,
ond þonne geþencan   hu we þider cumen;
ond we þonne eac tilien,   þæt we to moten
in þa ecan   eadignesse,   120
þær is lif gelong   in lufan Dryhtnes,
hyht in heofonum.   Þæs sy þam Halgan þonc,
þæt he usic geweorþade,   wuldres Ealdor,
ece Dryhten,   in ealle tid.   Amen.

The Wife's Lament

Ic þis giedd wrece   bi me ful geomorre,
minre sylfre sið.   Ic þæt secgan mæg,
hwæt Ic yrmþa gebad   siþþan Ic up weox,
niwes oþþe ealdes,   no ma þonne nu.
A Ic wite wonn   minra wræcsiþa.   5
   Ærest min hlaford gewat   heonan of leodum
ofer yþa gelac;   hæfde Ic uhtceare
hwær min leodfruma   londes wære.
Ða Ic me feran gewat   folgað secan,
wineleas wræcca   for minre weaþearfe.   10
Ongunnon þæt þæs monnes   magas hycgan
þurh dyrne geþoht   þæt hy todælden unc,
þæt wit gewidost   in woruldrice,
lifdon laðlicost;   ond mec longade.
   Het mec hlaford min   her heard niman.   15
Ahte Ic leofra lyt   on þissum londstede,
holdra freonda;   forþon is min hyge geomor.
Ða Ic me ful gemæcne   monnan funde
heardsæligne,   hygegeomorne,
mod miþendne,   morþor hycgendne,   20
bliþe gebæro.   Ful oft wit beotedan
þæt unc ne gedælde   nemne deað ana,
owiht elles;   eft is þæt onhworfen.
Is nu   swa hit no wære
freondscipe uncer.   Sceal Ic feor ge neah   25

Blessed is the man who lives humbly: the favour of heaven will come to him.
God establishes that spirit in him because he believes in his power.
A man must control a headstrong spirit and hold that firmly,
reliable in his pledges and clean in his ways.   110
Every man should act with restraint
towards both friend and foe,
although he might want him filled with fire,
or consumed on the pyre,
this friend that he has made. Fate is greater,   115
the Lord more mighty than any man's conception.
   Let us consider where we might have a home,
and then reflect upon how we could come there
and then we may also strive so that we should come there
into that eternal blessedness,   120
where there is life to be obtained in the love of God,
hope in heaven. Thanks be to the Holy One
that he has exalted us, Prince of glory,
eternal Lord, through all time.   Amen.

The Wife's Lament

I relate this very mournful riddle about myself,
about my own journey. I am able to relate
those miseries that I endured since I grew up,
of new and old ones, never more than now.
Forever I have suffered the torment of my exile.   5
   First my lord went away from the people
over tossing waves; I had anxiety at dawn
about where in the land my leader of the people might be.
Then I departed on my journey to seek a refuge,
a friendless exile because of my woeful need.   10
The kinsmen of the man began to think,
through secret consideration, that they would separate us,
so that we two would live furthest apart in this worldly kingdom,
most hatefully; and yearning occupied me.
   My cruel lord commanded me to be taken here.   15
I possessed few dear ones in this region,
loyal friends; because of that my mind is mournful.
Then I found a very well suited man to me
ill-fated, sad at heart,
having a concealing mind, intending violent crime,   20
but with a cheerful bearing. Very often, we two vowed
that nothing would part the two of us
except death alone; afterwards, that has turned around.
It is now as if it never were
the friendship of us two. Far and near I shall endure   25

mines felaleofan   fæhðu dreogan.
  Heht mec mon wunian   on wuda bearwe,
under actreo   in þam eorðscræfe.
Eald is þes eorðsele;   eal Ic eom oflongad.
Sindon dena dimme,   duna uphea,   30
bitre burgtunas   brerum beweaxne:
wic wynna leas.   Ful oft mec her wraþe begeat
fromsiþ frean.   Frynd sind on eorþan,
leofe lifgende,   leger weardiað,
þonne Ic on uhtan   ana gonge   35
under actreo   geond þas eorðscrafu.
Þær Ic sittan mot   sumorlangne dæg
þær Ic wepan mæg   mine wræcsiþas,
earfoþa fela;   forþon Ic æfre ne mæg
þære modceare   minre gerestan,   40
ne ealles þæs longaþes   þe mec on þissum life begeat.
  A scyle geong mon   wesan geomormod,
heard heortan geþoht,   swylce habban sceal
bliþe gebæro   eac þon breostceare,
sinsorgna gedreag,   sy æt him sylfum gelong   45
eal his worulde wyn,   sy ful wide fah
feorres folclondes,   þæt min freond siteð
under stanhliþe   storme behrimed,
wine werigmod,   wætre beflowen
on dreorsele.   Dreogeð se min wine   50
micle modceare;   he gemon to oft
wynlicran wic.   Wa bið þam þe sceal
of langoþe   leofes abidan.

that feud of my beloved.
    He commanded me to dwell in the wood's grove
under an oak tree in the earth-cave.
Old is this hall in the earth; I am all worn out with longing.
There are dark valleys, high hills,   30
bitter enclosures overgrown with briars:
a dwelling place deprived of joy. Very often here the departure of my lord
cruelly laid hold of me. Beloved ones are on the earth,
loved ones living, occupying a bed,
while I walk alone at dawn   35
under the oak tree through these earth-dwellings.
There I must sit the summer-long day,
where I can only weep about my exile,
about many hardships; because of this I cannot ever
rest from the sadness of my heart,   40
or from all the longing which takes hold of me in this life.
    The young man may always be sad in mind,
hard-hearted in thought, just as he must have
a happy appearance despite the grief in his breast
of a multitude of perpetual sorrows, whether it is that all his   45
joy in the world is at his own disposal, or whether far and wide
he is outlawed in a distant country, so that my beloved sits
under rocky cliffs assaulted by a storm,
a lord sad at heart, surrounded by water,
in a dismal hall. My beloved suffers   50
much mental torment; he remembers too often
a more joyful dwelling. It is misery for those who, longing,
have to wait for a loved one.

From the Vercelli Book

The Dream of the Rood

Hwæt, Ic swefna cyst   secgan wylle
hwæt me gemætte   to midre nihte,
syðþan reordberend   reste wunedon.
Þuhte me þæt Ic gesawe   syllicre treow
on lyft lædan,   leohte bewunden,   5
beama beorhtost.   Eall þæt beacen wæs
begoten mid golde;   gimmas stodon
fægere æt foldan sceatum,   swylce þær fife wæron
uppe on þam eaxlegespanne.   Beheoldon þær engel Dryhtnes ealle
fægere þurh forðgesceaft.   Ne wæs ðær huru fracodes gealga;   10
ac hine þær beheoldon   halige gastas,
men ofer moldan   ond eall þeos mære gesceaft.
Syllic wæs se sigebeam   ond Ic synnum fah,
forwunded mid wommum.   Geseah Ic wuldres treow
wædum geweorðode,   wynnum scinan,   15
gegyred mid golde;   gimmas hæfdon
bewrigene weorðlice   wealdes treow.
    Hwæðre, Ic þurh þæt gold   ongytan meahte
earmra ærgewin,   þæt hit ærest ongan
swætan on þa swiðran healfe.   Eall Ic wæs mid sorgum gedrefed.   20
Forht Ic wæs for þære fægran gesyhðe;   geseah Ic þæt fuse beacen
wendan wædum ond bleom: hwilum hit wæs mid wætan bestemed,
beswyled mid swates gange;   hwilum mid since gegyrwed.
Hwæðre Ic þær licgende   lange hwile,
beheold hreowcearig   Hælendes treow,   25
oððæt Ic gehyrde   þæt hit hleoðrode;
ongan þa word sprecan   wudu selesta:
    'Þæt wæs geara iu,   Ic þæt gyta geman,
þæt Ic wæs aheawen   holtes on ende,
astyred of stefne minum.   Genaman me ðær strange feondas,   30
geworhton him þær to wæfersyne,   heton me heora wergas hebban.
Bæron me ðær beornas on eaxlum,   oððæt hie me on beorg asetton,
gefæstnodon me þær feondas genoge.   Geseah Ic þa Frean mancynnes
efstan elne mycle   þæt he me wolde on gestigan.
Þær Ic þa ne dorste   ofer Dryhtnes word   35
bugan oððe berstan,   þa Ic bifian geseah

The Dream of the Rood

Listen, I will tell the best of visions,
what came to me in the middle of the night,
when voice-bearers dwelled in rest.
   It seemed to me that I saw a more wonderful tree
lifted in the air, wound round with light,   5
the brightest of beams. That beacon was entirely
cased in gold; beautiful gems stood
at the corners of the earth, likewise there were five
upon the cross-beam. All those fair through creation
gazed on the angel of the Lord there. There was certainly no gallows of the wicked;
but the holy spirits beheld it there,
men over the earth and all this glorious creation.
Wondrous was the victory-tree, and I stained with sins,
wounded with guilts. I saw the tree of glory,
honoured with garments, shining with joys,   15
covered with gold; gems had
covered magnificently the tree of the forest.
   Nevertheless, I was able to perceive through that gold
the ancient hostility of wretches, so that it first began
to bleed on the right side. I was all drenched with sorrows.   20
I was frightened by the beautiful vision; I saw that urgent beacon
change its covering and colours: sometimes it was soaked with wetness,
stained with the coursing of blood; sometimes adorned with treasure.
Yet as I lay there a long while
I beheld sorrowful the tree of the Saviour,   25
until I heard it utter a sound;
it began to speak words, the best of wood:
   'That was very long ago, I remember it still,
that I was cut down from the edge of the wood,
ripped up by my roots. They seized me there, strong enemies,   30
made me a spectacle for themselves there, commanded me to raise up their criminals.
Men carried me there on their shoulders, until they set me on a hill,
enemies enough fastened me there. I saw then the Saviour of mankind
hasten with great zeal, as if he wanted to climb up on me.
There I did not dare, against the word of the Lord,   35
bow or break, when I saw the

eorðan sceatas. Ealle Ic mihte
feondas gefyllan; hwæðre Ic fæste stod.
Ongyrede hine þa geong hæleð – þæt wæs God ælmihtig –
strang ond stiðmod; gestah he on gealgan heanne,   40
modig on manigra gesyhðe, þa he wolde mancyn lysan.
Bifode Ic þa me se beorn ymbclypte; ne dorste Ic hwæðre bugan to eorðan,
feallan to foldan sceatum, ac Ic sceolde fæste standan.
Rod wæs Ic aræred. Ahof Ic ricne Cyning,
heofona Hlaford; hyldan me ne dorste.   45
Þurhdrifan hi me mid deorcan næglum; on me syndon þa dolg gesiene,
opene inwidhlemmas; ne dorste Ic hira nænigum sceððan.
Bysmeredon hie unc butu ætgædere. Eall Ic wæs mid blode bestemed
begoten of þæs guman sidan siððan he hæfde his gast onsended.
    Feala Ic on þam beorge gebiden hæbbe   50
wraðra wyrda. Geseah Ic weruda God
þearle þenian. Þystro hæfdon
bewrigen mid wolcnum Wealdendes hræw,
scirne sciman. Sceadu forð eode
wann under wolcnum. Weop eal gesceaft,   55
cwiðdon Cyninges fyll. Crist wæs on rode.
    Hwæðere þær fuse feorran cwoman
to þam æðelinge; Ic þæt eall beheold.
Sare Ic wæs mid sorgum gedrefed; hnag Ic hwæðre þam secgum to handa,
eaðmod elne mycle. Genamon hie þær ælmihtigne God,   60
ahofon hine of ðam hefian wite. Forleton me þa hilderincas,
standan steame bedrifenne; eall Ic wæs mid strælum forwundod.
Aledon hie ðær limwerigne, gestodon him æt his lices heafdum,
beheoldon hie ðær heofenes Dryhten, ond he hine ðær hwile reste,
meðe æfter ðam miclan gewinne. Ongunnon him þa moldern wyrcan,   65
beornas on banan gesyhðe; curfon hie ðæt of beorhtan stane,
gesetton hie ðæron sigora Wealdend. Ongunnon him þa sorhleoð galan
earme on þa æfentide; þa hie woldon eft siðian
meðe fram þam mæran Þeodne. Reste he ðær mæte weorode.
    Hwæðere we ðær reotende gode hwile   70
stodon on staðole, syððan stefn up gewat
hilderinca. Hræw colode,
fæger feorgbold. Þa us man fyllan ongan
ealle to eorðan: þæt wæs egeslic wyrd.
Bedealf us man on deopan seaþe; hwæðre me þær Dryhtnes þegnas,   75
freondas gefrunon,
gyredon me gold ond seolfre.
    Nu þu miht gehyran, hæleð min se leofa,
þæt Ic bealuwara weorc gebiden hæbbe,
sarra sorga. Is nu sæl cumen   80
þæt me weorðiað wide ond side
menn ofer moldan ond eall þeos mære gesceaft,
gebiddaþ him to þyssum beacne. On me Bearn Godes
þrowode hwile; forþan Ic þrymfæst nu,

corners of the earth tremble. I might have
felled all the enemies; even so, I stood fast.
He stripped himself then, young hero – that was God almighty –
strong and resolute; he ascended on the high gallows,   40
brave in the sight of many, when he wanted to ransom mankind.
I trembled when the warrior embraced me; even then I did not dare to bow to earth,
fall to the corners of the earth, but I had to stand fast.
I was reared a cross. I raised up the powerful King,
the Lord of heaven; I did not dare to bend.   45
They pierced me with dark nails; on me are the wounds visible,
the open wounds of malice; I did not dare to injure any of them.
They mocked us both together. I was all drenched with blood
poured out from that man's side after he had sent forth his spirit.
    I have experienced on that hillside many   50
cruelties of fate. I saw the God of hosts
violently stretched out. Darkness had
covered with clouds the Ruler's corpse,
the gleaming light. Shadows went forth
dark under the clouds. All creation wept,   55
lamented the King's fall. Christ was on the cross.
    Yet there eager ones came from afar
to that noble one; I beheld all that.
I was all drenched with sorrow; nevertheless I bowed down to the hands of the men,
humble, with great eagerness. There they took almighty God,   60
lifted him from that oppressive torment. The warriors forsook me then
standing covered with moisture; I was all wounded with arrows.
They laid the weary-limbed one down there, they stood at the head of his body,
they beheld the Lord of heaven there, and he himself rested there a while,
weary after the great battle. They began to fashion a tomb for him,   65
warriors in the sight of the slayer; they carved that from bright stone,
they set the Lord of victories in there. They began to sing the sorrow-song for him,
wretched in the evening-time; then they wanted to travel again,
weary from the glorious Lord. He rested there with little company.
    Nevertheless, weeping, we stood there a good while   70
in a fixed position, after the voice departed up
of the warriors. The corpse grew cold,
the fair life-dwelling. Then men began to fell us
all to the ground: that was a terrible fate.
Men buried us in a deep pit; nevertheless the Lord's thanes,   75
friends, discovered me there,
adorned me with gold and silver.
    Now you might hear, my beloved hero,
that I have experienced the work of evil-doers,
grievous sorrows. Now the time has come   80
that I will be honoured far and wide
by men over the earth and all this glorious creation;
they will pray to this beacon. On me the Son of God
suffered for a while; because of that I am glorious now,

hlifige under heofenum,   ond Ic hælan mæg   85
æghwylcne anra   þara þe him bið egesa to me.
Iu Ic wæs geworden   wita heardost,
leodum laðost,   aerþan Ic him lifes weg
rihtne gerymde,   reordberendum.
Hwæt, me þa geweorðode   wuldres Ealdor   90
ofer holmwudu,   heofonrices Weard,
swylce swa he his modor eac,   Marian sylfe,
ælmihtig God,   for ealle menn
geweorðode   ofer eall wifa cynn.
    Nu Ic þe hate,   hæleð min se leofa,   95
þæt ðu þas gesyhðe   secge mannum:
onwreoh wordum   þæt hit is wuldres beam
se ðe ælmihtig God   on þrowode
for mancynnes   manegum synnum
ond Adomes   ealdgewyrhtum.   100
Deað he þær byrigde;   hwæðere eft Dryhten aras
mid his miclan mihte   mannum to helpe.
He ða on heofenas astag.   Hider eft fundaþ
on þysne middangeard   mancynn secan
on domdæge   Dryhten sylfa,   105
ælmihtig God,   ond his englas mid,
þæt he þonne wile deman,   se ah domes geweald,
anra gehwylcum   swa he him ærur her
on þyssum lænum   life geearnaþ.
Ne mæg þær ænig   unforht wesan   110
for þam worde   þe se Wealdend cwyð:
frineð he for þære mænige   hwær se man sie,
se ðe for Dryhtnes naman   deaðes wolde
biteres onbyrigan,   swa he ær on ðam beame dyde.
Ac hie þonne forhtiað   ond fea þencaþ   115
hwæt hie to Criste   cweðan onginnen.
Ne þearf ðær þonne ænig   unforht wesan
þe him ær in breostum bereð   beacna selest.
Ac ðurh ða rode sceal   rice gesecan
of eorðwege   æghwylc sawl   120
seo þe mid Wealdende   wunian þenceð.'
    Gebæd Ic me þa to þan beame   bliðe mode,
elne mycle,   þær Ic ana wæs
mæte werede.   Wæs modsefa
afysed on forðwege;   feala ealra gebad   125
langunghwila.   Is me nu lifes hyht
þæt Ic þone sigebeam   secan mote
ana oftor   þonne ealle men,
well weorþian.   Me is willa to ðam
mycel on mode,   ond min mundbyrd is   130
geriht to þære rode.   Nah Ic ricra feala
freonda on foldan;   ac hie forð heonon

towering under the heavens, and I am able to heal   85
each one of those who is in awe of me.
Formerly I was made the hardest of punishments,
most hateful to the people, before I opened for them,
for the voice-bearers, the true way of life.
Listen, the Lord of glory, the Guardian of the kingdom of heaven,   90
then honoured me over the forest trees,
just as he, almighty God, also honoured
his mother, Mary herself, for all men,
over all womankind.
   Now I urge you, my beloved man,   95
that you tell men about this vision:
reveal with words that it is the tree of glory
on which almighty God suffered
for mankind's many sins
and Adam's ancient deeds.   100
Death he tasted there; nevertheless, the Lord rose again
with his great might to help mankind.
He ascended into heaven. He will come again
to this earth to seek mankind
on doomsday, the Lord himself,   105
almighty God, and his angels with him,
so that he will then judge, he who has the power of judgement,
each one of them, for what they themselves have
earned here earlier in this transitory life.
Nor may any of them be unafraid there   110
because of the words which the Saviour will speak:
he will ask in front of the multitude where the person might be
who for the Lord's name would
taste bitter death, just as he did before on that tree.
But then they will be fearful and little think   115
what they might begin to say to Christ.
Then there will be no need for any of those to be very afraid
who bear before them in the breast the best of trees.
But by means of the rood each soul
who thinks to dwell with the Ruler   120
must seek the kingdom from the earthly way.'
   I prayed to the tree with a happy spirit then,
with great zeal, there where I was alone
with little company. My spirit was
inspired with longing for the way forward; I experienced in all   125
many periods of longing. It is now my life's hope
that I might seek the tree of victory
alone more often than all men,
to honour it well. My desire for that is
great in my mind, and my hope of protection is   130
directed to the cross. I do not have many wealthy
friends on earth; but they have gone forward from here,

gewiton of worulde dreamum,   sohton him wuldres Cyning;
lifiaþ nu on heofenum   mid Heahfædere,
wuniaþ on wuldre.   Ond Ic wene me   135
daga gehwylce   hwænne me Dryhtnes rod,
þe Ic her on eorðan   ær sceawode,
on þysson lænan   life gefetige
ond me þonne gebringe   þær is blis mycel,
dream on heofonum,   þær is Dryhtnes folc   140
geseted to symle,   þær is singal blis;
ond he þonne asette   þær Ic syþþan mot
wunian on wuldre   well mid þam halgum
dreames brucan.   Si me Dryhten freond,
se ðe her on eorþan   ær þrowode   145
on þam gealgtreowe   for guman synnum.
He us onlysde   ond us lif forgeaf,
heofonlicne ham.   Hiht wæs geniwad
mid bledum on mid blisse   þam þe þær bryne þolodan.
Se Sunu wæs sigorfæst   on þam siðfate,   150
mihtig ond spedig,   þa he mid manigeo com,
gasta weorode,   on Godes rice,
Anwealda ælmihtig,   englum to blisse
ond eallum ðam halgum   þam þe on heofonum ær,
wunedon on wuldre,   þa heora Wealdend cwom,   155
ælmihtig God,   þær his eðel wæs.

passed from the joys of this world, sought for themselves the King of glory;
they live now in heaven with the High Father,
they dwell in glory. And I myself hope   135
each day for when the Lord's cross,
that I looked at here on earth,
will fetch me from this transitory life,
and then bring me where there is great bliss,
joy in heaven, where the Lord's people   140
are set in feasting, where there is unceasing bliss;
and then he will set me where I might afterwards
dwell in glory fully with the saints
to partake of joy. May the Lord be a friend to me,
he who here on earth suffered previously   145
on the gallows-tree for the sins of man.
He redeemed us, and gave us life,
a heavenly home. Hope was renewed
with dignity and with joy for those who suffered burning there.
The Son was victorious in that undertaking,   150
powerful and successful, when he came with the multitudes,
a troop of souls, into God's kingdom,
the one Ruler almighty, to the delight of angels
and all the saints who were in heaven before,
who dwelled in glory, when their Ruler came,   155
almighty God, to where his native land was.

The Battle of Maldon

... brocen wurde.
Het þa hyssa hwæne   hors forlætan,
feor afysan   and forð gangan,
hicgan to handum   and to hige godum.
Þa þæt Offan mæg   ærest onfunde   5
þæt se eorl nolde   yrhðo geþolian,
he let him þa of handon   leofne fleogan
hafoc wið þæs holtes,   and to þære hilde stop;
be þam man mihte oncnawan   þæt se cniht nolde
wacian æt þam wige,   þa he to wæpnum feng.   10
Eac him wolde Eadric   his ealdre gelæstan,
frean to gefeohte,   ongan þa forð beran
gar to guþe.   He hæfde god geþanc
þa hwile þe he mid handum   healdan mihte
bord and brad swurd;   beot he gelæste   15
þa he ætforan his frean   feohtan sceolde.

Ða þær Byrhtnoð ongan   beornas trymian,
rad and rædde,   rincum tæhte
hu hi sceoldon standan   and þone stede healdan,
and bæd þæt hyra randas   rihte heoldon   20
fæste mid folman,   and ne forhtedon na.
Þa he hæfde þæt folc   fægere getrymmed,
he lihte þa mid leodon   þær him leofost wæs,
þær he his heorðwerod   holdost wiste.

Þa stod on stæðe,   stiðlice clypode   25
wicinga ar,   wordum mælde,
se on beot abead   brimliþendra
ærænde to þam eorle,   þær he on ofre stod:
'Me sendon to þe   sæmen snelle,
heton ðe secgan   þæt þu most sendan raðe   30
beagas wið gebeorge;   and eow betere is
þæt ge þisne garræs   mid gafole forgyldon
þon we swa hearde   hilde dælon.
Ne þurfe we us spillan,   gif ge spedaþ to þam;
we willað wið þam golde   grið fæstnian.   35
Gyf þu þat gerædest,   þe her ricost eart,
þæt þu þine leoda   lysan wille,
syllan sæmannum –   on hyra sylfra dom –

      . . . may have become broken.
Then he commanded each one of the warriors to let his horse go,
to drive it far away and to advance on foot,
to turn thoughts to hands and to be of good courage.
Then when Offa's kinsman first found   5
that the earl would not endure cowardice
he let fly from his hands his beloved
hawk into the wood, and stepped into battle;
by that a man might perceive that the warrior would not
weaken at that battle when he took up his weapons.   10
In addition to him, Eadric wanted to serve his leader,
his lord in the fight, so he began then to carry forward
his spear into battle. He had a firm mind
as long as he could hold with his hands
his shield and broad sword; he fulfilled his boast   15
when he was obliged to fight in front of his lord.
    Then Byrhtnoth began to encourage the warriors there,
he rode about and gave them advice, taught the warriors
how they should stand and maintain the position,
and urged them to hold their shields properly,   20
securely with their hands, and not to be afraid at all.
When he had suitably arrayed that host,
he dismounted among the men where it was most pleasing to him to be,
where he knew his retainers to be most loyal.
    Then there stood on the bank, and fiercely called out   25
a messenger of the Vikings, he spoke with words,
he announced in a boast a message of the seafarers
to the earl where he stood on the bank of the river:
'Bold seamen have sent me to you,
they command me to tell you that you must quickly send   30
rings in return for protection; and it will be better for you
that you buy off this storm of spears with a tribute
than that we should take part in such a hard battle.
We will not need to destroy one another if you are sufficiently wealthy;
we will establish a truce in exchange for that gold.   35
If you, the one who is most powerful here, decide upon this,
that you want to ransom your people,
give the seamen – what they judge for themselves –

feoh wið freode,   and niman frið æt us,
we willaþ mid þam sceattum   us to scype gangan,   40
on flot feran,   and eow friþes healdan.'
Byrhtnoð maþelode;   bord hafenode,
wand wacne æsc,   wordum mælde
yrre and anræd,   ageaf him andsware:
'Gehyrst þu, sælida,   hwæt þis folc segeð?   45
Hi willað eow to gafole   garas syllan,
ættrynne ord   and ealde swurd,
þa heregeatu   þe eow æt hilde ne deah.
Brimmanna boda,   abeod eft ongean,
sege þinum leodum   miccle laþre spell: 50
þæt her stynt unforcuð   eorl mid his werode,
þe wile gealgean   eþel þysne,
Æþelredes eard,   ealdres mines,
folc and foldan.   Feallan sceolon
hæþene æt hilde.   To heanlic me þinceð   55
þæt ge mid urum sceattum   to scype gangon
unbefohtene   nu ge þus feor hider
on urne eard   in becomon.
Ne sceole ge swa softe   sinc gegangan:
us sceal ord and ecg   ær geseman,   60
grim guðplega,   ær we gofol syllon.'
   Het þa bord beran,   beornas gangan,
þæt hi on þam easteðe   ealle stodon.
Ne mihte þær for wætere   werod to þam oðrum;
þær com flowende   flod æfter ebban   65
lucon lagustreamas.   To lang hit him þuhte
hwænne hi togædere   garas beron.
Hi þær Pantan stream   mid prasse bestodon,
Eastseaxena ord   and se æschere;
ne mihte hyra ænig   oþrum derian   70
buton hwa þurh flanes flyht   fyl genam.
Se flod ut gewat;   þa flotan stodon gearowe,
wicinga fela,   wiges georne.
Het þa hæleða hleo   healdan þa bricge
wigan wigheardne   se wæs haten Wulfstan,   75
cafne mid his cynne   (þæt wæs Ceolan sunu)
þe ðone forman man   mid his francan ofsceat
þe þær baldlicost   on þa bricge stop.
Þær stodon mid Wulfstane   wigan unforhte,
Ælfere and Maccus,   modige twegen,   80
þa noldon æt þam forda   fleam gewyrcan,
ac hi fæstlice   wið ða fynd weredon
þa hwile þe hi wæpna   wealdan moston.
Þa hi þæt ongeaton   and georne gesawon
þæt hi þær bricgweardas   bitere fundon,   85
ongunnon lytegian,   þa   laðe gystas:

money for peace, and accept protection from us,
and we will go to our ships with that tribute,   40
set sail and maintain that peace with you.'
Byrthnoth made a speech; he lifted his shield,
shook his slender ash spear, spoke forth with words
angry and resolute, and gave him an answer:
'Do you hear, seafarer, what this army says?   45
They will give you spears as tribute,
the poisoned spear-tip and ancient swords,
that war-gear that will not be of use to you in battle.
Messenger of the seamen, report back again,
tell your people a much more hateful message: 50
that here stands, with his troop, an earl of untainted reputation,
who will defend this native land,
the country of Æthelred, my lord's
people and ground. The heathens
will fall in battle. It seems too shameful to me   55
that you should go to your ships with our tribute
without a fight now that you have come this far
here into our land.
You shall not get treasure so easily:
weapon-tip and edge shall arbitrate between us first,   60
the fierce game of battle, before we give you tribute.'
    Then he commanded the warriors to advance bearing shields,
so that they all stood on the bank of the river.
One army could not get at the other because of the water there;
where the tide came flowing after the ebb   65
streams of water enclosed the land. It seemed too long to them
until they could brandish spears together.
They stood there alongside the River Pante in military formation,
the East Saxon vanguard and the Viking army;
not one of them was able to injure any other   70
unless someone received death from the flight of a missile.
The tide went out; the seamen stood ready,
many Vikings, eager for battle.
Then the protector of the heroes commanded the causeway to be defended
by a warrior fierce in war called Wulfstan,   75
as brave as all his family (he was Ceola's son),
who with his spear shot the first man
who stepped most boldly onto that causeway.
There stood with Wulfstan fearless warriors,
Ælfere and Maccus, two brave men,   80
who would not take flight from that ford,
but they firmly resisted the enemy
as long as they were able to brandish their weapons.
When the Vikings perceived this and saw plainly
that they had found there fierce causeway-defenders,   85
they began to use cunning, the hateful strangers:

bædon þæt hi upgangan   agan moston,
ofer þone ford faran,   feþan lædan.
Ða se eorl ongan   for his ofermode
alyfan landes to fela   laþere ðeode.   90
Ongan ceallian þa   ofer cald wæter,
Byrhtelmes bearn –   beornas gehlyston:
'Nu eow is gerymed,   gað ricene to us
guman to guþe;   God ana wat
hwa þære wælstowe   wealdan mote.'   95
    Wodon þa wælwulfas;   for wætere ne murnon
wicinga werod.   West ofer Pantan,
ofer scir wæter,   scyldas wegon;
lidmen to lande   linde bæron.
Þær ongean gramum   gearowe stodon   100
Byrhtnoð mid beornum.   He mid bordum het
wyrcan þone wihagan   and þæt werod healdan
fæste wiþ feondum.   Þa wæs feohte neh,
tir æt getohte;   wæs seo tid cumen
þæt þær fæge men   feallan sceoldon.   105
Þær wearð hream ahafen;   hremmas wundon,
earn æses georn;   wæs on eorþan cyrm.
Hi leton þa of folman   feolhearde speru,
gegrundene   garas fleogan;
bogan wæron bysige,   bord ord onfeng.   110
Biter wæs se beaduræs;   beornas feollon
on gehwæðere hand,   hyssas lagon.
Wund wearð Wulfmær,   wælræste geceas,
Byrhtnoðes mæg;   he mid billum wearð,
his swuster sunu,   swiðe forheawen.   115
Þær wærð wicingum   wiþerlean agyfen.
Gehyrde Ic þæt Eadweard   anne sloge
swiðe mid his swurde –   swenges ne wyrnde –
þæt him æt fotum feoll   fæge cempa,
þæs him his ðeoden   þanc gesæde,   120
þam burþene,   þa he byre hæfde.
Swa stemnetton   stiðhicgende,
hysas æt hilde,   hogodon georne
hwa þær mid orde   ærost mihte
on fægean men   feorh gewinnan,   125
wigan mid wæpnum.   Wæl feol on eorðan.
Stodon stædefæste;   stihte hi Byrhtnoð,
bæd þæt hyssa gehwylc   hogode to wige
þe on Denon wolde   dom gefeohtan.
    Wod þa wiges heard,   wæpen up ahof,   130
bord to gebeorge,   and wið þæs beornes stop.
Eode swa anræd   eorl to þam ceorle:
ægþer hyra oðrum   yfeles hogode.
Sende ða se særinc   suþerne gar

they requested that they should be allowed a passage to land,
to travel over the ford, to lead the foot-soldiers.
Then the earl, because of his pride, began
to allow too much land to a more hateful nation.   90
He began to call out then over the cold water,
this son of Byrhtelm – the warriors listened:
'Now a passage is granted to you, come quickly to us
as men to battle; God alone knows
who will be allowed to control the place of slaughter.'   95
    The wolves of slaughter advanced; they did not care about the water,
that host of Vikings. West over the Pante,
over the shining water, they bore their shields;
the sailors carried their lime-wood shields to land.
There against the hostile ones stood ready   100
Byrhtnoth with his men. He commanded the army
to make a battle-wall with shields and to hold fast
against the enemies. The battle was near then,
glory in the fray; the time had come
that fated men should fall there.   105
An outcry was raised there; ravens circled in the air,
the eagle eager for carrion; there was uproar on earth.
Then from their hands they let fly spears as hard as files,
sharpened missiles;
bows were busy, the shield received the sword-point.   110
Bitter was the rush of battle; warriors fell
on either side, soldiers lay dead.
Wulfmær was wounded, he chose death in battle,
the kinsman of Byrhtnoth, son of his sister:
he was cruelly cut down with swords.   115
Requital was given to the Vikings there.
I heard that Eadweard killed one
fiercely with his sword – he did not withhold the blow –
so that at his feet a doomed warrior fell,
for which his lord gave thanks   120
to his chamberlain when he had the chance.
So those resolute in purpose stood firm,
young warriors in battle, eagerly they concentrated there
on whoever might win the life of a doomed man
first with the spear-point,   125
those soldiers with their weapons. The dead of battle fell to the earth.
They stood steadfast; Byrhtnoth urged them on,
he asked that each soldier should focus on the battle,
whoever wished to get glory from the Danes in battle.
    Then one fierce in battle advanced, raised his weapon up,   130
used his shield as protection, and marched towards that man.
The earl moved towards that peasant just as resolutely:
each of them intended ill-harm to the other.
Then the Viking threw a spear of southern make

þæt gewundod wearð   wigena hlaford;   135
he sceaf þa mid ðam scylde   þæt se sceaft tobærst,
and þæt spere sprengde   þæt hit sprang ongean.
Gegremod wearð se guðrinc;   he mid gare stang
wlancne wicing   þe him þa wunde forgeaf.
Frod wæs se fyrdrinc;   he let his francan wadan   140
þurh ðæs hysses hals;   hand wisode
þæt he on þam færsceaðan   feorh geræhte.
Ða he oþerne   ofstlice sceat,
þæt seo byrne tobærst;   he wæs on breostum wund
þurh ða hringlocan;   him æt heortan stod   145
ætterne ord.   Se eorl wæs þe bliþra.
Hloh þa, modi man,   sæde Metode þanc
ðæs dægweorces   þe him Drihten forgeaf.
Forlet þa drenga sum   daroð of handa,
fleogan of folman,   þæt se to forð gewat   150
þurh ðone æþelan   Æþelredes þegen.
Him be healfe stod   hyse unweaxen,
cniht on gecampe,   se full caflice
bræd of þam beorne   blodigne gar,
Wulfstanes bearn,   Wulfmær se geonga.   155
Forlet forheardne   faran eft ongean;
ord in gewod   þæt se on eorþan læg
þe his þeoden ær   þearle geræhte.
   Eode þa gesyrwed   secg to þam eorle;
he wolde þæs beornes   beagas gefecgan,   160
reaf and hringas   and gerenod swurd.
Þa Byrhtnoð bræd   bill of sceðe,
brad and bruneccg,   and on þa byrnan sloh.
To raþe hine gelette   lidmanna sum,
þa he þæs eorles   earm amyrde.   165
Feoll þa to foldan   fealohilte swurd;
ne mihte he gehealdan   heardne mece,
wæpnes wealdan.   Þa gyt þæt word gecwæð
har hilderinc,   hyssas bylde,
bæd gangan forð   gode geferan.   170
Ne mihte þa on fotum leng   fæste gestandan;
he to heofenum wlat:
'Geþance þe,   ðeoda Waldend,
ealra þæra wynna   þe Ic on worulde gebad.
Nu Ic ah, milde Metod,   mæste þearfe   175
þæt þu minum gaste   godes geunne,
þæt min sawul to ðe   siðian mote
on þin geweald,   Þeoden engla,
mid friþe ferian.   Ic eom frymdi to þe
þæt hi helsceaðan   hynan ne moton.'   180
Ða hine heowon   hæðene scealcas,
and begen þa beornas   þe him big stodon,

so that the lord of the warriors was wounded;   135
he shoved with his shield then so that the shaft shattered
and that spear quivered as it sprang back out.
The warrior became enraged; he struck with a spear
the proud Viking who had given him that wound.
That warrior was old and wise; he made his spear go   140
through the neck of the soldier; his hand guided it
so that he took the life from that sudden attacker.
Then he quickly threw another
so that his mail-coat burst; he was wounded in the breast
through the ringmail shirt; positioned in his heart   145
was the poison-tipped spear. The earl was the happier.
The bold man laughed then, he gave thanks to the Creator
for the day's work that the Lord had granted to him.
Then a certain warrior sent a light spear from his hands,
let it fly from his clutches, so that it went forwards   150
through the noble thane of Æthelred.
By his side stood a youth not fully grown,
a boy in the battle, who very bravely
pulled out the bloody spear from that warrior,
this was the son of Wulfstan, the young Wulfmær.   155
He let the exceedingly hard spear journey back again;
the point penetrated so that he who had severely wounded
his lord before lay dead on the ground.
    Then the armed man went towards the earl;
he wanted to fetch the warrior's ornaments,   160
the armour and rings, and decorated sword.
Then Byrhtnoth pulled his sword from its sheath
broad and shiny edged, and struck against the mail-coat.
Too swiftly one of the Vikings prevented him,
when he wounded the earl's arm.   165
The golden-hilted sword fell to the ground:
he could not hold the hard blade,
or wield his weapon. And yet the hoary warrior
said these words, encouraged the young soldiers,
urged them to go forwards as good companions.   170
He could not stand fast on his feet any longer;
he looked up to heaven:
'I thank you, Lord of nations,
for all of the joys that I have experienced in this world.
Now I have, merciful God, most need   175
that you grant a benefit to my spirit,
that my soul might journey to you
into your power, Lord of angels,
to travel in peace. I beg you
that thieves from hell will not be permitted to injure it.'   180
The heathen warriors cut him down,
and both the men who stood beside him,

Ælfnoð and Wulmær   begen lagon,
ða onemn hyra frean   feorh gesealdon.
    Hi bugon þa fram beaduwe   þe þær beon noldon.   185
Þær wurdon Oddan bearn   ærest on fleame,
Godric fram guþe,   and þone godan forlet
þe him mænigne oft   mear gesealde.
He gehleop þone eoh   þe ahte his hlaford,
on þam gerædum,   þe hit riht ne wæs,   190
and his broðru mid him   begen ærndon,
Godwine and Godwig: guþe ne gymdon,
ac wendon fram þam wige   and þone wudu sohton,
flugon on þæt fæsten   and hyra feore burgon,
and manna ma   þonne hit ænig mæð wære,   195
gyf hi þa geearnunga   ealle gemundon
þe he him to duguþe   gedon hæfde.
Swa him Offa on dæg   ær asæde
on þam meþelstede,   þa he gemot hæfde,
þæt þær modelice   manega spræcon   200
þe eft æt þearfe   þolian noldon.
    Þa wearð afeallen   þæs folces ealdor,
Æþelredes eorl;   ealle gesawon
heorðgeneatas   þæt hyra heorra læg.
    Þa ðær wendon forð   wlance þegenas,   205
unearge men   efston georne:
hi woldon þa ealle   oðer twega,
lif forlætan   oððe leofne gewrecan.
Swa hi bylde forð   bearn Ælfrices,
wiga wintrum geong,   wordum mælde,   210
Ælfwine þa cwæð,   he on ellen spræc:
'Gemunaþ þa mæla   þe we oft æt meodo spræcon,
þonne we on bence   beot ahofon,
hæleð on healle,   ymbe heard gewinn;
nu mæg cunnian   hwa cene sy.   215
Ic wylle mine æþelo   eallum gecyþan,
þæt Ic wæs on Myrcon   miccles cynnes;
wæs min ealda fæder   Ealhelm haten,
wis ealdorman,   woruldgesælig.
Ne sceolon me on þære þeode   þegenas ætwitan   220
þæt Ic of ðisse fyrde   feran wille
eard gesecan,   nu min ealdor ligeð
forheawen æt hilde.   Me is þæt hearma mæst:
he wæs ægðer min mæg   and min hlaford.'
Þa he forð eode,   fæhðe gemunde,   225
þæt he mid orde   anne geræhte
flotan on þam folce,   þæt se on foldan læg
forwegen mid his wæpne.   Ongan þa winas manian,
frynd and geferan,   þæt hi forð eodon.
Offa gemælde,   æscholt asceoc: 230

Ælfnoð and Wulmær both lay slain,
they gave their lives beside their lord.
    Then those who did not want to be there turned away from battle.   185
There the sons of Odda became the first to flee,
Godric turned from the battle, and abandoned the good man
who had often given him many a horse.
He leapt onto the horse that his lord had owned,
into those trappings, which was not right,   190
and his brothers, Godwine and Godwig,
both ran with him: they did not care about the battle,
but escaped from that fight and sought the woods,
fled into the place of safety and saved their own lives,
as did many more than was in any way appropriate,   195
if they recalled all the benefits
that Byrhtnoth had done to their advantage.
So earlier in the day Offa had said
in that meeting place, when they held a council,
that many spoke bravely there   200
who would not hold out afterwards when there was need.
    So the leader of the people had fallen,
Æthelred's earl; the retainers
all saw that their lord lay dead.
Then proud thanes came forward there,   205
the undaunted men hastened eagerly:
they all wanted one of two things,
to give up their life or to avenge their beloved lord.
The son of Ælfric urged them forth,
a warrior young in years, spoke words,   210
Ælfwine then said, and he bravely uttered:
'Remember the words that we often spoke over mead,
when we raised a vow at our bench,
heroes in the hall, about the hard battle;
now it will be tested who is brave.   215
I will reveal my noble lineage to everyone,
that I was from a great family in Mercia;
my grandfather was called Ealhelm,
a wise ealdorman, prosperous and happy in this world.
The thanes of that people will not reproach me   220
that I want to go from this army
to seek my homeland, now that my lord lies dead
cut down in battle. To me that is the greatest of sorrows:
he was both my kinsman and my lord.'
Then he stepped forward, mindful of the feud,   225
so that with his spear he reached one
Viking in that army, such that he lay dead on the ground
killed by his weapon. Then he began to exhort his comrades,
friends and companions, that they should go forward.
Offa spoke, the ash spear shook: 230

'Hwæt þu, Ælfwine,   hafast ealle gemanode
þegenas to þearfe.   Nu ure þeoden lið,
eorl on eorðan,   us is eallum þearf
þæt ure æghwylc   oþerne bylde,
wigan to wige,   þa hwile þe he wæpen mæge   235
habban and healdan,   heardne mece,
gar and god swurd.   Us Godric hæfð,
earh Oddan bearn,   ealle beswicene:
wende þæs formoni man,   þa he on meare rad,
on wlancan þam wicge,   þæt wære hit ure hlaford;   240
forþan wearð her on felda   folc totwæmed,
scyldburh tobrocen.   Abreoðe his angin,
þæt he her swa manigne   man aflymde!'
Leofsunu gemælde,   and his linde ahof,
bord to gebeorge;   he þam beorne oncwæð: 245
'Ic þæt gehate,   þæt Ic heonon nelle
fleon fotes trym,   ac wille furðor gan
wrecan on gewinne   minne winedrihten.
Ne þurfon me embe Sturmere   stedefæste hælæð
wordum ætwitan   nu min wine gecranc,   250
þæt Ic hlafordleas   ham siðie,
wende fram wige;   ac me sceal wæpen niman,
ord and iren.'   He ful yrre wod,
feaht fæstlice;   fleam he forhogode.
Dunnere þa cwæð,   daroð acwehte,   255
unorne ceorl,   ofer eall clypode,
bæd þæt beorna gehwylc   Byrhtnoð wræce:
'Ne mæg na wandian   se þe wrecan þenceð
frean on folce   ne for feore murnan.'
Þa hi forð eodon,   feores hi ne rohton.   260
Ongunnon þa hiredmen   heardlice feohtan,
grame garberend,   and God bædon
þæt hi moston gewrecan   hyra winedrihten
and on hyra feondum   fyl gewyrcan.
Him se gysel ongan   geornlice fylstan;   265
he wæs on Norðhymbron   heardes cynnes,
Ecglafes bearn,   him wæs Æscferð nama.
He ne wandode na   æt þam wigplegan,
ac he fysde forð   flan genehe;
hwilon he on bord sceat,   hwilon beorn tæsde;   270
æfre embe stunde   he sealde sume wunde
þa hwile ðe he wæpna   wealdan moste.
Þa gyt on orde stod   Eadweard se langa;
gearo and geornful,   gylpwordum spræc
þæt he nolde fleogan   fotmæl landes,   275
ofer bæc bugan,   þa his betera leg.
He bræc þone bordweall   and wið þa beornas feaht,
oðþæt he his sincgyfan   on þam sæmannum

'Indeed, Ælfwine, you have exhorted all
the thanes at this time of need. Now our lord lies dead,
the earl on the ground, there is a need for us all
that each of us encourage the other,
warriors into battle, as long as he may   235
have and hold a weapon, the hard blade,
a spear and good sword. Godric,
the cowardly son of Odda, has betrayed us all:
very many men thought, when he rode away on that horse,
on that noble steed, that it was our lord;   240
therefore the army on this field became divided,
the shield-wall broken. May his venture fail,
that he caused so many men to flee here!'
Leofsunu spoke out, and he raised his lime-wood shield
as protection; he answered the warrior: 245
'I pledge this, that from here I shall not
flee one footstep, but I mean to go further onwards
to avenge my beloved lord in battle.
The resolute heroes around Sturmer will have no need
to condemn me with words, now my lord has died,   250
that I should go home lordless,
turn away from battle; rather a weapon shall take me,
the spear-tip and iron sword.' Very angry, he advanced,
fought bravely; he scorned flight.
Dunnere then spoke, he shook his light spear,   255
a simple peasant, he called out over everyone,
and urged that each warrior should avenge Byrhtnoth:
'He who thinks to avenge his lord upon that people
cannot draw back or fear for his life.'
They went forwards then, they did not care about their lives.   260
The retainers started to fight fiercely,
hostile spear-carriers, and prayed God
that they could avenge their beloved lord
and bring death to their enemies.
The hostage eagerly began to help them;   265
he was from a hardy family from Northumbria,
the son of Ecglaf, his name was Æscferth.
He did not draw back at all in that battle-game,
but he frequently shot forth darts;
sometimes he shot into a shield, sometimes he lacerated a warrior;   270
always within a short time he caused some wound
as long as he was able to wield weapons.
Also in the vanguard stood Eadweard the tall;
ready and eager, he spoke determined words
that he would not flee one foot of ground,   275
retreat back, while his better man lay dead.
He broke the shield-wall and fought against the warriors,
until, among those Vikings, he avenged his treasure-giver

wurðlice wrec,   ær he on wæle læge.
Swa dyde Æþeric,   æþele gefera,   280
fus and forðgeorn,   feaht eornoste,
Sibyrhtes broðor,   and swiðe mænig oþer,
clufon cellod bord,   cene hi weredon.
Bærst bordes lærig,   and seo byrne sang
gryreleoða sum.   Þa æt guðe sloh   285
Offa þone sælidan   þæt he on eorðan feoll,
and ðær Gaddes mæg   grund gesohte.
Raðe wearð æt hilde   Offa forheawen;
he hæfde ðeah geforþod   þæt he his frean gehet,
swa he beotode ær   wið his beahgifan   290
þæt hi sceoldon begen   on burh ridan,
hale to hame,   oððe on here crincgan,
on wælstowe   wundum sweltan.
He læg ðegenlice   ðeodne gehende.
    Ða wearð borda gebræc.   Brimmen wodon,   295
guðe gegremode.   Gar oft þurhwod
fæges feorhhus.   Forð ða eode Wistan,
Þurstanes suna,   wið þas secgas feaht;
he wæs on geþrang   hyra þreora bana,
ær him Wigelmes bearn   on þam wæle læge.   300
Þær wæs stið gemot.   Stodon fæste
wigan on gewinne.   Wigend cruncon,
wundum werige;   wæl feol on eorþan.
Oswold and Eadwold   ealle hwile,
begen þa gebroþru,   beornas trymedon,   305
hyra winemagas   wordon bædon
þæt hi þær æt ðearfe   þolian sceoldon,
unwaclice   wæpna neotan.
Byrhtwold maþelode,   bord hafenode,
se wæs eald geneat,   æsc acwehte;   310
he ful baldlice   beornas lærde:
'Hige sceal þe heardra,   heorte þe cenre,
mod sceal þe mare,   þe ure mægen lytlað.
Her lið ure ealdor   eall forheawen,
god on greote.   A mæg gnornian   315
se ðe nu fram þis wigplegan   wendan þenceð.
Ic eom frod feores;   fram Ic ne wille,
ac Ic me be healfe   minum hlaforde,
be swa leofan men,   licgan þence.'
Swa hi Æþelgares bearn   ealle bylde,   320
Godric to guþe.   Oft he gar forlet,
wælspere windan   on þa wicingas,
swa he on þam folce   fyrmest eode,
heow and hynde,   oðþæt he on hilde gecranc.
Næs þæt na se Godric   þe ða guðe forbeah.   325

honourably, before he himself lay among the dead.
So did Ætheric, a noble companion,   280
keen and eager to advance, he fought committedly,
this brother of Sigebryht, and very many others,
they split the embossed shield, they defended themselves bravely.
The rim of the shield burst, and the mail-coat sang
a song of terror. Then in the battle   285
Offa struck a Viking so that he fell dead on the earth,
and there this kinsman of Gad sought the ground.
Offa was quickly cut down in battle;
he had, though, accomplished what he promised his lord,
when he pledged before with his ring-giver   290
that they should both ride into the nobleman's dwelling,
ride unharmed into the home, or fall in conflict,
die from wounds in the place of slaughter.
He lay loyally next to his lord.
    Then shields were broken. The seafarers advanced   295
incensed by the battle. The spear often pierced
the body of the fated man. Wistan then went forward,
the son of Thurstan, he fought against the men;
he was the slayer of three of them in the throng
before Wigelm's son lay before him among the dead.   300
It was a fierce encounter there. They stood fast,
warriors in the battle. Warriors died
overcome by wounds; the slain fell to the ground.
Oswold and Eadwold all the while,
the two brothers, encouraged the warriors,   305
they entreated their dear kinsmen with their words
that they should hold out there in this time of need,
use their weapons unfailingly.
Byrhtwold spoke out, raised his shield,
he was an old retainer, he shook his ash spear;   310
very boldly he instructed the men:
'The mind must be tougher, the heart the bolder,
resolve shall be greater, as our strength becomes less.
Here lies our lord all cut down,
a good man in the dust. He who thinks to turn away   315
from this battle-play now will always regret it.
I am experienced in life; I will not go away,
but by the side of my lord,
of such a dear man, I intend to lie.'
Godric, Æthelgar's son, likewise encouraged them all   320
to battle. He sent a spear often,
a deadly spear to fly into the Vikings;
so he advanced first into that army;
he cut down and killed, until he perished in that conflict.
He was not that Godric who fled from the battle.   325

From the Beowulf Manuscript

From *Beowulf*

X

Ða him Hroþgar gewat   mid his hæleþa gedryht,
eodur Scyldinga   ut of healle;
wolde wigfruma   Wealhþeo secan
cwen to gebeddan.   Hæfde Kyning-wuldor   665
Grendle togeanes,   swa guman gefrungon,
seleweard aseted;   sundornytte beheold
ymb aldor Dena,   eotonweard abead.
Huru Geata leod   georne truwode
modgan mægnes,   Metodes hyldo.   670
   Ða he him of dyde   isernbyrnan,
helm of hafelan,   sealde his hyrsted sweord
irena cyst   ombihtþegne,
ond gehealdan het   hildegeatwe.
Gespræc þa se goda   gylpworda sum,   675
Beowulf Geata,   ær he on bed stige:
'No Ic me an herewæsmun   hnagran talige
guþgeweorca   þonne Grendel hine;
forþan Ic hine sweorde   swebban nelle,
aldre beneotan,   þeah Ic eal mæge.   680
Nat he þara goda,   þæt he me ongean slea,
rand geheawe,   þeah ðe he rof sie
niþgeweorca;   ac wit on niht sculon
secge ofersittan,   gif he gesecean dear
wig ofer wæpen,   ond siþðan witig God   685
on swa hwæþere hond,   halig Dryhten,
mærðo deme,   swa him gemet þince.'
   Hylde hine þa heaþodeor;   hleorbolster onfeng
eorles andwlitan,   ond hine ymb monig
snellic særinc   selereste gebeah.   690
Nænig heora þohte   þæt he þanon scolde
eft eardlufan   æfre gesecean,
folc oþðe freoburh   þær he afeded wæs;
ac hie hæfdon gefrunen   þæt hie ær to fela micles
in þæm winsele   wældeað fornam,   695
Denigea leode.   Ac him Dryhten forgeaf

From *Beowulf*

X

Then Hrothgar departed with his company of men,
the protector of the Scyldings went out of the hall;
the war-leader wanted to go to Wealhtheow
as a bed-fellow to the queen. The King of glory,   665
as men heard, had appointed a hall-guardian
against Grendel; he fulfilled a special task
for the lord of the Danes, offered a guard against the giant.
Indeed, the Geatish man firmly trusted
in his brave strength, the favour of the Creator.   670
    Then he took off his iron mail-coat,
and the helmet from his head, gave his decorated sword
of the best iron to an attendant thane,
and commanded him to guard the war-equipment.
The good man, Beowulf of the Geats,   675
uttered some vaunting words before he climbed into bed:
'I do not consider myself in warlike stature and in battle-deeds
any poorer than Grendel himself;
therefore I do not wish to kill him with a sword,
to deprive him of life so, though I easily could do that.   680
He does not know the skills, inasmuch as he might strike against me,
cut through a shield, even though he may be strong
in hostile deeds; but tonight we two shall
forgo the sword, if he dares to seek
battle without a weapon, and afterwards, the wise God   685
the holy Lord, will judge glory
on whichever side, as it seems fitting to him.'
    Then the man brave in battle lay down; the pillow
received the face of the warrior, and around him many
brave seamen lay down on beds in the hall.   690
None of them thought that he would ever
reach his beloved homeland again,
his people and noble stronghold where he was brought up;
but they had learned that far too many before them
had been carried off in slaughter from that wine-hall,   695
from among the Danish people. But the Lord granted to them,

wigspeda gewiofu,   Wedera leodum,
frofor ond fultum,   þæt hie feond heora
ðurh anes cræft   ealle ofercomon,
selfes mihtum.   Soð is gecyþed,   700
þæt mihtig God   manna cynnes
weold wideferhð.   Com on wanre niht
scriðan sceadugenga.   Sceotend swæfon,
þa þæt hornreced   healdan scoldon,
ealle buton anum.   Þæt wæs yldum cuþ   705
þæt hie ne moste,   þa Metod nolde,
se scynscaþa   under sceadu bregdan;
ac he wæccende   wraþum on andan,
bad bolgenmod   beadwa geþinges.

XI

Ða com of more   under misthleoþum   710
Grendel gongan.   Godes yrre bær.
Mynte se manscaða   manna cynnes
sumne besyrwan   in sele þam hean.
Wod under wolcnum   to þæs þe he winreced,
goldsele gumena   gearwost wisse,   715
fættum fahne.   Ne wæs þæt forma sið
þæt he Hroþgares   ham gesohte;
næfre he on aldordagum,   ær ne siþðan,
heardran hæle   healðegnas fand.
    Com þa to recede   rinc siðian,   720
dreamum bedæled.   Duru sona onarn,
fyrbendum fæst,   syþðan he hire folmum gehran.
Onbræd þa bealohydig,   ða he gebolgen wæs,
recedes muþan.   Raþe æfter þon
on fagne flor   feond treddode,   725
eode yrre-mod;   him of eagum stod
ligge gelicost   leoht unfæger.
Geseah he in recede   rinca manige,
swefan sibbegedriht   samod ætgædere,
magorinca heap.   Þa his mod ahlog;   730
mynte þæt he gedælde,   ærþon dæg cwome,
atol aglæca,   anra gehwylces
lif wið lice   þa him alumpen wæs
wistfylle wen.   Ne wæs þæt wyrd þa gen
þæt he ma moste   manna cynnes   735
ðicgean ofer þa niht.   Þryðswyð beheold
mæg Higelaces   hu se manscaða
under færgripum   gefaran wolde.
Ne þæt se aglæca   yldan þohte,
ac he gefeng hraðe   forman siðe   740
slæpendne rinc,   slat unwearnum,
bat banlocan,   blod edrum dranc,

the people of the Geats, the fortune of success in war,
comfort and aid, so that they entirely overcame
their enemy through the power of one man,
and his own might. The truth is well known,   700
that mighty God rules the race of men
for ever. In the dark night came
stalking a walker in shadows. The warriors slept,
those who had to guard the gabled hall,
all except one. It was known to men   705
that the demonic ravager could not,
when the Creator did not wish it, drag them under the shadows;
but he, watching, hostile in anger,
enraged awaited the outcome of battle.

XI

Then from the moor under the misty slopes came   710
Grendel advancing. He bore God's anger.
The evil ravager intended to ensnare one
of the race of men in that lofty hall.
He advanced under the clouds to where he most clearly recognized
the wine-hall, the gold-hall of men,   715
gleaming with gold plating. Nor was that the first time
that he had come to Hrothgar's home;
never in the days of his life, before or after,
did he meet hall-thanes with worse fortune.
    He came then to the hall, a warrior making his way,   720
deprived of joys. The door sprang open,
the secure forged bars, when he touched it with his hands.
He was enraged then, intending destruction,
he pulled open the door of the hall. Quickly after that
the enemy stepped on the decorated floor,   725
he advanced angry at heart; from his eyes gleamed
an ugly light, most like a flame.
He saw many warriors in the hall,
a sleeping band of kinsman all together,
a troop of young warriors. Then his spirit laughed;   730
the terrible monster intended to sever
the life from the body of each one
before day came since the expectation of a lavish feast
had presented itself to him. But it was not fated
that he would be permitted to take still more   735
of the race of men after that night. The mighty kinsman of Hygelac
waited to see how the wicked ravager
would proceed with the sudden grip of attack.
Nor did that fierce assailant intend to delay,
but at the first opportunity he quickly seized   740
a sleeping warrior, tore at him without restraint,
bit into the muscles, drank the blood from the veins,

synsnædum swealh;   sona hæfde
unlyfigendes   eal gefeormod,
fet ond folma.   Forð near ætstop,   745
nam þa mid handa   higeþihtigne,
rinc on ræste,   ræhte ongean
feond mid folme;   he onfeng hraþe
inwitþancum   ond wið earm gesæt.
Sona þæt onfunde   fyrena hyrde   750
þæt he ne mette   middangeardes,
eorþan sceata,   on elran men
mundgripe maran.   He on mode wearð
forht on ferhðe;   no þy ær fram meahte.
Hyge wæs him hinfus,   wolde on heolster fleon   755
secan deofla gedræg;   ne wæs his drohtoð þær
swylce he on ealderdagum   ær gemette.
   Gemunde þa se goda   mæg Higelaces,
æfenspræce,   uplang astod
ond him fæste wiðfeng;   fingras burston –   760
eoten wæs utweard –   eorl furþur stop.
Mynte se mæra,   þær he meahte swa,
widre gewindan,   ond on weg þanon
fleon on fenhopu;   wiste his fingra geweald
on grames grapum.   Þæt wæs geocor sið   765
þæt se hearmscaþa   to Heorute ateah!
Dryhtsele dynede;   Denum eallum wearð,
ceasterbuendum,   cenra gehwylcum,
eorlum ealuscerwen.   Yrre wæron begen,
reþe renweardas.   Reced hlynsode: 770
þa wæs wundor micel   þæt se winsele
wiðhæfde heaþodeorum,   þæt he on hrusan ne feol,
fæger foldbold;   ac he þæs fæste wæs
innan ond utan   irenbendum
searoþoncum besmiþod.   Þær fram sylle abeag   775
medubenc monig,   mine gefræge,
golde geregnad,   þær þa graman wunnon.
Þæs ne wendon ær   witan Scyldinga
þæt hit a mid gemete   manna ænig,
betlic ond banfag,   tobrecan meahte,   780
listum tolucan,   nymþe liges fæþm
swulge on swaþule.   Sweg up astag
niwe geneahhe;   Norð-Denum stod
atelic egesa,   anra gehwylcum
þara þe of wealle   wop gehyrdon,   785
gryreleoð galan   Godes ondsacan,
sigeleasne sang,   sar wanigean
helle hæfton.   Heold hine fæste,
se þe manna wæs   mægene strengest
on þæm dæge   þysses lifes.   790

swallowed the sinful morsels; soon he had
completely consumed the unliving man,
feet and hands. Forward nearer he stepped,   745
seized with his hands the strong-hearted man,
the warrior in bed, the fiend reached out
with his hands; Beowulf quickly seized him
with hostile purpose and sat up, leaning on his arm.
At once the master of evil deeds discovered that   750
he had not encountered in the world,
in the regions of the earth, another man
with a greater hand-grip. He became in his heart
fearful in spirit; none the sooner could he get away.
His mind was eager to escape, he wanted to flee into the darkness,   755
to seek the company of devils; nor was his experience there
such as he had encountered before in the days of his life.
　　When the brave kinsman of Hygelac remembered
the evening's speech, he stood upright
and grasped him firmly; fingers cracked –   760
the giant was trying to escape – the warrior stepped closer.
The infamous one intended, if he was able,
to escape further off, and flee from there on his way
to his fen-retreat; he knew the power of those fingers
in the grasp of the hostile man. That was a bitter journey   765
that the grievous foe undertook to Heorot!
The noble hall resounded; to all of the Danes,
the fortress-dwellers, among each of the brave,
the warriors, there were ale-showers. Both were furious,
fierce guardians of the hall. The hall echoed: 770
it was a great wonder that the wine-hall
withstood those brave in battle, that the beautiful building
did not fall to the ground; but it was so securely
and skilfully forged inside and out
with iron bands. Many mead-benches there   775
were turned over on the floor, as I have heard,
gold-adorned, where the hostile ones fought.
The wise men of the Scyldings did not previously think
that any one of humankind would ever shatter it,
by any means, excellent and adorned with bones at it was,   780
or by cunning destroy it, unless the embrace of fire
swallowed it in flames. Sound rose up
anew often; horrible terror came upon
the North-Danes, on each one of them
who heard the wailing from the wall,   785
God's adversary chanted a song of terror,
a song without victory, the captive of hell
bewailing his wound. He held him firmly,
he who of men was the strongest in strength
in those days of this life.   790

XII

Nolde eorla hleo   ænige þinga
þone cwealmcuman   cwicne forlætan,
ne his lifdagas   leoda ænigum
nytte tealde.   Þær genehost brægd
eorl Beowulfes   ealde lafe;   795
wolde freadrihtnes   feorh ealgian,
mæres þeodnes,   ðær hie meahton swa.
Hie þæt ne wiston   þa hie gewin drugon
heardhicgende   hildemecgas
ond on healfa gehwone   heawan þohton   800
sawle secan,   þone synscaðan
ænig ofer eorþan   irenna cyst,
guðbilla nan,   gretan nolde;
ac he sigewæpnum   forsworen hæfde
ecga gehwylcre.   Scolde his aldorgedal   805
on ðæm dæge   þysses lifes
earmlic wurðan,   ond se ellorgast
on feonda geweald   feor siðian.

   Ða þæt onfunde,   se þe fela æror
modes myrðe   manna cynne,   810
fyrene gefremede   – he fag wið God –
þæt him se lichoma   læstan nolde,
ac hine se modega   mæg Hygelaces
hæfde be honda;   wæs gehwæþer oðrum
lifigende lað.   Licsar gebad   815
atol æglæca: him on eaxle wearð
syndolh sweotol,   seonowe onsprungon,
burston banlocan.   Beowulfe wearð
guðhreð gyfeþe;   scolde Grendel þonan
feorhseoc fleon   under fenhleoðu   820
secean wynleas wic;   wiste þe geornor
þæt his aldres wæs   ende gegongen,
dogera dægrim.   Denum eallum wearð
æfter þam wælræse   willa gelumpen:
hæfde þa gefælsod   se þe ær feorran com,   825
snotor ond swyðferhð,   sele Hroðgares,
genered wið niðe;   nihtweorce gefeh,
ellenmærþum.   Hæfde East-Denum
Geatmecga leod   gilp gelæsted,
swylce oncyþðe   ealle gebette   830
inwidsorge   þe hie ær drugon,
ond for þreanydum   þolian scoldon,
torn unlytel.   Þæt wæs tacen sweotol,
syþðan hildedeor   hond alegde,
earm ond eaxle   – þær wæs eal geador   835
Grendles grape –   under geapne hrof.

XII

The warriors' protector would not by any means
let the murderous visitor go alive,
nor did any of the people consider his life-days
to be of use. There many of Beowulf's men
brandished ancient heirlooms;   795
they wanted to protect their lord's life,
the renowned prince, if they were able to do so.
These warriors resolute in mind did not know
when they engaged in the conflict
and thought to strike on each side   800
to seek its life, that the evil ravager
could not be touched by any war-sword
or by any of the finest swords on earth;
but he had made weapons of victory, every blade,
useless by a spell. His severing from life   805
in those days of this existence would
needs be miserable, and the alien being
was to make a journey far away into the power of fiends.
    Then he discovered, he who had previously
committed many afflictions of the heart, wicked deeds   810
against mankind – he fought against God –
that his body would not be of service,
but the courageous kinsman of Hygelac
had him in his hands; each was loathsome to the other
while living. The terrible fierce assailant   815
suffered physical pain: in his shoulder was
made visible a mortal wound, sinews sprang apart,
muscles burst. To Beowulf was granted
triumph in battle; Grendel had to flee from there
fatally wounded under the fenland slopes   820
to go to a joyless dwelling; he knew the more surely
that his life had reached its end,
his days were numbered. The desire of the Danes
had been fulfilled after that deadly onslaught:
he who had come from far away,   825
wise and resolute, had cleansed Hrothgar's hall,
saved it from the affliction; he rejoiced in the night's work,
in the heroic deeds. The leader of the Geats
had fulfilled his vow to the East-Danes,
he also entirely remedied the grief,   830
for those who had previously endured evil sorrows,
and been forced to suffer dire distresses,
no small affliction. That was a clear sign,
when the man brave in battle placed the hand,
the arm and shoulder – there all together was   835
Grendel's grasp – under the broad roof.

XIII

Ða wæs on morgen,   mine gefræge,
ymb þa gifhealle   guðrinc monig;
ferdon folctogan   feorran ond nean
geond widwegas   wundor sceawian,   840
laþes lastas.   No his lifgedal
sarlic þuhte   secga ænegum
þara þe tirleases   trode sceawode,
hu he werig-mod   on weg þanon,
niða ofercumen,   on nicera mere   845
fæge ond geflymed   feorhlastas bær.
Ðær wæs on blode   brim weallende,
atol yða geswing   eal gemenged
haton heolfre,   heorodreore weol;
deaðfæge deog   siððan dreama leas   850
in fenfreoðo   feorh alegde
hæþene sawle;   þær him hel onfeng.
   Þanon eft gewiton   ealdgesiðas,
swylce geong manig   of gomenwaþe
fram mere modge   mearum ridan,   855
beornas on blancum.   Ðær wæs Beowulfes
mærðo mæned;   monig oft gecwæð
þætte suð ne norð   be sæm tweonum,
ofer eormengrund   oþer nænig
under swegles begong   selra nære   860
rondhæbbendra,   rices wyrðra;
ne hie huru winedrihten   wiht ne logon,
glædne Hroðgar,   ac þæt wæs god cyning.
Hwilum heaþorofe   hleapan leton,
on geflit faran   fealwe mearas   865
ðær him foldwegas   fægere þuhton
cystum cuðe.   Hwilum cyninges þegn,
guma gilphlæden,   gidda gemyndig,
se ðe ealfela   ealdgesegena
worn gemunde,   word oþer fand   870
soðe gebunden.   Secg eft ongan
sið Beowulfes   snyttrum styrian,
ond on sped wrecan   spel gerade,
wordum wrixlan.   Welhwylc gecwæð
þæt he fram Sigemunde   secgan hyrde,   875
ellendædum,   uncuþes fela,
Wælsinges gewin,   wide siðas,
þara þe gumena bearn   gearwe ne wiston,
fæhðe ond fyrena,   buton Fitela mid hine,
þonne he swulces hwæt   secgan wolde,   880
eam his nefan,   swa hie a wæron
æt niða gehwam   nydgesteallan;
hæfdon ealfela   eotena cynnes

XIII

Then in the morning, as I have heard,
around the gift-hall were many warriors;
the leaders of the people travelled far and near
through the distant regions to look at the wonder,   840
the tracks of the hostile one. His severing from life
did not seem at all painful to any of the men
who looked at the footprints of the inglorious one,
how he, weary-hearted on the way from there,
overcome in battle, bore his life-tracks   845
into the mere of water-monsters, doomed and put to flight.
There the water was surging with blood,
the terrible swirling of waves all mingled
with hot blood, welled up with battle-gore;
the one who was doomed to die when deprived of joy hid,   850
he laid down his life in the fen-refuge,
heathen soul; there hell received him.
    The old retainers departed again from there,
also many young ones from the joyous journey,
rode on their horses from the lake, high-spirited,   855
heroes on horses. There Beowulf's glory
was related; many often said
that south or north between the seas,
over the spacious earth none other
under the expanse of the sky was ever a better   860
shield-bearer, more worthy of a kingdom;
nor indeed did they find fault with the friend and lord,
gracious Hrothgar, but that was a good king.
At times, those brave in battle were allowed to gallop,
to ride in a contest of the bay mares   865
where the paths seemed attractive to them
and were known for their excellence. At times the king's thane,
a man filled with eloquent speech, recalling stories,
he who could remember a multitude, many
traditional tales, devised other words   870
truly linked. The man began again
to recite Beowulf's exploit with skill,
and to compose a skilful tale with success,
to vary it with words. He recounted everything
that he had heard said about Sigemund,   875
of brave deeds, of many things not known,
of Wælsing's conflict, of far journeys,
of things the children of men did not know fully,
except for Fitela who was with him, of feuds and wicked deeds,
when he wanted to say something of such a matter,   880
as uncle to his nephew, so they were always
comrades at need in every battle;
they had killed with swords very many

sweordum gesæged.   Sigemunde gesprong
æfter deaðdæge   dom unlytel,   885
syþðan wiges heard   wyrm acwealde,
hordes hyrde.   He under harne stan,
æþelinges bearn,   ana geneðde
frecne dæde,   ne wæs him Fitela mid.
Hwæþre him gesælde   ðæt þæt swurd þurhwod   890
wrætlicne wyrm   þæt hit on wealle ætstod,
dryhtlic iren;   draca morðre swealt.
Hæfde aglæca   elne gegongen
þæt he beahhordes   brucan moste
selfes dome;   sæbat gehleod,   895
bær on bearm scipes   beorhte frætwa,
Wælses eafera.   Wyrm hat gemealt.
Se wæs wreccena   wide mærost
ofer werþeode,   wigendra hleo
ellendædum   (he þæs ær onðah),   900
siððan Heremodes   hild sweðrode,
eafoð ond ellen.   He mid Eotenum wearð
on feonda geweald   forð forlacen,
snude forsended.   Hine sorhwylmas
lemede to lange.   He his leodum wearð,   905
eallum æþellingum   to aldorceare;
swylce oft bemearn   ærran mælum
swiðferhþes sið   snotor ceorl monig,
se þe him bealwa to   bote gelyfde,
þæt þæt ðeodnes bearn   geþeon scolde,   910
fæderæþelum onfon,   folc gehealdan,
hord ond hleoburh,   hæleþa rice,
eþel Scyldinga.   He þær eallum wearð
mæg Higelaces   manna cynne
freondum gefægra;   hine fyren onwod.   915
   Hwilum flitende   fealwe stræte
mearum mæton.   Ða wæs morgenleoht
scofen ond scynded.   Eode scealc monig
swiðhicgende   to sele þam hean
searowundor seon;   swylce self cyning   920
of brydbure,   beahhorda weard,
tryddode tirfæst   getrume micle,
cystum gecyþed,   ond his cwen mid him
medostigge mæt   mægþa hose.

                              XIIII
Hroðgar maþelode,   he to healle geong,   925
stod on stapole,   geseah steapne hrof
golde fahne,   ond Grendles hond:
'Ðisse ansyne   Alwealdan þanc
lungre gelimpe.   Fela Ic laþes gebad

grynna æt Grendle.   A mæg God wyrcan   930
wunder æfter wundre,   wuldres Hyrde.
Ðæt wæs ungeara   þæt Ic ænigra me
weana ne wende   to widan feore
bote gebidan,   þonne blode fah
husa selest   heorodreorig stod,   935
wea widscofen   witena gehwylcum,
ðara þe ne wendon   þæt hie wideferhð
leoda landgeweorc   laþum beweredon,
scuccum ond scinnum.   Nu scealc hafað
þurh Drihtnes miht   dæd gefremede   940
ðe we ealle   ær ne meahton
snyttrum besyrwan.   Hwæt, þæt secgan mæg
efne swa hwylc mægþa   swa ðone magan cende
æfter gumcynnum,   gyf heo gyt lyfað,
þæt hyre Ealdmetod   este wære   945
bearngebyrdo.   Nu Ic, Beowulf, þec,
secg betsta,   me for sunu wylle
freogan on ferhþc;   heald forð tela
niwe sibbe;   ne bið þe nænigre gad
worolde wilna   þe Ic geweald hæbbe.   950
Ful oft Ic for læssan   lean teohhode,
hordweorþunge   hnahran rince,
sæmran æt sæcce.   Þu þe self hafast
dædum gefremed   þæt þin dom lyfað
awa to aldre.   Alwalda þec   955
gode forgylde,   swa he nu gyt dyde.'
   Beowulf maþelode,   bearn Ecþeowes:
'We þæt ellenweorc   estum miclum,
feohtan fremedon,   frecne geneððon
eafoð uncuþes.   Uþe Ic swiþor   960
þæt ðu hine selfne   geseon moste
feond on frætewum   fylwerigne.
Ic hine hrædlice   heardan clammum
on wælbedde   wriþan þohte
þæt he for mundgripe   minum scolde   965
licgean lifbysig,   butan his lic swice.
Ic hine ne mihte,   þa Metod nolde,
ganges getwæman,   no Ic him þæs georne ætfealh,
feorhgeniðlan;   wæs to foremihtig
feond on feþe.   Hwæþere he his folme forlet   970
to lifwraþe   last weardian,
earm ond eaxle.   No þær ænige swa þeah
feasceaft guma   frofre gebohte;
no þy leng leofað   laðgeteona,
synnum geswenced,   ac hyne sar hafað   975
mid nidgripe   nearwe befongen,
balwon bendum;   ðær abidan sceal

of the race of giants. Sigemund's glory
spread forth not a little after his death-day,
since, hardened in war, he killed a dragon,
a guardian of treasure. Under a grey stone he,
the son of a prince, alone ventured on
the daring deed, nor was Fitela with him.
Nevertheless, it happened to him that the sword pierced through
the wondrous serpent so that it remained fast in the skin,
the lordly sword; the dragon had died by violent assault.
The fierce warrior had brought it about with courage
that he was able to enjoy the treasure-hord
at his own choice; he loaded the sea-vessel,
carried bright adornments into the hold of the ship,
this son of Wæls. The serpent had melted away in the heat.
He was the most famous of exiles far and wide
over the nations, the protector of warriors,
because of his deeds of courage (he had prospered from that previously),
since Heremod's prowess in battle diminished,
his strength and bravery. He was betrayed, along with the Jutes,
into the power of the enemies,
quickly put to death. Surging sorrows
oppressed him for too long. He became to his people,
to all the noblemen, a great anxiety;
also many wise men had often lamented in earlier times
at the way of life of the strong-minded man,
many a man who had counted on him to remedy afflictions,
and that this son of a prince should have prospered,
received a father's nobility, protected his people,
the treasure and stronghold, the kingdom of heroes,
the native land of the Scyldings. There
the kinsman of Hygelac became the dearer to friends
and to all the race of people; sin entered Heremod's heart.
  At times competing on the sandy road
they travelled on horses. Then the morning light was
advanced and hastened. Many a retainer went
resolute in mind to the hall of the high man
to see the curious wonder; also the king himself,
the guardian of the hoard of rings, stepped from the marriage-chamber
glorious with his great troop,
renowned for his good attributes, and his queen with him
crossed the path to the mead-hall with a troop of women.

XIIII

Hrothgar spoke, he went to the hall,
stood on the steps, saw the lofty roof
gleaming with gold, and Grendel's hand:
'For this sight thanks to the Ruler of all
should be given at once. I have endured many hateful

afflictions from Grendel. God always brings about 930
wonder after wonder, the Shepherd of glory.
It was only recently that I did not ever expect
myself to live to see a remedy for any of the miseries,
when, stained with blood,
the best of houses stood gory from battle, 935
a widespread misery to each of the wise ones,
of those who did not expect that they would ever
defend the people's stronghold from enemies,
demons and evil spirits. Now a warrior,
has carried out the deed through the power of the Lord 940
which we all could not previously
accomplish with our skills. Indeed, it might be said
that whichever woman gave birth to this son
among the race of men, if she is still living,
that the God of old was gracious to her 945
in child-bearing. Now Beowulf,
the best of men, I will love you as my son
in my heart; I will from now on keep well
the new kinship; nor will you lack any
desirable things of the world over which I have control. 950
Very often I have assigned reward for less,
honouring with gifts a more lowly man,
a weaker one in battle. You yourself have
performed deeds so that your glory will live
for ever and ever. The Ruler of all 955
will reward your goodness, as he even now has done.'
  Beowulf, the son of Ecgtheow, spoke:
'We carried out that courageous deed,
that fight, with good will, daringly risked against
the strength of the unknown. I should have wished rather 960
that you yourself could have seen
the enemy in trappings wearied to the point of death.
I thought to bind him quickly with
a tight grip upon his death-bed
so that he should lie struggling for life 965
because of my hand-grip, unless his body escaped.
I could not prevent him from going,
the Creator did not wish it, neither could I grasp him firmly enough,
the deadly foe; he was too powerful
an enemy in going. However, he left his hand 970
to remain behind in order to protect his life,
his arm and shoulder. Even so the wretched being
will not have gained any comfort there;
nor will the hateful ravager live the longer,
afflicted with sins, for his pain will have 975
seized him tightly in its inexorable grip,
its deadly fetters; there he must await

maga mane fah   miclan domes,
hu him scir Metod   scrifan wille.'
    Ða wæs swigra secg,   sunu Eclafes,   980
on gylpspræce   guðgeweorca,
siþðan æþelingas   eorles cræfte
ofer heanne hrof   hand sceawedon,
feondes fingras;   foran æghwær wæs
stedenægla gehwylc   style gelicost,   985
hæþenes handsporu   hilderinces
eg unheoru.   Æghwylc gecwæð
þæt him heardra nan   hrinan wolde
iren ærgod   þæt ðæs ahlæcan
blodge beadufolme   onberan wolde.   990

                          XV
Ða wæs haten hreþe   Heort innanweard
folmum gefrætwod;   fela þæra wæs
wera ond wifa   þe þæt winreced
gestsele gyredon.   Goldfag scinon
web æfter wagum,   wundorsiona fela   995
secga gehwylcum   þara þe on swylc starað.
Wæs þæt beorhte bold   tobrocen swiðe,
eal inneweard   irenbendum fæst,
heorras tohlidene;   hrof ana genæs
ealles ansund   þe se aglæca   1000
fyrendædum fag   on fleam gewand,
aldres orwena.   No þæt yðe byð
to befleonne   (fremme se þe wille),
ac gesecan sceal   sawlberendra
nyde genydde   niþða bearna,   1005
grundbuendra   gearwe stowe,
þær his lichoma   legerbedde fæst
swefeþ æfter symle.   Þa wæs sæl ond mæl
þæt to healle gang   Healfdenes sunu;
wolde self cyning   symbel þicgan.   1010
Ne gefrægen Ic þa mægþe   maran weorode
ymb hyra sincgyfan   sel gebæran.
Bugon þa to bence   blædagande,
fylle gefægon;   fægere geþægon
medoful manig   magas þara   1015
swiðhicgende   on sele þam hean,
Hroðgar ond Hroþulf.   Heorot innan wæs
freondum afylled;   nalles facenstafas
Þeod-Scyldingas   þenden fremedon.
Forgeaf þa Beowulfe   brand Healfdenes,   1020
segen gyldenne   sigores to leane,
hroden hildecumbor,   helm ond byrnan;
mære maðþumsweord   manige gesawon

the great judgement, a man stained with crime,
how the resplendent Creator will judge him.'
    Then the man, the son of Ecgtheow was more silent   980
in vaunting speech of warlike deeds,
after the noblemen looked at the hand,
the strength of the warrior, on the high roof,
the enemy's fingers; at every position of the tip
each of the firm nails was most similar to steel,   985
the heathen warrior's claw
a monstrous spike. Each of the hardy men
said that no sword of proven worth
would touch him or would injure that
bloody battle-hand of the fierce assailant.   990

XV

Then orders were quickly given that Heorot
should be decorated inside by hands; many
men and women prepared that wine-hall
and guest-hall. Tapestries shone,
adorned with gold along the walls, a number of wondrous sights   995
for each person who gazed on them.
That bright building was much damaged,
though it was all secured within by iron bands,
hinges sprang apart; the roof alone survived
wholly unharmed when the fierce assailant   1000
stained with wicked deeds turned in flight,
despairing of his life. Nor was it that easy
to flee (let him try it who will),
but compelled by necessity, he is obliged to seek out
the place prepared for the children of men,   1005
for earth-dwellers having a soul,
where his body held fast in the death-bed
sleeps after the feast. Then it was the season and time
that the son of Healfdene went to the hall;
the king himself wanted to participate in the feast.   1010
I have not heard of a greater company of people
behaving better around their treasure-giver.
They sat down on benches enjoying glory,
rejoiced at the feast; the resolute kinsmen,
Hrothgar and Hrothulf, graciously accepted   1015
many a cup of mead
in that lofty hall. The inside of Heorot
was filled with friends; not then were the
people of the Scyldings engaged in wicked acts at all.
Then Hrothgar gave Beowulf Healfdene's sword,   1020
a golden standard as a reward for victory,
a decorated battle-banner, a helmet and corslet;
many saw the renowned treasure-sword

beforan beorn beran.   Beowulf geþah
ful on flette;   no he þære feohgyfte   1025
for sceotendum   scamigan ðorfte.
Ne gefrægn Ic freondlicor   feower madmas
golde gegyrede   gummanna fela
in ealobence   oðrum gesellan.
Ymb þæs helmes hrof   heafodbeorge   1030
wirum bewunden   wala utan heold,
þæt him fela laf   frecne ne meahton
scurheard sceþðan   þonne scyldfreca
ongean gramum   gangan scolde.
   Heht ða eorla hleo   eahta mearas   1035
fætedhleore   on flet teon
in under eoderas;   þara anum stod
sadol searwum fah   since gewurþad.
Þæt wæs hildesetl   heahcyninges,
ðonne sweorda gelac   sunu Healfdenes   1040
efnan wolde;   næfre on ore læg
widcuþes wig   ðonne walu feollon.
Ond ða Beowulfe   bega gehwæþres
eodor Ingwina   onweald geteah,
wicga ond wæpna;   het hine wel brucan.   1045
Swa manlice   mære þeoden,
hordweard hæleþa,   heaþoræsas geald
mearum ond madmum   swa hy næfre man lyhð
se þe secgan wile   soð æfter rihte.

XVI

Ða gyt æghwylcum   eorla drihten   1050
þara þe mid Beowulfe   brimlade teah
on þære medubence   maþðum gesealde,
yrfelafe,   ond þone ænne heht
golde forgyldan   þone ðe Grendel ær
mane acwealde,   swa he hyra ma wolde,   1055
nefne him witig God   wyrd forstode
ond ðæs mannes mod.   Metod eallum weold
gumena cynnes,   swa he nu git deð.
Forþan bið andgit   æghwær selest,
ferhðes foreþanc;   fela sceal gebidan   1060
leofes ond laþes   se þe longe her
on ðyssum windagum   worolde bruceð.
   Þær wæs sang ond sweg   samod ætgædere
fore Healfdenes   hildewisan,
gomenwudu greted,   gid oft wrecen   1065
ðonne healgamen   Hroþgares scop
æfter medobence   mænan scolde
Finnes eaferum.   Ða hie se fær begeat,
hæleð Healf-Dena,   Hnæf Scyldinga,

carried before the warrior. Beowulf drank
from a cup in the hall; nor did he need to feel ashamed there   1025
of the costly gifts given in front of the warriors.
I have not heard of four treasures
adorned with gold given by many men to another
on the ale-benches in a more friendly way.
Around the crown of that helmet as a head-guard, a crest   1030
bound with wires gave protection on the exterior,
so that the remnants of files, hard in battle,
might not injure him severely when the shield-warrior
had to advance against hostile men.
　　The protector of warriors then ordered eight horses   1035
with gold-plated bridles to be led in onto the floor
through the courtyard; on one of them was
a saddle decorated with skill, enriched with treasure.
That had been the battle-seat of the high king,
when Healfdene's son wanted to engage in   1040
the contests of swords; the courage of the renowned man
never failed in the front when those killed fell.
And so the protector of the Ingwine conferred both of the things
into the possession of Beowulf,
the horses and weapons; he told him to enjoy them well.   1045
Thus, manfully, the famous lord,
treasure-guarder of the warriors, repaid the storms of battle
with horses and treasures so that no one would ever find fault with them
among those who are inclined in fairness to speak the truth.

XVI

Furthermore, the lord of warriors gave treasures,   1050
an heirloom, to each of those on the mead-benches
who undertook the sea-passage with Beowulf,
and ordered that one man
should pay compensation of gold for the one whom Grendel
had previously killed through wickedness, as he would have done   1055
to more of them if the wise God and the courage of that man
had not prevented that fate. The Creator had power over all
of the race of men, as he does even now.
Therefore, the best thing is always to have understanding,
forethought of mind; he who long partakes   1060
of these days of strife within the world here
shall experience much that is dear and hateful.
　　There was song and music together
in the presence of Healfdene's battle-leader,
the mirth-wood was touched, a tale often recited   1065
when Hrothgar's scop related the entertainment in the hall
along the mead-benches
concerning the sons of Finn. When the sudden attack came upon them,
the hero of the Half-Danes, Hnæf of the Scyldings,

in Freswæle   feallan scolde.   1070
Ne huru Hildeburh   herian þorfte
Eotena treowe;   unsynnum wearð
beloren leofum   æt þam lindplegan,
bearnum ond broðrum;   hie on gebyrd hruron,
gare wunde.   Þæt wæs geomuru ides.   1075
Nalles holinga   Hoces dohtor
meotodsceaft bemearn   syþðan morgen com,
ða heo under swegle   geseon meahte
morþorbealo maga   þær heo ær mæste heold
worolde wynne.   Wig ealle fornam   1080
Finnes þegnas   nemne feaum anum,
þæt he ne mehte   on þæm meðelstede
wig Hengeste   wiht gefeohtan,
ne þa wealafe   wige forþringan
þeodnes ðegne.   Ac hig him geþingo budon   1085
þæt hie him oðer flet   eal gerymdon,
healle ond heahsetl,   þæt hie healfre geweald,
wið Eotena bearn   agan moston;
ond æt feohgyftum   Folcwaldan sunu
dogra gehwylce   Dene weorþode,   1090
Hengestes heap   hringum wenede,
efne swa swiðe   sincgestreonum
fættan goldes,   swa he Fresena cyn
on beorsele   byldan wolde.
Ða hie getruwedon   on twa healfa   1095
fæste frioðuwære.   Fin Hengeste
elne unflitme   aðum benemde
þæt he þa wealafe   weotena dome
arum heolde,   þæt ðær ænig mon
wordum ne worcum   wære ne bræce,   1100
ne þurh inwitsearo   æfre gemænden,
ðeah hie hira beaggyfan   banan folgedon
ðeodenlease,   þa him swa geþearfod wæs;
gyf þonne Frysna hwylc   frecnan spræce
ðæs morþorhetes   myndgiend wære,   1105
þonne hit sweordes ecg   syððan scolde.
    Að wæs geæfned   ond icge gold
ahæfen of horde.   Here-Scyldinga
betst beadorinca   wæs on bæl gearu;
æt þæm ade wæs   eþgesyne   1110
swatfah syrce,   swyn ealgylden,
eofer irenheard,   æþeling manig
wundum awyrded;   sume on wæle crungon.
Het ða Hildeburh   æt Hnæfes ade
hire selfre sunu   sweoloðe befæstan,   1115
banfatu bærnan,   ond on bæl don
eame on eaxle.   Ides gnornode,

was to perish in the Frisian slaughter. 1070
Indeed, Hildeburh had no need to praise
the loyalty of the Jutes; guiltless, she was
deprived of her dear sons and brothers
in that shield-play; fated, they fell
wounded by the spear. That was a sad woman. 1075
Not at all without cause did the daughter of Hoc
mourn the decree of fate when the morning came,
when she was able to see under the sky
the slaughter of kinsmen where she had previously had
the greatest joy in the world. The war had taken away 1080
all the retainers of Finn except for a few only,
so that in that meeting-place he could not fight the battle to a finish
with Hengest, the prince's thane,
or force out in war those that remained
from the disaster. But they offered them a truce, 1085
that they would completely clear out another building for them,
a hall and a high-seat, so that they might control half of it,
could possess it along with the sons of the Jutes;
and that at the treasure-givings the son of Folcwalda
should honour the Danes each time, 1090
should present rings to the company of Hengest,
treasures plated with gold,
just as he would encourage the people of the Frisians
in the beer-hall in the same way.
Then on the two sides they confirmed 1095
the peace-treaty firmly. Finn declared
oaths with undisputed courage to Hengest
that he would honourably hold to the judgement of counsellors
from among the disaster's survivors, that there no man
would break the treaty with words or deeds, 1100
or ever complain through malice,
although they served the murderer of their ring-giver
without a prince, which was imposed on them by necessity;
if a certain one of the Frisians spoke recklessly then
and was reminded of the murderous hate, 1105
then afterwards it had to be the sword's edge.
   The oath was carried out, and splendid gold
was brought from the hoard. The best of the warriors
of the Scylding army was prepared for the pyre;
easily visible at that funeral pyre was 1110
the bloodstained mail-coat, the all-gold boar image,
the boar as hard as iron, and many a nobleman
destroyed by wounds: some men fallen in slaughter.
Hildeburh then requested her own son
to be committed to the blaze at Hnæf's pyre, 1115
to burn the bodies, and in the fire to be placed
at his uncle's shoulder. The woman mourned,

geomrode giddum.   Guðrinc astah.
Wand to wolcnum   wælfyra mæst,
hlynode for hlawe.   Hafelan multon,   1120
bengeato burston   ðonne blod ætspranc,
laðbite lices.   Lig ealle forswealg,
gæsta gifrost,   þara ðe þær guð fornam
bega folces;   wæs hira blæd scacen.

XVII

Gewiton him ða wigend   wica neosian,   1125
freondum befeallen,   Frysland geseon,
hamas ond heaburh.   Hengest ða gyt
wælfagne winter   wunode mid Finne
eal unhlitme;   eard gemunde,
þeah þe he ne meahte   on mere drifan   1130
hringedstefnan.   Holm storme weol,
won wið winde;   winter yþe beleac
isgebinde   oþðæt oþer com
gear in geardas,   swa nu gyt deð,
þa ðe syngales   sele bewitiað   1135
wuldortorhtan weder.   Ða wæs winter scacen:
fæger foldan bearm;   fundode wrecca,
gist of geardum;   he to gyrnwræce
swiðor þohte   þonne to sælade,
gif he torngemot   þurhteon mihte   1140
þæt he Eotena bearn   inne gemunde.
Swa he ne forwyrnde   woroldrædenne
þonne him Hunlafing   hildeleoman,
billa selest   on bearm dyde
þæs wæron mid Eotenum   ecge cuðe.   1145
Swylce ferhðfrecan   Fin eft begeat
sweordbealo sliðen   æt his selfes ham,
siþðan grimne gripe   Guðlaf ond Oslaf
æfter sæsiðe   sorge mændon,
ætwiton weana dæl;   ne meahte wæfre mod   1150
forhabban in hreþre.   Ða wæs heal roden
feonda feorum,   swilce Fin slægen,
cyning on corþre,   ond seo cwen numen.
Sceotend Scyldinga   to scypon feredon
eal ingesteald   eorðcyninges,   1155
swylce hie æt Finnes ham   findan meahton
sigla searogimma.   Hie on sælade
drihtlice wif   to Denum feredon,
læddon to leodum.   Leoð wæs asungen,
gleomannes gyd.   Gamen eft astah,   1160
beorhtode bencsweg,   byrelas sealdon
win of wunderfatum.   Þa cwom Wealhþeo forð
gan under gyldnum beage   þær þa godan twegen

lamented a dirge. The warrior was raised aloft.
The greatest of funeral fires curled to the clouds,
roared in front of the burial mound. The heads melted,   1120
wound-gashes, the grievous wounds of the body, burst
when the blood spurted out. The fire, the greediest of spirits,
completely swallowed up those who had been carried off in war there
from both nations; their glory had passed away.

XVII

The warriors departed, deprived of friends,   1125
to go to their dwelling-places, to see Friesland,
their homes and great strongholds. Hengest still
remained the slaughter-stained winter with Finn
entirely ill-fated; he thought of his homeland,
although he was not able to sail his ring-prowed ship   1130
on the sea. The sea surged with storms,
contended with winds; winter locked the waves
in icy bonds until another year came
to the dwellings, as it still does,
and those times of gloriously bright weather always observe   1135
their proper seasons. Then the winter departed:
the bosom of the earth grew beautiful; the exile and stranger
longed to go from those dwellings; he thought more
about revenge for injury than upon the sea-journey,
if he could bring about a hostile encounter   1140
so that he could bear in mind the sons of the Jutes.
So it was that he did not refuse the law of the world
when Hunlafing placed on his lap
a battle-light, the best of swords,
the edges of which were known to the Jutes.   1145
Thus, a cruel death by the sword afterwards
befell the bold-spirited Finn at his own home,
when Guthlaf and Oslaf, after their sea-journey,
spoke of the savage attack and their sorrows,
blamed him for their share of woes; nor could his restless spirit   1150
be restrained within his heart. Then the hall was made red
with the lives of the enemies, Finn was also killed,
the king among his troop, and the queen was taken.
The Scylding warriors carried to their ships
all of the property belonging to that country's king,   1155
whatever precious gems and jewels they could find
at Finn's home. They carried the noble lady
on a sea-journey to the Danes,
brought her to her people. A lay was sung,
the tale of a minstrel. Revelry arose again,   1160
the noise of the benches resounded brightly, the cup-bearers gave
wine from wondrous vessels. Then Wealhtheow came forward
under a golden circlet to where the two good men,

sæton suhtergefæderan;   þa gyt wæs hiera sib ætgædere,
æghwylc oðrum trywe.   Swylce þær Unferþ þyle   1165
æt fotum sæt frean Scyldinga;   gehwylc hiora his ferhþe treowde –
þæt he hæfde mod micel –   þeah þe he his magum nære
arfæst æt ecga gelacum.   Spræc ða ides Scyldinga:

'Onfoh þissum fulle,   freodrihten min,
sinces brytta.   Þu on sælum wes,   1170
goldwine gumena,   ond to Geatum spræc
mildum wordum,   swa sceal man don.
Beo wið Geatas glæd,   geofena gemyndig
nean ond feorran   þe þu nu hafast.
Me man sægde   þæt þu ðe for sunu wolde   1175
hererinc habban.   Heorot is gefælsod,
beahsele beorhta;   bruc þenden þu mote
manigra medo,   ond þinum magum læf
folc ond rice   þonne ðu forð scyle
metodsceaft seon.   Ic minne can   1180
glædne Hroþulf   þæt he þa geogoðe wile
arum healdan   gyf þu ær þonne he,
wine Scildinga,   worold oflætest;
wene Ic þæt he mid gode   gyldan wille
uncran eaferan,   gif he þæt eal gemon,   1185
hwæt wit to willan   ond to worðmyndum
umborwesendum ær   arna gefremedon.'
    Hwearf þa bi bence   þær hyre byre wæron,
Hreðric ond Hroðmund,   ond hæleþa bearn,
giogoð ætgædere;   þær se goda sæt,   1190
Beowulf Geata,   be þæm gebroðrum twæm.

XVIII

Him wæs ful boren,   ond freondlaþu
wordum bewægned,   ond wunden gold
estum geeawed: earmreade twa,
hrægl ond hringas,   healsbeaga mæst   1195
þara þe Ic on foldan   gefrægen hæbbe.
Nænigne Ic under swegle   selran hyrde
hordmaðum hæleþa,   syþðan Hama ætwæg
to þære byrhtan byrig   Brosinga mene,
sigle ond sincfæt;   searoniðas fealh   1200
Eormenrices;   geceas ecne ræd.
Þone hring hæfde   Higelac Geata,
nefa Swertinges,   nyhstan siðe
siðþan he under segne   sinc ealgode,
wælreaf werede;   hyne wyrd fornam   1205
syþðan he for wlenco   wean ahsode:
fæhðe to Frysum.   He þa frætwe wæg,
eorclanstanas   ofer yða ful

nephew and uncle, sat; there was peace between them still,
each was true to the other. The spokesman Unferth was also there   1165
sat at the feet of the lord of the Scyldings; each of them trusted his spirit –
that he had great courage – even though he had not been
merciful to his kinsmen in the play of the sword's edge. The lady of the
    Scyldings spoke:
  'Take this cup, my noble lord,
giver of treasure. Be joyful,   1170
gold-giving friend of men, and speak to the Geats
with well-disposed words, as a man should do.
Be gracious to the Geats, mindful of the gifts
that you now have from near and afar.
Someone told me that you would have this warrior   1175
as a son. Heorot is cleansed,
the bright ring-hall; make use of the many rewards
while you can, and leave the people and kingdom
to your kinsmen when you have to pass on
to discover your destiny. I know that   1180
my gracious Hrothulf will treat the youths
honourably if you leave the world
earlier than he does, friend of the Scyldings;
I believe that he will generously repay our sons
with goodness, if he recalls it all,   1185
what we two previously did in the way of favours
for pleasure and for honour when he was a child.'
  Then she turned to the bench where her two sons were,
Hrethric and Hrothmund, and the sons of warriors,
a band of young warriors together; the good man,   1190
Beowulf of the Geats, sat there by the two brothers.

XVIII

The cup was carried to him, and a friendly invitation
was offered in words, and twisted gold
was presented with good will: two arm-ornaments,
a garment and rings, the greatest neck-ring   1195
on earth that I have heard of.
I have not heard of better heroes' treasures
under the sky, since Hama carried off
the Brosings' necklace, the jewel and precious setting,
to the magnificent city; he endured the cunning hostility   1200
of Eormenric; he chose eternal gain.
Hygelac of the Geats, grandson of Swerting,
had that necklace with him on his last expedition
when he defended the treasure under the standard,
protected the booty from the slain; fate carried him off   1205
after he sought out trouble because of his pride:
a feud with the Frisians. The mighty prince took those adornments,
those precious stones over the cup of the waves;

rice þeoden;   he under rande gecranc.
Gehwearf þa in Francna fæþm   feorh cyninges,   1210
breostgewædu   ond se beah somod;
wyrsan wigfrecan   wæl reafeden
æfter guðsceare;   Geata leode,
hreawic heoldon.   Heal swege onfeng.
Wealhðeo maþelode;   heo fore þæm werede spræc: 1215
'Bruc ðisses beages,   Beowulf leofa,
hyse, mid hæle,   ond þisses hrægles neot,
þeodgestreona,   ond geþeoh tela,
cen þec mid cræfte,   ond þyssum cnyhtum wes
lara liðe.   Ic þe þæs lean geman.   1220
Hafast þu gefered   þæt ðe feor ond neah
ealne wideferhþ   weras ehtigað,
efne swa side   swa sæ bebugeð,
windgeard weallas.   Wes þenden þu lifige
æþeling eadig.   Ic þe an tela   1225
sincgestreona.   Beo þu suna minum
dædum gedefe,   dream healdende.
Her is æghwylc eorl   oþrum getrywe,
modes milde,   mandrihtne hold;
þegnas syndon geþwære,   þeod ealgearo,   1230
druncne dryhtguman,   doð swa Ic bidde.'
    Eode þa to setle.   Þær wæs symbla cyst,
druncon win weras.   Wyrd ne cuþon,
geosceaft grimne,   swa hit agangen wearð
eorla manegum   syþðan æfen cwom   1235
ond him Hroþgar gewat   to hofe sinum
rice to ræste.   Reced weardode
unrim eorla,   swa hie oft ær dydon.
Bencþelu beredon;   hit geondbræded wearð
beddum ond bolstrum.   Beorscealca sum   1240
fus ond fæge   fletræste gebeag.
Setton him to heafdon   hilderandas,
bordwudu beorhtan;   þær on bence wæs
ofer æþelinge   yþgesene
heaþosteapa helm,   hringed byrne,   1245
þrecwudu þrymlic.   Wæs þeaw hyra
þæt hie oft wæron   an wig gearwe,
ge æt ham ge on herge   ge gehwæþer þara
efne swylce mæla   swylce hira mandryhtne
þearf gesælde.   Wæs seo þeod tilu.   1250

he died under his shield.
The body of the king passed into the hands of the Franks,   1210
the corslet and the circlet too;
less worthy warriors plundered those killed
after the slaughter of battle; the people of the Geats
occupied the place of corpses. The hall was filled with sound.
Wealhtheow made a speech; she spoke before the company: 1215
'Enjoy this circlet, beloved young Beowulf,
and with luck, use this mail-coat,
the people's treasure, and prosper well,
show yourself with strength, and be kind to my boys
with your advice. I shall remember your reward for this.   1220
You have brought it about that you will be praised among men
near and far for ever,
even as widely as the sea, the home of the wind,
flows round the cliffs. Be fortunate for as long as you live,
prince. I wish well for you   1225
a wealth of treasures. Be kind in the things you do
for my sons, joyful man.
Here, every warrior is true to the other,
kind in heart, loyal to their liege lord;
the thanes are united, the troop is fully prepared,   1230
the noble warriors, having drunk to it, will do as I ask.'
     Then she went to her seat. There was the best of feasts,
men drank wine. They did not know the fate,
the grim destiny, that was to come about
for many of the warriors once evening came,   1235
and once Hrothgar, the powerful one, had gone
to his dwelling to his place of rest. The hall was guarded
by a countless number of warriors, just as they had often done before.
The benches were cleared; bedding and pillows
were spread over the floor. One beer-drinker,   1240
ripe for death, lay down on a couch in the hall.
They set their shields by their heads,
their shining shields; there on the bench,
above a nobleman, was clearly seen
a helmet towering in battle, a corslet formed of rings,   1245
and a mighty spear. It was their custom
that they should be constantly ready for war,
both at home and abroad, and any time,
wherever their liege lord
had need of them. It was a good nation.   1250

Judith

   ...tweode gifena
in ðys ginnan grunde;   heo ðær ða gearwe funde
mundbyrd æt ðam mæran Þeodne,   þa heo ahte mæste þearfe
hyldo þæs hehstan Deman,   þæt he hie wið þæs hehstan brogan
gefriðode, frymða Waldend.   Hyre ðæs Fæder on roderum   5
torhtmod tiðe gefremede,   þe heo ahte trumne geleafan
a to ðam Ælmihtigan.   Gefrægen Ic ða Olofernus
winhatan wyrcean georne   ond eallum wundrum þrymlic
girwan up swæsendo;   to ðam het se gumena baldor
ealle ða yldestan ðegnas.   Hie ðæt ofstum miclum   10
ræfndon rondwiggende;   comon to ðam rican þeodne
feran, folces ræswan.   Þæt wæs þy feorðan dogore
þæs ðe Judith hyne,   gleaw on geðonce,
ides ælfscinu,   ærest gesohte.

X

Hie ða to ðam symble   sittan eodon,   15
wlance to wingedrince,   ealle his weagesiðas,
bealde byrnwiggende.   Þær wæron bollan steape
boren æfter bencum gelome,   swylce eac bunan ond orcas
fulle fletsittendum.   Hie þæt fæge þægon,
rofe rondwiggende,   þeah ðæs se rica ne wende,   20
egesful eorla dryhten.   Ða wearð Olofernus,
goldwine gumena,   on gytesalum.
Hloh ond hlydde,   hlynede ond dynede,
þæt mihten fira bearn   feorran gehyran
hu se stiðmoda   styrmde ond gylede;   25
modig ond medugal,   manode geneahhe
bencsittende   þæt hi gebærdon wel.
Swa se inwidda,   ofer ealne dæg,
dryhtguman sine   drencte mid wine,
swiðmod sinces brytta,   oðþæt hie on swiman lagon,   30
oferdrencte his duguðe ealle,   swylce hie wæron deaðe geslegene,
agotene goda gehwylces.   Swa het se gumena aldor
fylgan fletsittendum,   oðþæt fira bearnum
nealæhte niht seo þystre.   Het ða niða geblonden
þa eadigan mægð   ofstum fetigan   35
to his bedreste,   beagum gehlæste,
hringum gehrodene.   Hie hraðe fremedon,
anbyhtscealcas,   swa him heora ealdor bebead,
byrnwigena brego.   Bearhtme stopon
to ðam gysterne   þær hie Judithe   40
fundon ferhðgleawe,   ond ða fromlice
lindwiggende   lædan ongunnon
   ꞇ torhtan mægð   to træfe þam hean,

Judith

... She doubted
gifts in this wide earth; there she readily found
protection from the glorious Lord, when she had most need
of favour from the highest Judge, so that he, the Lord of creation,
defended her against the greatest terror. The glorious Father in the skies   5
granted her request, since she always possessed true faith
in the Almighty. I have heard then that Holofernes
eagerly issued invitations to a feast and provided all types of
magnificent wonders for the banquets; to it the lord of men summoned
the most experienced retainers. The warriors obeyed   10
with great haste; they came to the powerful lord and
proceeded to the leader of people. That was the fourth day
after Judith, prudent in mind,
this woman of elfin beauty, first visited him.

X

They went into the feast to sit down,   15
proud men at the wine-drinking, bold mail-coated warriors,
all his companions in misfortune. There, along the benches,
deep bowls were carried frequently; full cups and pitchers
were also carried to the sitters in the hall. They received those, doomed to die,
brave warriors, though the powerful man did not expect it,   20
that terrible lord of heroes. Then Holofernes,
the gold-giving friend of his men, became joyous from the drinking.
He laughed and grew vociferous, roared and clamoured,
so that the children of men could hear from far away,
how the fierce one stormed and yelled;   25
arrogant and excited by mead, he frequently admonished
the guests that they enjoy themselves well.
So, for the entire day, the wicked one,
the stern dispenser of treasures,
drenched his retainers with wine until they lay unconscious,   30
the whole of his troop were as drunk as if they had been struck down in death,
drained of every ability. So, the men's lord commanded
the guests to be served, until the dark night approached
the children of men. Then corrupted by evil,
he commanded that the blessed maiden should be hastily fetched   35
to his bed, adorned with bracelets,
decorated with rings. The retainers quickly did
as their lord, the ruler of warriors,
commanded them. They stepped into the tumult
of the guest-hall where they found the wise Judith,   40
and then quickly
the warriors began to lead the
illustrious maiden to the lofty tent,

þær se rica hyne   reste on symbel
nihtes inne,   Nergende lað,   45
Olofernus.   Þær wæs eallgylden
fleohnet fæger   ymbe þæs folctogan
bed ahongen,   þæt se bealofulla
mihte wlitan þurh,   wigena baldor,
on æghwylcne   þe ðærinne com   50
hæleða bearna,   ond on hyne nænig
monna cynnes,   nymðe se modiga hwæne
niðe rofra   him þe near hete
rinca to rune gegangan.   Hie ða on reste gebrohton
snude ða snoteran idese.   Eodon ða stercedferhðe,   55
hæleð heora hearran cyðan   þæt wæs seo halige meowle
gebroht on his burgetelde.   Þa wearð se brema on mode
bliðe, burga ealdor: þohte ða beorhtan idese
mid widle ond mid womme besmitan.   Ne wolde þæt wuldres Dema
geðafian, þrymmes Hyrde,   ac he him þæs ðinges gestyrde,   60
Dryhten, dugeða Waldend.   Gewat ða se deofulcunda,
galferhð gumena ðreate
bealofull his beddes neosan,   þær he sceolde his blæd forleosan
ædre binnan anre nihte.   Hæfde ða his ende gebidenne
on eorðan unswæslicne,   swylcne he ær æfter worhte,   65
þearlmod ðeoden gumena,   þenden he on ðysse worulde
wunode under wolcna hrofe.   Gefeol ða wine swa druncen
se rica on his reste middan,   swa he nyste ræda nanne
on gewitlocan.   Wiggend stopon
ut of ðam inne   ofstum miclum,   70
weras winsade,   þe ðone wærlogan,
laðne leodhatan,   læddon to bedde
nehstan siðe.   Þa wæs Nergendes
þeowen þrymful   þearle gemyndig
hu heo þone atolan   eaðost mihte   75
ealdre benæman,   ær se unsyfra,
womfull, onwoce.   Genam ða wundenlocc
Scyppendes mægð,   scearpne mece,
scurum heardne,   ond of sceaðe abræd
swiðran folme.   Ongan ða swegles Weard   80
be naman nemnan,   Nergend ealra
woruldbuendra,   ond þæt word acwæð:
    'Ic ðe, frymða God   ond frofre Gæst,
Bearn Alwaldan,   biddan wylle
miltse þinre   me þearfendre,   85
Ðrynesse ðrym.   Þearle ys me nu ða
heorte onhæted,   ond hige geomor,
swyðe mid sorgum gedrefed.   Forgif me, swegles Ealdor,
sigor ond soðne geleafan   þæt Ic mid þys sweorde mote
geheawan þysne morðres bryttan.   Geunne me minra gesynta,   90
þearlmod Þeoden gumena: nahte Ic þinre næfre

where the powerful man Holofernes, hateful to the Saviour,
rested himself during the night.   45
There was a beautiful
all-golden fly-net that the commander
had hung around the bed, so that the wicked one
the lord of warriors, could look through
on each of those sons of men who came in there,   50
but not one of the race of mankind could look
on him, unless, brave man, he commanded one
of his very iniquitous men to come
nearer to him for secret consultation. They quickly brought to bed
the prudent woman. Then the resolute heroes   55
went to inform their lord that the holy maiden
had been brought into his tent. Then the notorious one, that lord of cities,
became happy in his mind: he intended to violate
the bright woman with defilement and with sin. The Judge of glory,
the majestic Guardian, the Lord, Ruler of hosts, would not consent to that,   60
but he prevented him from that thing. Then the diabolical one,
the wanton and wicked man, departed
with a troop of his men to find his bed, where he would lose his life
forthwith within that one night. He had attained his violent end
on earth, just as he had previously deserved,   65
this severe lord of men, since he had dwelled under the roof
of clouds in this world. The mighty man then fell into the middle
of his bed, so drunk with wine that he possessed no sense
in his mind. The warriors stepped
out from that place with great haste,   70
men sated with wine, who led the traitor,
that hateful tyrant, to bed
for the last time. Then the Saviour's
glorious handmaiden was very mindful
of how she could deprive the terrible one   75
of life most easily, before the impure and
foul one awoke. Then the Creator's maiden,
with her braided locks, took a sharp sword,
a hard weapon in the storms of battle, and drew it from the sheath
with her right hand. She began to call the Guardian of heaven   80
by name, the Saviour of all
the inhabitants of earth, and said these words:
    'God of creation, Spirit of comfort,
Son of the Almighty, I want to beseech you
for your mercy on me in my time of need,   85
glorious Trinity. My heart is intensely
inflamed within me now, and my mind is troubled,
greatly afflicted with sorrows. Give me, Lord of heaven,
victory and true belief so I might cut down this bestower of torment
with this sword. Grant me my salvation,   90
mighty Lord of men: I have never had more need

miltse þon maran þearfe.   Gewrec nu, mihtig Dryhten,
torhtmod tires Brytta,   þæt me ys þus torne on mode,
hate on hreðre minum.'   Hi ða se hehsta Dema
ædre mid elne onbryrde,   swa he deð anra gehwylcne   95
herbuendra   þe hyne him to helpe seceð
mid ræde ond mid rihte geleafan.   Þa wearð hyre rume on mode,
haligre hyht geniwod.   Genam ða þone hæðenan mannan
fæste be feaxe sinum,   teah hyne folmum wið hyre weard
bysmerlice,   ond þone bealofullan   100
listum alede,   laðne mannan,
swa heo ðæs unlædan   eaðost mihte
wel gewealdan.   Sloh ða wundenlocc
þone feondsceaðan   fagum mece,
heteþoncolne,   þæt heo healfne forcearf   105
þone sweoran him,   þæt he on swiman læg,
druncen ond dolhwund.   Næs ða dead þa gyt,
ealles orsawle.   Sloh ða eornoste
ides ellenrof   oþre siðe
þone hæðenan hund,   þæt him þæt heafod wand   110
forð on ða flore.   Læg se fula leap
gesne beæftan;   gæst ellor hwearf
under neowelne næs   ond ðær genyðerad wæs,
susle gesæled   syððan æfre,
wyrmum bewunden,   witum gebunden,   115
hearde gehæfted   in hellebryne
æfter hinsiðe.   Ne ðearf he hopian no,
þystrum forðylmed,   þæt he ðonan mote
of ðam wyrmsele,   ac ðær wunian sceal
awa to aldre   butan ende forð   120
in ðam heolstran ham,   hyhtwynna leas.

XI

Hæfde ða gefohten   foremærne blæd
Judith æt guðe,   swa hyre God uðe,
swegles Ealdor,   þe hyre sigores onleah.
Þa seo snotere mægð   snude gebrohte   125
þæs herewæðan   heafod swa blodig
on ðam fætelse   þe hyre foregenga,
blachleor ides,   hyra begea nest;
ðeawum geðungen   þyder on lædde,
ond hit þa swa heolfrig   hyre on hond ageaf,   130
higeþoncolre,   ham to berenne,
Judith gingran sinre.   Eodon ða gegnum þanonne
þa idesa ba   ellenþriste,
oðþæt hie becomon,   collenferhðe,
eadhreðige mægð,   ut of ðam herige   135
þæt hie sweotollice   geseon mihten
þære wlitegan byrig   weallas blican,

of your mercy than now. Avenge now, mighty Lord,
eminent Bestower of glory, that which is so grievous in my mind,
so fervent in my heart.' Then the highest Judge
inspired her immediately with great zeal, as he does to each   95
of the dwellers on earth who seek help from him
with reason and with true faith. Then she felt relief in her mind,
hope was renewed for the holy woman. She seized the heathen man
securely by his hair, pulled him shamefully towards her
with her hands, and skilfully placed   100
the wicked and loathsome man
so that she could most easily manage the miserable one
well. Then, the woman with braided locks struck
the enemy, that hostile one,
with the shining sword, so that she cut through half   105
of his neck, such that he lay unconscious,
drunk and wounded. He was not dead yet,
not entirely lifeless. The courageous woman
struck the heathen hound energetically
another time so that his head rolled   110
forwards on the floor. The foul body lay
behind, dead; the spirit departed elsewhere
under the deep earth and was oppressed there
and fettered in torment forever after,
wound round with serpents, bound with punishments,   115
cruelly imprisoned in hell-fire
after his departure. Enveloped in darkness,
he had no need at all to hope that he should get out from
that serpent-hall, but there he must remain
always and forever, henceforth without end,   120
in that dark home deprived of the joy of hope.

XI

Judith had won illustrious glory
in the battle as God, the Lord of heaven,
granted it so when he gave her her victory.
Then the prudent woman immediately placed   125
the warrior's head still bloody
into the sack in which her attendant,
a woman of pale complexion, an excellent handmaiden,
had brought food for them both; and then Judith
put it, all gory, into the hands of her   130
thoughtful servant to carry home.
Then both the courageous women
went from there straightaway,
until the triumphant women, elated,
got away out from that army   135
so that they could clearly see
the beautiful city walls of Bethulia

Bethuliam. Hie ða beahhrodene
feðelaste   forð onettan,
oð hie glædmode   gegan hæfdon   140
to ðam wealgate. Wiggend sæton,
weras wæccende   wearde heoldon
in ðam fæstenne,   swa ðam folce ær
geomormodum   Judithe bebead,
searoðoncol mægð,   þa heo on sið gewat,   145
ides ellenrof. Wæs ða eft cumen
leof to leodum,   ond ða lungre het
gleawhydig wif   gumena sumne
of ðære ginnan byrig   hyre togeanes gan,
ond hi ofostlice   in forlæton   150
þurh ðæs wealles geat;   ond þæt word acwæð
to ðam sigefolce: 'Ic eow secgan mæg
þoncwyrðe þing   þæt ge ne þyrfen leng
murnan on mode. Eow ys Metod bliðe,
cyninga Wuldor. Þæt gecyðed wearð   155
geond woruld wide   þæt eow ys wuldorblæd
torhtlic toweard   ond tir gifeðe
þara læðða   þe ge lange drugon.'
    Þa wurdon bliðe   burhsittende
syððan hi gehyrdon   hu seo halige spræc   160
ofer heanne weall. Here wæs on lustum,
wið þæs fæstengeates   folc onette,
weras wif somod,   wornum ond heapum,
ðreatum ond ðrymmum   þrungon ond urnon
ongean ða Þeodnes mægð   þusendmælum,   165
ealde ge geonge. Æghwylcum wearð
men on ðære medobyrig   mod areted
syððan hie ongeaton   þæt wæs Judith cumen
eft to eðle;   ond ða ofostlice
hie mid eaðmedum   in forleton.   170
    þa seo gleawe het,   golde gefrætewod,
hyre ðinenne   þancolmode
þæs herewæðan   heafod onwriðan
ond hyt to behðe   blodig ætywan
þam burhleodum   hu hyre æt beaduwe gespeow.   175
Spræc ða seo æðele   to eallum þam folce:
'Her ge magon sweotole,   sigerofe hæleð,
leoda ræswan,   on ðæs laðestan
hæðenes heaðorinces   heafod starian,
Olofernus   unlyfigendes,   180
þe us monna mæst   morðra gefremede,
sarra sorga,   ond þæt swyðor gyt
ycan wolde;   ac him ne uðe God
lengran lifes   þæt he mid læððum us
eglan moste. Ic him ealdor oðþrong   185

glitter. Then, ring-adorned,
they hurried forwards along the path
until, glad at heart, they had reached   140
the rampart gate. Warriors were sitting,
men watching, and keeping guard
in that stronghold, just as Judith the wise maiden
had asked, when she had previously
departed from the sorrowful people,   145
the courageous woman. The beloved woman had returned again
to the people, and the prudent woman
soon asked one of the men
from the spacious city to come towards her,
and hastily to let them in   150
through the gate of the city-wall; and she spoke these words
to the victorious people: 'I am able to tell you
a memorable thing so that you need no longer
mourn in your minds. The Ruler, the Glory of kings,
is well disposed towards you. It has become revealed   155
throughout this wide world that glorious and triumphant success
is approaching and that honour has been granted by fate to you
because of the afflictions that you have long suffered.'
      Then the city-dwellers were joyful
when they heard how the holy one spoke   160
over the high city-wall. The army was joyous
and people hurried to the fortress gate,
men and women, in multitudes and crowds,
groups and troops pressed forward and ran
towards the Lord's maiden in their thousands,   165
old and young. The mind of each one of the people
in that rejoicing city was gladdened
when they perceived that Judith had returned
to her native land; and then hastily
and reverently, they let her in.   170
      Then the prudent woman, adorned with gold, asked
her attentive handmaiden
to uncover the warrior's head
and to display it, bloodied, as proof
to the citizens of how she had been helped in battle.   175
Then the noble woman spoke to all the people:
'Victorious heroes, here you can gaze clearly
on the leader of the people, on this head
of the most hateful of heathen warriors,
of the unliving Holofernes,   180
who, among men, inflicted on us the worst torments,
grievous afflictions, and wished to add to these
even more; but God would not grant him
a longer life so that he could plague us
with wrongs. I deprived him of life   185

þurh Godes fultum.   Nu Ic gumena gehwæne
þyssa burgleoda   biddan wylle,
randwiggendra,   þæt ge recene eow
fysan to gefeohte,   syððan frymða God,
arfæst Cyning,   eastan sende   190
leohtne leoman.   Berað linde forð,
bord for breostum   ond byrnhomas,
scire helmas,   in sceaðena gemong;
fyllan folctogan   fagum sweordum,
fæge frumgaras.   Fynd syndon eowere   195
gedemed to deaðe,   ond ge dom agon,
tir æt tohtan,   swa eow getacnod hafað
mihtig Dryhten   þurh mine hand.'
     Þa wearð snelra werod   snude gegearewod,
cenra to campe.   Stopon cynerofe   200
secgas ond gesiðas;   bæron sigeþufas;
foron to gefeohte   forð on gerihte,
hæleð under helmum,   of ðære haligan byrig
on ðæt dægred sylf.   Dynedan scildas,
hlude hlummon.   Þæs se hlanca gefeah   205
wulf in walde,   ond se wanna hrefn,
wælgifre fugel;   wistan begen
þæt him ða þeodguman   þohton tilian
fylle on fægum;   ac him fleah on last
earn ætes georn,   urigfeðera,   210
salowigpada;   sang hildeleoð,
hyrnednebba.   Stopon heaðorincas,
beornas to beadowe,   bordum beðeahte,
hwealfum lindum,   þa ðe hwile ær
elþeodigra   edwit þoledon,   215
hæðenra hosp.   Him þæt hearde wearð
æt ðam æscplegan   eallum forgolden,
Assyrium,   syððan Ebreas
under guðfanum   gegan hæfdon
to ðam fyrdwicum.   Hie ða fromlice   220
leton forð fleogan   flana scuras,
hildenædran   of hornbogan,
strælas stedehearde.   Styrmdon hlude
grame guðfrecan,   garas sendon
in heardra gemang.   Hæleð wæron yrre,   225
landbuende,   laðum cynne,
stopon styrnmode,   stercedferhðe,
wrehton unsofte   ealdgeniðlan
medowerige.   Mundum brugdon
scealcas of sceaðum   scirmæled swyrd,   230
ecgum gecoste,   slogon eornoste
Assiria   oretmæcgas,
niðhycgende.   Nanne ne sparedon

through God's help. Now I intend to ask
each of the men of these citizens,
each of the warriors, that you immediately
hasten to battle, as soon as the God of creation,
that glorious King, sends his radiant beam of light   190
from the east. Go forward carrying shields,
shields in front of your breasts and corslets,
gleaming helmets, into the troop of enemies;
fell the commanders, those leaders doomed to die
with shining swords. Your enemies   195
are condemned to death, and you will possess glory,
honour in conflict, just as mighty God has
given you that sign by my hand.'
        Then a host of brave and keen men prepared quickly
for the battle. Noble warriors and retainers   200
stepped out; they carried triumphant banners;
heroes in helmets went forward to battle straightaway
from that holy city
at dawn of that same day. Shields clashed,
resounded loudly. The lean wolf rejoiced   205
in the forest, as did the dark raven,
a bloodthirsty bird: they both knew
that the warriors intended to provide them
with a feast from those doomed to die; but behind them flew
the eagle eager for food, dewy-winged   210
with dark plumage; the horn-beaked bird
sang a battle-song. The warriors advanced,
men to battle, protected by shields,
hollow wooden shields, those who previously
had suffered the insolence of foreigners,   215
the insult of heathens. In the spear-play,
that was all grievously requited to
the Assyrians, when the Israelites
under their battle-banners had gone
to that camp. Then they boldly   220
let showers of arrows fly forwards,
battle arrows from horned bows,
firm arrows. Angry warriors
roared loudly, sent spears
into the midst of the cruel ones. The native heroes   225
were angry against the hateful race,
resolute, they marched, determined,
they violently aroused their ancient enemies
who were drunk with mead. With their hands,
the retainers drew brightly adorned swords from their sheaths,   230
excellent sword-edges, zealously killed
the Assyrian warriors,
those evil schemers. They did not spare one

þæs herefolces,   heanne ne ricne,
cwicera manna   þe hie ofercuman mihton.   235

XII

Swa ða magoþegnas   on ða morgentid
ehton elðeoda   ealle þrage,
oðþæt ongeaton   ða ðe grame wæron,
ðæs herefolces   heafodweardas,
þæt him swyrdgeswing   swiðlic eowdon   240
weras Ebrisce.   Hie wordum þæt
þam yldestan   ealdorþegnum
cyðan eodon,   wrehton cumbolwigan
ond him forhtlice   færspel bodedon,
medowerigum   morgencollan,   245
atolne ecgplegan.   Þa Ic ædre gefrægn
slegefæge hæleð   slæpe tobredon,
ond wið þæs bealofullan   burgeteldes
weras werigferhðe   hwearfum þringan,
Olofernus.   Hogedon aninga   250
hyra hlaforde   hilde bodian,
ær ðon ðe him se egesa   on ufan sæte,
mægen Ebrea.   Mynton ealle
þæt se beorna brego   ond seo beorhte mægð
in ðam wlitegan træfe   wæron ætsomne: 255
Judith seo æðele,   ond se galmoda,
egesfull ond afor.   Næs ðeah eorla nan
þe ðone wiggend   aweccan dorste
oððe gecunnian   hu ðone cumbolwigan
wið ða halgan mægð   hæfde geworden,   260
Metodes meowlan.   Mægen nealæhte,
folc Ebrea;   fuhton þearle
heardum heoruwæpnum,   hæste guldon
hyra fyrngeflitu,   fagum swyrdum,
ealde æfðoncan.   Assyria wearð   265
on ðam dægeweorce   dom geswiðrod,
bælc forbiged.   Beornas stodon
ymbe hyra þeodnes træf   þearle gebylde,
sweorcendferhðe.   Hi ða somod ealle
ongunnon cohhetan,   cirman hlude   270
ond gristbitian,   gode orfeorme,
mid toðon torn þoligende.   Þa wæs hyra tires æt ende,
eades ond ellendæda.   Hogedon þa eorlas
aweccan hyra winedryhten;   him wiht ne speow.
    Þa wearð sið ond late   sum to ðam arod   275
þara beadorinca   þæt he in þæt burgeteld
niðheard neðde,   swa hyne nyd fordraf.
Funde ða on bedde   blacne licgan
his goldgifan   gæstes gesne,

man's life from that army, neither the
lowly nor the powerful whom they could overcome.   235

XII

So, in the morning, the retainers
pursued the foreign people the entire time,
until the chief leaders of that army,
of those who were the enemies, perceived
that the Hebrew men had shown violent sword-brandishing   240
to them. They went to reveal
all that in words to the most
senior retainers, and they aroused the warriors
and announced fearfully to those drunk with mead
the dreadful news, the morning's terror,   245
the terrible battle. Then, I have heard, immediately
the warriors, doomed to perish, cast off sleep,
and the subdued men thronged in crowds
to the tent of the wicked man,
Holofernes. They intended to announce   250
the battle to their lord at once,
before the terrible force of the Israelites
came down on them. They all supposed
that the leader of the warriors and the bright maiden
were together in that beautiful tent: 255
Judith the noble one, and the licentious one,
terrible and fierce. There was not a single one of the men
who dared to wake the warrior
or inquire how the warrior
had got on with the holy maiden,   260
the Lord's woman. The armed force of the Israelites
approached; they fought vigorously
with hard swords, violently requited
their ancient grudges, that old conflict,
with shining swords. The Assyrians'   265
glory was destroyed in that day's work,
their pride humbled. Warriors stood
about their lord's tent very uneasy
and sombre in spirit. Then together they all
began to cough, to cry out loudly,   270
to gnash their teeth, suffering grief,
to no avail. Then their glory, success and brave deeds
were at an end. The men considered how to awaken
their lord; it did them no good.

    It got later and later when one of the warriors   275
became bold in that he daringly risked going
into the tent, as need compelled him to.
He found on the bed his pale lord,
lying deprived of spirit,

lifes belidenne.   He þa lungre gefeoll   280
freorig to foldan,   ongan his feax teran,
hreoh on mode,   ond his hrægl somod,
ond þæt word acwæð   to ðam wiggendum
þe ðær unrote   ute wæron:
'Her ys geswutelod   ure sylfra forwyrd,   285
toweard getacnod,   þæt þære tide ys
mid niðum neah geðrungen,   þe we sculon nu losian,
somod æt sæcce forweorðan.   Her lið sweorde geheawen,
beheafdod healdend ure.'   Hi ða hreowigmode
wurpon hyra wæpen ofdune,   gewitan him werigferhðe,   290
on fleam sceacan.   Him mon feaht on last,
mægeneacen folc,   oð se mæsta dæl
þæs heriges læg   hilde gesæged
on ðam sigewonge,   sweordum geheawen
wulfum to willan   ond eac wælgifrum   295
fuglum to frofre.   Flugon ða ðe lyfdon,
laðra linde.   Him on laste for
sweot Ebrea,   sigore geweorðod,
dome gedyrsod.   Him feng Dryhten God
fægre on fultum,   Frea ælmihtig.   300
Hi ða fromlice   fagum swyrdum,
hæleð higerofe,   herpað worhton
þurh laðra gemong;   linde heowon,
scildburh scæron.   Sceotend wæron
guðe gegremede,   guman Ebrisce,   305
þegnas on ða tid   þearle gelyste
gargewinnes.   Þær on greot gefeoll
se hyhsta dæl   heafodgerimes
Assiria   ealdorduguðe,
laðan cynnes.   Lythwon becom   310
cwicera to cyððe.   Cirdon cynerofe,
wiggend on wiðertrod,   wælscel on innan,
reocende hræw.   Rum wæs to nimanne
londbuendum   on ðam laðestan,
hyra ealdfeondum   unlyfigendum   315
heolfrig herereaf,   hyrsta scyne,
bord ond bradswyrd,   brune helmas,
dyre madmas.   Hæfdon domlice
on ðam folcstede   fynd oferwunnen
eðelweardas,   ealdhettende,   320
swyrdum aswefede.   Hie on swaðe reston,
þa ðe him to life   laðost wæron
cwicera cynna.   Þa seo cneoris eall,
mægða mærost,   anes monðes fyrst,
wlanc, wundenlocc,   wægon ond læddon   325
to ðære beorhtan byrig   Bethuliam,
helmas ond hupseax,   hare byrnan,

devoid of life. Immediately, he fell   280
frozen to the floor, and began to tear at his hair
and clothing, wild in mind,
and he spoke these words to the warriors
who were outside, dejected:
'Here our own destruction is made clear,   285
the future signified, that the time of troubles
is pressing near when we shall now lose,
shall perish at the battle together. Here lies our protector
cut down and beheaded by the sword.' Sorrowful, they
threw their weapons down then, and departed from him weary-spirited   290
to hasten in flight. The mighty people
fought them from behind, until the greatest part
of the army lay destroyed in battle
on that field of victory, cut down by swords
as a pleasure for the wolves and also as a joy   295
to bloodthirsty birds. Those who still lived fled
from the wooden weapons of their enemies. Behind them
came the army of the Hebrews, honoured with victory,
glorified with that judgement. The Lord God, the almighty Lord,
helped them generously with his aid.   300
Then quickly the valiant heroes
made a war-path through the hateful enemies
with their shining swords; cut down shields,
and penetrated the shield-wall. The Hebrew missile-throwers
were enraged in the battle,   305
the retainers at that time greatly desired
a battle of spears. There in the sand fell
the greatest part of the total number
of leaders of the Assyrians,
that hateful nation. Few returned   310
alive to their native land. The brave warriors
turned back to retreat among the carnage,
the reeking corpses. There was an opportunity for
the native inhabitants to seize from the most hateful
ancient enemies, the unliving ones,   315
bloody plunder, beautiful ornaments,
shield and broad sword, shining helmets,
precious treasures. The guardians of the country
had gloriously conquered their foes,
the ancient enemy, on that battlefield,   320
executed them with swords. Those who had been
the most hateful of living men while alive
rested in their tracks. Then the entire nation,
the greatest of tribes, the proud braided-haired ones,
for the space of one month carried and led   325
to the bright city of Bethulia
helmets and hip-swords, grey corslets,

guðsceorp gumena   golde gefrætewod,
mærra madma   ma þonne mon ænig
asecgan mæge   searoþoncelra.   330
Eal þæt ða ðeodguman   þrymme geeodon,
cene under cumblum   ond compwige
þurh Judithe   gleawe lare,
mægð modigre.   Hi to mede hyre
of ðam siðfate   sylfre brohton,   335
eorlas æscrofe   Olofernes
sweord ond swatigne helm,   swylce eac side byrnan
gerenode readum golde,   ond eal þæt se rinca baldor
swiðmod sinces ahte   oððe sundoryrfes,
beaga ond beorhtra maðma;   hi þæt þære beorhtan idese   340
ageafon gearoþoncolre.   Ealles ðæs Judith sægde
wuldor weroda Dryhtne,   þe hyre weorðmynde geaf,
mærðe on moldan rice,   swylce eac mede on heofonum,
sigorlean in swegles wuldre,   þæs ðe heo ahte soðne geleafan
to ðam Ælmihtigan.   Huru æt ðam ende ne tweode   345
þæs leanes þe heo lange gyrnde.   Þæs sy ðam leofan Dryhtne
wuldor to widan aldre,   þe gesceop wind ond lyfte,
roderas ond rume grundas,   swylce eac reðe streamas
ond swegles dreamas   þurh his sylfes miltse.

men's armour decorated with gold,
more illustrious treasures than any man
among the wise could say.   330
All of that was earned by the warriors' glory,
bold under the banners and in battle
through the prudent counsel of Judith,
the daring maiden. The brave warriors
brought as her reward from that expedition   335
the sword of Holofernes and his gory helmet,
and likewise his ample mail-coat
adorned with red gold, and everything that the arrogant
lord of warriors owned by way of treasures or personal heirlooms,
rings and bright riches; they gave that to the bright   340
and ready-witted woman. For all of this Judith said
thanks to the Lord of hosts, who had given her honour
and glory in the kingdom of this earth, and also as her reward in heaven,
the reward of victory in heaven's glory, because she possessed true faith
in the Almighty. Indeed, at the end she did not doubt   345
in the reward which she had long yearned for. For that be glory
to the beloved Lord for ever and ever, who created wind and air,
the heavens and spacious earth, likewise the raging seas
and joys of heaven through his own individual grace.

From London, British Library, Cotton Caligula A.IX

The Owl and the Nightingale

Ich was in one sumere dale,
In one suþe diȝele hale,
Iherde Ich holde grete tale
An Hule and one Niȝtingale.
Þat plait was stif and starc and strong,   5
Sum wile softe and lud among;
An aiþer aȝen oþer sval,
And let þat uvole mod ut al.
And eiþer seide of oþeres custe
Þat alre-worste þat hi wuste: 10
And hure and hure of oþeres songe
Hi holde plaiding suþe stronge.
   Þe Niȝtingale bigon þe speche
In one hurne of one breche,
And sat up one vaire boȝe,   15
Þar were abute blosme inoȝe,
In ore waste þicke hegge
Imeind mid spire and grene segge.
Ho was þe gladur vor þe rise,
And song a vele cunne wise: 20
Bet þuȝte þe dreim þat he were
Of harpe and pipe þan he nere;
Bet þuȝte þat he were ishote
Of harpe and pipe þan of þrote.
   Þo stod on old stoc þar biside,   25
Þar þo Ule song hire tide,
And was mid ivi al bigrowe.
Hit was þare Hule eardingstowe.
   Þe Niȝtingale hi iseȝ,
And hi bihold and overseȝ,   30

---

1 valley. 2 very secluded nook. 3 held; debate. 5 pleading; violent. 7 either; swelled up angrily.
8 offensive; temper. 9 character. 10 she; knew. 11 especially. 12 law-suit. 14 corner.
16 enough. 17 one. 18 Interspersed; reeds; sedge. 19 She; branch. 20 sang in many kinds of
song. 21 rather; seemed; sound. 22 than otherwise. 23 shot forth. 24 throat. 25 tree-stump.
26 canonical hours. 28 dwelling-place. 30 looked down on.

And þuȝte wel vul of þare Hule,
For me hi halt lodlich and fule.
'Unwiȝt,' ho sede, 'awei þu flo!
Me is þe wurs þat Ich þe so.
Iwis for þine vule lete,   35
Wel oft Ich mine song forlete;
Min horte atfliþ and falt mi tonge,
Wonne þu art to me iþrunge.
Me luste bet speten þane singe
Of þine fule ȝoȝelinge.'   40
    Þos Hule abod fort hit was eve,
Ho ne miȝte no leng bileve,
Vor hire horte was so gret
Þat wel neȝ hire fnast atschet,
And warp a word þarafter longe;   45
'Hu þincþe nu bi mine songe?
Wenst þu þat Ich ne cunne singe
Þeȝ Ich ne cunne of writelinge?
Ilome þu dest me grame,
And seist me boþe tone and schame.   50
Ȝif Ich þe holde on mine vote –
So hit bitide þat Ich mote –
And þu were ut of þine rise,
Þu sholdest singe anoþer wise.'
    Þe Niȝtingale ȝaf answare: 55
'Ȝif Ich me loki wit þe bare,
And me schilde wit þe blete,
Ne reche Ich noȝt of þine þrete;
Ȝif Ich me holde in mine hegge,
Ne recche Ich never what þu segge.   60
Ich wot þat þu art unmilde
Wiþ hom þat ne muȝe from þe schilde;
And þu tukest wroþe and uvele
Whar þu miȝt, over smale fuȝele.
Vorþi þu art loþ al fuelkunne,   65
And alle ho þe driveþ honne,
And þe bischricheþ and bigredet,
And wel narewe þe biledet;
And ek forþe þe sulve mose,
Hire þonkes wolde þe totose.   70

---

31 seemed; loathsome. **32** men; her; hold. **33** Monster. **34** see. **35** Indeed; behaviour. **37** flies
aways; fails. **38** when you thrust yourself on me. **39** spit. **40** hooting. **41** waited until. **42** hold
back. **44** breath; shot out. **45** threw out. **48** warbling. **49** Often; injury. **50** vex. **51** feet.
52 only it so happened that I could. **53** branch. **54** manner. **56** guard; open. **57** against;
being exposed. **58** care. **61** unmerciful. **62** those who cannot. **63** pluck. **64** birds. **65** Because;
types of birds. **67** screech around; cry out at. **68** pursue. **69** titmouse itself. **70** willingly; rip to
shreds.

Þu art lodlich to biholde,
And þu art loþ in monie volde:
Þi bodi is short, þi swore is smal,
Grettere is þin heved þan þu al;
Þin eȝene boþ col-blake and brode,   75
Riȝt swo ho weren ipeint mid wode;
Þu starest so þu wille abiten
Al þat þu miȝt mid clivre smiten.
Þi bile is stif and scharp and hoked,
Riȝt so an owel þat is croked;   80
Þarmid þu clackest oft and longe,
And þat is on of þine songe.
Ac þu þretest to mine fleshe,
Mid þine clivres woldest me meshe.
Þe were icundur to one frogge   85
Þat sit at mulne under cogge
Snailes, mus, and fule wiȝte,
Boþ þine cunde and þine riȝte.
Þu sittest adai and fliȝst aniȝt,
Þu cuþest þat þu art on unwiȝt.   90
Þu art lodlich and unclene,
Bï þine neste Ich hit mene,
And ek bi þine fule brode,
Þu fedest on hom a wel ful fode.
Uel wostu þat hi doþ þarinne: 95
Hi fuleþ hit up to þe chinne,
Ho sitteþ þar so hi bo bisne.
Þarbi men segget a vorbisne:
"Dahet habbe þat ilke best
Þat fuleþ his owe nest."   100
Þat oþer ȝer a faukun bredde,
His nest noȝt wel he ne bihedde.
Þarto þu stele in o dai,
And leidest þaron þi fole ey.
Þo hit bicom þat he haȝte,   105
And of his eyre briddes wraȝte;
Ho broȝte his briddes mete,
Bihold his nest, iseȝ hi ete;
He iseȝ bi one halve
His nest ifuled uthalve.   110
Þe faucun was wroþ wit his bridde,
And lude ȝal and sterne chidde:

72 in many respects. 73 neck. 74 head. 75 big. 76 woad. 77 bite to death. 78 claws.
79 beak. 80 hook. 81 With that. 84 crush. 85 You; more natural. 86 mill; cog-wheel.
87 creatures. 88 Accord with your nature. 89 at night. 90 monster. 93 foul brood. 94 off-
spring. 97 blind. 98 proverb. 99 Bad luck to those. 104 foul egg. 105 hatched. 106 eggs;
chicks; had brought to life. 108 saw. 110 on the outside. 112 yelled.

"Segget me, wo havet þis ido?
Ou nas never icunde þarto.
Hit was idon ov a loþe custe.   115
Seggeþ me ʒif ʒe hit wiste."
Þo quaþ þat on and quad þat oþer:
"Iwis it was ure oʒer broþer,
Þe ʒond þat haved þat grete heved:
Wai þat hi nis þarof bireved!   120
Worp hit ut mid þe alre wurste
Þat his necke him to-berste!"
Þe faucun ilefde his bridde,
And nom þat fule brid amidde,
And warp hit of þan wilde bowe,   125
Þar pie and crowe hit todrowe.
Herbi men segget a bispel,
Þeʒ hit ne bo fuliche spel;
Also hit is bi þan ungode
Þat is icumen of fule brode,   130
And is meind wit fro monne,
Ever he cuþ þat he com þonne,
Þat he com of þan adel eye,
Þeʒ he a fro neste leie.
Þeʒ appel trendli from þon trowe   135
Þar he and oþer mid growe,
Þeʒ he bo þarfrom bicume,
He cuþ wel whonene he is icume.'
    Þos word aʒaf þe Niʒtingale,
And after þare longe tale   140
He song so lude and so scharpe,
Riʒt so me grulde schille harpe.
Þos Hule luste þiderward,
And hold hire eʒe noþerward,
And sat tosuolle and ibolwe,   145
Also ho hadde one frogge isuolʒe,
For ho wel wiste and was iwar
Þat ho song hire a-bisemar.
And noþeles ho ʒaf andsuare:
'Whi neltu flon into þe bare,   150
And sewi ware unker bo
Of briʒter howe, of vairur blo?'
    'No, þu havest wel scharpe clawe,

---

113 who. 114 You; natural inclination. 115 way. 120 It's a pity; deprived. 121 Throw; worst of all. 123 believed. 124 took. 126 magpie. 127 moral tale. 128 fully; fiction. 129 low-born person. 131 brought together; noble. 133 addled egg. 134 noble. 135 might roll. 142 plucked. 143 listened. 144 downwards. 145 swollen. 146 swallowed. 148 in mockery of her. 150 open. 151 which of us both. 152 fairer; complexion.

Ne kep Ich noȝt þat þu me clawe.
Þu havest clivers suþe stronge,   155
Þu tuengst þarmid so doþ a tonge.
Þu þoȝtest, so doþ þine ilike,
Mid faire worde me biswike.
Ich nolde don þat þu me raddest,
Ich wiste wel þat þu me misraddest.   160
Schamie þe for þin unrede.
Unwroȝen is þi suikelhede!
Schild þine suikeldom vram þe liȝte,
And hud þat woȝe among þe riȝte.
Þane þu wilt þin unriȝt spene,   165
Loke þat hit ne bo isene.
Vor suikedom haved schome and hete,
Ȝif hit is ope and underȝete.
Ne speddestu noȝt mid þine unwrenche,
For Ich am war and can wel blenche.   170
Ne helpþ noȝt þat þu bo to þriste:
Ich wolde viȝte bet mid liste
Þan þu mid al þine strengþe.
Ich habbe, on brede and eck on lengþe,
Castel god on mine rise: 175
"Wel fiȝt þat wel fliȝt," seiþ þe wise.
Ac lete we awei þos cheste,
Vor suiche wordes boþ unwreste;
And fo we on mid riȝte dome,
Mid faire worde and mid ysome.   180
Þeȝ we ne bo at one acorde,
We muȝe bet mid fayre worde,
Witute cheste, and bute fiȝte,
Plaidi mid foȝe and mid riȝte;
And mai hure eiþer wat hi wile   185
Mid riȝte segge and mid sckile.'
        Þo quaþ þe Hule: 'Wu schal us seme,
Þat kunne and wille riȝt us deme?'
        'Ich wot wel,' quaþ þe Niȝtingale,
'Ne þaref þarof bo no tale.   190
Maister Nichole of Guldeforde,
He is wis an war of worde;
He is of dome suþe gleu,

---

154 I have no wish. **156** pinch; tongs. **158** betray. **159** advised. **160** misadvised. **161** poor advice. **162** Revealed; deceitfulness. **163** deceit. **164** hide the crookedness. **165** wickedness; put to use. **166** be. **168** perceived. **169** did you succeed; trickery. **170** get out of the way. **171** bold. **172** cunning. **174** also. **176** fights; takes flight. **177** brawling. **178** petty. **179** let us begin; judgement. **180** peaceable words. **182** rather. **184** Plead; relevance. **186** reason. **187** reconcile. **188** will be able; judge. **190** There's no need. **192** careful. **193** very prudent.

And him is loþ evrich unþeu.
He wot insiʒt in eche songe,   195
Wo singet wel, wo singet wronge;
And he can schede vrom þe riʒte
Þat woʒe, þat þuster from þe liʒte.'
    Þo Hule one wile hi biþoʒte,
And after þan þis word upbroʒte: 200
'Ich granti wel þat he us deme,
Vor þeʒ he were wile breme,
And lof him were Niʒtingale,
And oþer wiʒte gente and smale,
Ich wot he is nu suþe acoled.   205
Nis he vor þe noʒt afoled,
Þat he, for þine olde luve,
Me adun legge and þc buve;
Ne schaltu nevre so him queme,
Þat he for þe fals dom deme.   210
He is him ripe and fastrede,
Ne lust him nu to none unrede;
Nu him ne lust na more pleie,
He wile gon a riʒte weie.'
    Þe Niʒtingale was al ʒare,   215
Ho hadde ilorned wel aiware:
'Hule,' ho sede, 'seie me soþ,
Wi dostu þat unwiʒtis doþ?
Þu singist aniʒt and noʒt adai,
And al þi song is "wailawai".   220
Þu miʒt mid þine songe afere
Alle þat ihereþ þine ibere.
Þu schrichest and ʒollest to þine fere,
Þat hit is grislich to ihere.
Hit þincheþ boþe wise and snepe   225
Noʒt þat þu singe, ac þat þu wepe.
Þu fliʒst aniʒt and noʒt adai:
Þarof Ich wundri and wel mai,
Vor evrich þing þat schuniet riʒt,
Hit luveþ þuster and hatiet liʒt;   230
And evrich þing þat is lof misdede,
Hit luveþ þuster to his dede.
A wis word, þeʒ hit bo unclene,
Is fele manne a muþe imene,

---

194 vice. 195 a deep understanding. 197 distinguish. 198 What is wrong, the dark. 202 wild for a while. 203 beloved. 204 high-born. 205 greatly cooled down. 206 because of; fooled. 208 lay down; raise up. 209 please. 211 mature; secure in advice. 212 does not like; foolishness. 216 everywhere. 217 truly. 218 monsters. 220 "woe and alas". 221 frighten. 222 cries. 223 screech; companions. 225 seems; to fools. 229 shuns. 230 darkness. 232 for. 234 many; common among.

For Alvred King hit seide and wrot: 235
"He schunet þat hine vul wot."
Ich wene þat þu dost also,
Vor þu fliȝst niȝtes ever mo.
An oþer þing me is a wene,
Þu havest aniȝt wel briȝte sene;   240
Bi daie þu art stareblind,
Þat þu ne sichst ne bou ne rind.
Adai þu art blind oþer bisne,
Þarbi men segget a vorbisne:
"Riȝt so hit farþ bi þan ungode   245
Þat noȝt ne suþ to none gode,
And is so ful of uvele wrenche
Þat him ne mai no man atprenche,
And can wel þane þustre wai,
And þane briȝte lat awai."   250
So doþ þat boþ of þine cunde:
Of liȝte nabbeþ hi none imunde.'
    Þos Hule luste suþe longe,
And was oftoned suþe stronge.
Ho quaþ: 'Þu hattest Niȝtingale,   255
Þu miȝtest bet hoten galegale,
Vor þu havest to monie tale.
Lat þine tunge habbe spale!
Þu wenest þat þes dai bo þin oȝe;
Lat me nu habbe mine þroȝe.   260
Bo nu stille and lat me speke,
Ich wille bon of þe awreke.
And lust hu Ich con me bitelle
Mid riȝte soþe, witute spelle.
    Þu seist þat Ich me hude adai,   265
Þarto ne segge Ich "nich" ne "nai".
And lust, Ich telle þe warevore,
Al wi hit is and warevore.
Ich habbe bile stif and stronge,
And gode clivers scharp and longe,   270
So hit bicumeþ to havekes cunne;
Hit is min hiȝte, hit is mi wune,
Þat Ich me draȝe to mine cunde,
Ne mai no man þarevore schende.
On me hit is wel isene,   275
Vor riȝte cunde Ich am so kene.

239 think. 240 vision. 241 quite blind. 242 bough nor bark. 243 or sightless. 245 goes.
246 sees.   247 tricks.   248 elude.   249 knows; dark. 250 abandons.   252 concern.
254 offended. 255 are called. 256 chatterbox. 258 rest. 259 own. 260 turn. 262 be;
avenged. 263 listen; defend. 264 fiction. 267 what for. 270 claws. 271 hawk's. 272 delight;
joy. 273 I take after. 274 put to shame. 276 nature; bold.

Vorþi Ich am loþ smale foȝle
Þat floþ bi grunde an bi þuvele:
Hi me bichermet and bigredeþ,
And hore flockes to me ledeþ.   280
Me is lof to habbe reste
And sitte stille in mine neste:
Vor nere Ich never no þe betere
Yif Ich mid chavling and mid chatere
Hom schende and mid fule worde,   285
So herdes doþ oþer mid schitworde.
Ne lust me wit þe screwen chide;
Forþi Ich wende from hom wide.
Hit is a wise monne dome,
And hi hit segget wel ilome,   290
Þat me ne chide wit þe gidie,
Ne wit þan ofne me ne ȝonie.
At sume siþe herde I telle
Hu Alvred sede on his spelle:
"Loke þat þu ne bo þare   295
Þar chavling boþ and cheste ȝare:
Lat sottes chide and vorþ þu go."
And Ich am wis and do also.
And ȝet Alvred seide an oþer side
A word þat is isprunge wide: 300
"Þat wit þe fule haveþ imene,
Ne cumeþ he never from him cleine."
Wenestu þat haveck bo þe worse
Þoȝ crowe bigrede him bi þe mershe,
And goþ to him mid hore chirme   305
Riȝt so hi wille wit him schirme?
Þe havec folȝeþ gode rede,
And fliȝt his wei and lat him grede.
   ȝet þu me seist of oþer þinge,
And telst þat Ich ne can noȝt singe;   310
Ac al mi rorde is woning,
And to ihire grislich þing.
Þat nis noȝt soþ, Ich singe efne,
Mid fulle dreme and lude stefne.
Þu wenist þat ech song bo grislich,   315
Þat þine pipinge nis ilich.
Mi stefne is bold and noȝt unorne;
Ho is ilich one grete horne,

278 fly; thicket. **279** scream at; cry out at. **283** would not. **284** bickering. **285** scolded. **286** shitty words. **287** like; shrewish; debate. **288** thus; turned. **289** judgement. **290** very often. **291** people; foolish. **292** oven; should one; gape. **293** occasion. **301** has dealings with. **303** Do you think. **304** cry out at. **305** screeching. **306** fight. **307** advice. **308** lets; cry. **311** voice; lamentation. **312** hear. **313** smoothly. **314** sound; voice. **316** like. **317** wretched.

And þin is ilich one pipe,
Of one smale wode unripe.   320
Ich singe bet þan þu dest:
Þu chaterest so doþ on Irish prost.
Ich singe an eve a riʒte time,
And soþþe won hit is bedtime,
Þe þridde siþe ad middelniʒte,   325
And so Ich mine song adiʒte.
Wone Ich iso arise vorre
Oþer dairim oþer daisterre.
Ich do god mid mine þrote,
And warni men to hore note.   330
Ac þu singest alle longe niʒt,
From eve fort hit is dailiʒt,
And evre seist þin o song
So longe so þe niʒt is long;
And evre croweþ þi wrecche crei,   335
Þat he ne swikeþ niʒt ne dai.
Mid þine pipinge þu adunest
Þas monnes earen þar þu wunest,
And makest þine song so unwurþ
Þat me ne telþ of þar noʒt wurþ.   340
Evrich murʒþe mai so longe ileste
Þat ho shal liki wel unwreste:
Vor harpe, and pipe, and fuʒeles song
Mislikeþ, ʒif hit is to long.
Ne bo þe song never so murie,   345
Þat he ne shal þinche wel unmurie
ʒef he ilesteþ over unwille:
So þu miʒt þine song aspille.
Vor hit is soþ, Alvred hit seide,
And me hit mai ine boke rede: 350
"Evrich þing mai losen his godhede
Mid unmeþe and mid overdede."
Mid este þu þe miʒt overquatie,
And overfulle makeþ wlatie;
An evrich mureʒþe mai agon,   355
ʒif me hit halt evre forþ in on,
Bute one, þat is Godes riche,
Þat evre is suete and evre iliche.
Þeʒ þu nime evre oþþan lepe,

320 half-grown. 324 after. 325 time. 326 prepare. 327 see; far away. 328 daybreak; morning
star. 330 advantage. 332 until. 333 one. 335 throat. 336 is not silent. 337 deafen.
338 dwell. 340 count it; value. 341 mirth; last. 342 badly. 347 beyond displeasure.
348 waste. 351 excellence. 352 excess. 353 gratification; overindulge. 354 superfluity; pro-
duces disgust. 355 pleasure; vanish. 356 one; persists; continually. 357 Except; kingdom.
358 the same. 359 take; basket.

Hit is evre ful bi hepe; 360
Wunder hit is of Godes riche,
Þat evre spenþ and ever is iliche.
3ut þu me seist anoþer shome:
Þat Ich am on mine e3en lome,
An seist, for þat Ich flo bi ni3te, 365
Þat Ich ne mai iso bi li3te.
Þu liest! On me hit is isene
Þat Ich habbe gode sene:
Vor nis non so dim þusternesse
Þat Ich ever iso þe lasse. 370
Þu wenest þat Ich ne mi3te iso,
Vor Ich bi daie no3t ne flo.
Þe hare luteþ al dai,
Ac noþeles iso he mai:
3if hundes urneþ to himward, 375
He gengþ wel suiþe awaiward,
And hokeþ paþes suiþe narewe,
And haveþ mid him his blenches 3arewe,
And hupþ and stard suþe cove,
An secheþ paþes to þe grove; 380
Ne sholde he vor boþe his e3e
So don, 3if he þe bet nise3e.
Ich mai ison so wel so on hare,
Þe3 Ich bi daie sitte an dare.
Þar a3te men boþ in worre, 385
An fereþ boþe ner an forre,
An overvareþ fele þode,
An doþ bi ni3te gode node,
Ich fol3i þan a3te manne,
An flo bi ni3te in hore banne.' 390
    Þe Ni3tingale in hire þo3te
Athold al þis and longe þo3te
Wat ho þarafter mi3te segge,
Vor ho ne mi3te no3t alegge
Þat þe Hule hadde hire ised, 395
Vor he spac boþe ri3t an red.
An hire ofþu3te þat ho hadde
Þe speche so for vorþ iladde,
An was oferd þat hire answare
Ne wurþe no3t ari3t ifare. 400
Ac noþeles he spac boldeliche,

---

360 fully heaped. 362 is used. 364 crippled. 366 see. 368 vision. 372 fly. 373 hides. 375 run towards it. 376 goes very quickly. 377 turns this way and that along. 378 dodges; prepared. 379 hops and leaps; fast. 382 could not see. 384 remain hidden. 385 valiant; are. 387 overrun; countries. 388 service. 390 troop. 392 Considered. 394 refute. 396 good sense. 398 led.

Vor he is wis þat hardeliche
Wiþ is vo berþ grete ilete,
Þat he vor areȝþe hit ne forlete:
Vor suich worþ bold ȝif þu fliȝst,   405
Þat wule flo ȝif þu isvicst;
Ȝif he isiþ þat þu nart areȝ,
He wile of bore wurchen bareȝ.
And forþi, þeȝ þe Niȝtingale
Were aferd, ho spac bolde tale.   410
'Hule,' ho seide, 'wi dostu so?
Þu singest a-winter "wolawo"!
Þu singest so doþ hen a snowe,
Al þat ho singeþ hit is for wowe.
A wintere þu singest wroþe and ȝomere,   415
An evre þu art dumb a sumere.
Hit is for þine fule niþe
Þat þu ne miȝt mid us bo bliþe,
Vor þu forbernest wel neȝ for onde
Wane ure blisse cumeþ to londe.   420
Þu farest so doþ þe ille,
Evrich blisse him is unwille:
Grucching and luring him boþ rade,
Ȝif he isoþ þat men boþ glade.
he wolde þat he iseȝe   425
Teres in evrich monnes eȝe;
Ne roȝte he þeȝ flockes were
Imeind bi toppes and bi here.
Also þu dost on þire side:
Vor wanne snou liþ þicke and wide,   430
An alle wiȝtes habbeþ sorȝe,
Þu singest from eve fort amorȝe.
    Ac Ich alle blisse mid me bringe,
Ech wiȝt is glad for mine þinge,
And blisseþ hit wanne Ich cume,   435
And hiȝteþ aȝen mine kume.
Þe blostme ginneþ springe and sprede,
Boþe ine tro and ek on mede:
Þe lilie mid hire faire wlite
Wolcumeþ me, þat þu hit wite,   440
Bit me mid hire faire blo
Þat ich shulle to hire flo.

---

402 resolutely. **403** enemy; puts on a great show. **404** cowardice; yield. **405** For such a one becomes. **406** fight. **407** coward. **408** boar; piglet. **413** as; in. **415** angrily and dolefully. **417** hatred. **418** happy. **419** are consumed; spite. **421** evil man. **423** grumbling and scowling. **427** would care. **428** Entangled; tufts; hair. **429** your. **431** creatures. **432** until morning. **436** anticipates with hope; arrival. **438** also; field. **439** appearance. **440** know. **441** Greets; complexion.

Þe rose also mid hire rude,
Þat cumeþ ut of þe þorne wode,
Bit me þat Ich shulle singe   445
Vor hire luve one skentinge.
And Ich so do þurȝ niȝt and dai,
Þe more Ich singe þe more I mai,
An skente hi mid mine songe,
Ac noþeles noȝt overlonge.   450
Wane Ich iso þat men boþ glade,
Ich nelle þat hi bon to sade.
Þan is ido vor wan Ich com,
Ich fare aȝen and do wisdom.
Wane mon hoȝeþ of his sheve,   455
An falew cumeþ on grene leve,
Ich fare hom and nime leve:
Ne recche ich noȝt of winteres reve.
Wan Ich iso þat cumeþ þat harde,
Ich fare hom to min erde,   460
An habbe boþe luve and þonc
Þat Ich her com and hider swonk.
Þan min erende is ido,
Sholde Ich bileve? Nai, warto?
Vor he nis noþer ȝep ne wis,   465
Þat longe abid þar him nod nis.'
    Þos Hule luste, and leide an hord
Al þis mot, word after word,
An after þoȝte hu he miȝte
Ansuere vinde best mid riȝte: 470
Vor he mot hine ful wel biþenche,
Þat is aferd of plaites wrenche.
    'Þu aishest me,' þe Hule sede,
'Wi Ich a winter singe and grede.
Hit is gode monne iwone,   475
An was from þe worlde frome,
Þat ech god man his frond icnowe,
An blisse mid hom sume þrowe
In his huse at his borde,
Mid faire speche and faire worde.   480
And hure and hure to Cristesmasse,
Þane riche and povre, more and lasse,
Singeþ cundut niȝt and dai;

443 red hue. 446 amusing song. 448 can. 449 amuse. 452 are too weary of it. 453 When
what I came here to do is done. 454 go. 455 considers; sheaves. 456 green leaves become
fallow. 457 take; my leave. 458 plunder. 459 hard season. 460 native land. 462 worked.
464 remain here; what for. 465 clever. 466 doesn't need to. 468 argument. 470 find.
471 ponder. 472 tricks of pleading. 473 ask. 474 cry out. 475 customary. 476 world's
beginning. 478 rejoice; for some time. 479 table. 481 especially. 483 carols.

Ich hom helpe what ich mai.
And ek Ich þenche of oþer þinge   485
Þane to pleien oþer to singe.
Ich habbe herto gode ansuare
Anon iredi and al ȝare:
Vor sumeres tide is al to wlonc,
An doþ misreken monnes þonk: 490
Vor he ne recþ noȝt of clennesse,
Al his þoȝt is of golnesse.
Vor none dor no leng nabideþ,
Ac evrich upon oþer rideþ;
Þe sulve stottes ine þe stode   495
Boþ boþe wilde and merewode.
And þu sulf art þar among,
For of golnesse is al þi song,
An aȝen þet þu wult teme
Þu art wel modi and wel breme.   500
Sone so þu havest itrede,
Ne miȝtu leng a word iqueþe;
Ac pipest also doþ a mose,
Mid chokeringe, mid stevne hose.
Ȝet þu singst worse þon þe heisugge,   505
Þat fliȝþ bi grunde among þe stubbe:
Wane þi lust is ago,
Þonne is þi song ago also.
A sumere chorles awedeþ
And vorcrempeþ and vorbredeþ: 510
Hit nis for luve noþeles,
Ac is þe chorles wode res;
Vor wane he haveþ ido his dede,
Ifallen is al his boldhede;
Habbe he istunge under gore,   515
Ne last his luve no leng more.
Also hit is on þine mode:
So sone so þu sittest a brode,
Þu forlost al þine wise.
Also þu farest on þine rise,   520
Wane þu havest ido þi gome,
Þi stevne goþ anon to shome.
     Ac wane niȝtes cumeþ longe,
And bringeþ forstes starke an stronge,

---

486 or. **488** prepared. **489** heedless. **490** to go astray; thoughts. **492** wantoness. **493** animal; will not wait. **495** horses themselves; stud. **496** Are; mad for the mares. **497** yourself. **499** expecting; breed. **500** full of spirit; wild. **501** As soon as; copulated. **502** longer; speak. **503** titmouse. **504** hoarse voice. **505** hedge-sparrow. **509** go mad. **510** cramp and contort themselves (i.e. have sex). **512** violent impulse. **514** valour. **515** poked; clothing. **519** lose; tunes. **520** branch. **521** sport. **522** voice; ruin. **524** frosts.

Þanne erest hit is isene   525
War is þe snelle, war is þe kene.
At þan harde me mai avinde
Wo geþ forþ, wo liþ bihinde.
Me mai ison at þare node,
Wan me shal harde wike bode.   530
Þanne Ich am snel and pleie and singe,
And hiȝte me mid mi skentinge:
Of none wintere Ich ne recche,
Vor Ich nam non asunde wrecche.
And ek Ich frouri vele wiȝte   535
Þat mid hom nabbed none miȝtte:
Hi boþ hoȝfule and uel arme,
An secheþ ȝorne to þe warme.
Oft Ich singe vor hom þe more
For lutli sum of hore sore.   540
Hu þincþ þe? Artu ȝut inume?
Artu mid riȝte overcume?'
        'Nay, nay!' sede þe Niȝtingale,
'Þu shalt ihere anoþer tale:
Ȝet nis þos speche ibroȝt to dome.   545
Ac bo wel stille, and lust nu to me.
Ich shal mid one bare worde
Do þat þi speche wurþ forworþe.'
        'Þat nere noht riȝt,' þe Hule sede,
'Þu havest bicloped also þu bede,   550
An Ich þe habbe iȝive ansuare;
Ac ar we to unker dome fare,
Ich wille speke toward þe
Also þu speke toward me;
An þu me ansuare ȝif þu miȝt.   555
    Seie me nu, þu wrecche wiȝt,
Is in þe eni oþer note
Bute þu havest schille þrote?
Þu nart noȝt to non oþer þinge,
Bute þu canst of chateringe: 560
Vor þu art lutel an unstrong,
An nis þi reȝel noþing long.
Wat dostu godes among monne?
Na mo þe deþ a wrecche wranne.
Of þe ne cumeþ non oþer god,   565
Bute þu gredest suich þu bo wod;

---

526 active one; bold one. **527** hard times; discover. **529** one; necessary time. **530** From whom; ask for service. **532** rejoice in myself. **533** care. **534** a feeble. **535** comfort; creatures. **536** in themselves; power. **537** anxious; wretched. **538** eagerly. **540** to lessen; sorrow. **541** answered. **545** judgement. **548** becomes worthless. **550** brought a charge; requested. **552** before; our. **558** Except; shrill. **562** dress. **563** of benefit. **564** wren. **566** cry out; are.

An bo þi piping overgo,
Ne boþ on þe craftes na mo.
Alvred sede, þat was wis –
He miȝte wel, for soþ hit is: 570
"Nis no man for is bare songe
Lof ne wurþ noȝt suþe longe:
Vor þat is a forworþe man
Þat bute singe noȝt ne can."
Þu nart bute on forworþe þing: 575
On þe nis bute chatering.
Þu art dim an of fule howe,
An þinchest a lutel soti clowe;
Þu nart fair, no þu nart strong,
No þu nart þicke, ne þu nart long;   580
Þu havest imist al of fairhede,
An lutel is al þi godede.
An oþer þing of þe Ich mene:
Þu nart vair, ne þu nart clene.
Wane þu comest to manne haȝe,   585
Þar þornes boþ and ris idraȝe,
Bi hegge and bi þicke wode,
Þar men goþ oft to hore node
Þarto þu draȝst, þarto þu wunest,
An oþer clene stede þu schunest.   590
Þan Ich flo niȝtes after muse,
I mai þe vinde ate rumhuse;
Among þe wode, among þe netle,
Þu sittest and singst bihinde þe setle.
Þar me mai þe ilomest finde,   595
Þar men worpeþ hore bihinde.
Ȝet þu atuitest me mine mete,
An seist þat Ich fule wiȝtes ete.
Ac wat etestu, þat þu ne liȝe,
Bute attercoppe and fule vliȝe,   600
An wormes, ȝif þu miȝte finde
Among þe volde of harde rinde?
Ȝet Ich can do wel gode wike,
Vor Ich can loki manne wike;
An mine wike boþ wel gode,   605
Vor Ich helpe to manne vode.
Ich can nimen mus at berne,

---

567 finished. 568 of skill; no more. 572 Praised or honoured. 573 useless. 574 other than; knows. 575 a. 578 seen like; sooty bundle. 581 missed out on; beauty. 582 excellence. 583 complain. 585 hedges. 586 branches drawn together. 588 need. 589 approach; dwell. 592 you; toilet. 594 seat. 595 most often. 596 thrust out; behinds. 597 upbraid. 598 foul creatures. 599 and don't you lie. 600 spiders; flies. 602 bark. 603 services. 604 protect; dwellings. 606 food. 607 catch.

An ek at chirche ine þe derne:
Vor me is lof to Cristes huse,
To clansi hit wiþ fule muse, 610
Ne schal þar nevre come to
Ful wiȝt, ȝif Ich hit mai ivo.
An ȝif me lust one mi skentinge
To wernen oþer wunienge,
Ich habbe at wude trou wel grete, 615
Mit þicke boȝe no þing blete,
Mid ivi grene al bigrowe,
Þat evre stont iliche iblowe,
An his hou never ne vorlost,
Wan hit sniuw ne wan hit frost. 620
Þarin Ich habbe god ihold,
A winter warm, a sumere cold.
Wane min hus stont briȝt and grene,
Of þine nis noþing isene.

  Ȝet þu me telst of oþer þinge, 625
Of mine briddes seist gabbinge:
Þat hore nest nis noȝt clene.
Hit is fale oþer wiȝte imene,
Vor hors a stable and oxe a stalle
Doþ al þat hom wule þar falle. 630
An lute children in þe cradele,
Boþe chorles an ek aþele,
Doþ al þat in hore ȝoeþe
Þat hi vorleteþ in hore duȝeþe.
Wat! Can þat ȝongling hit bihede? 635
Ȝif hit misdeþ, hit mod nede:
A vorbisne is of olde ivurne,
Þat node makeþ old wif urne.

    An ȝet Ich habbe anoþer andsware.
Wiltu to mine neste vare 640
An loki hu hit is idiȝt?
Ȝif þu art wis lorni þu miȝst.
Mi nest is holȝ and rum amidde,
So hit is softest mine bridde.
Hit is broiden al abute, 645
Vrom þe neste vor wiþute:
Þarto hi god to hore node;
Ac þat þu menest Ich hom forbode.

---

608 dark. **610** cleanse; from. **612** catch. **613** like. **614** reject; dwellings. **615** tree. **616** not at all bare. **618** in leaf. **619** appearance; changes. **621** refuge. **623** stands. **625** chicks; lies. **628** many; common. **630** Allow. **632** noble. **633** youth. **634** abandon; adulthood. **635** young one; prevent. **636** does wrong; must by necessity. **637** proverb; from ancient times. **638** necessity; run. **640** go. **641** made. **642** learn. **643** hollow; spacious. **645** woven. **647** go. **648** complain about; forbid.

We nimeþ ȝeme of manne bure,
An after þan we makeþ ure: 650
Men habbet, among oþer iwende,
A rumhus at hore bures ende,
Vor þat hi nelleþ to vor go,
An mine briddes doþ also.
Site nu stille, chaterestre!   655
Nere þu never ibunde vastre;
Herto ne vindestu never andsware.
Hong up þin ax! Nu þu miȝt fare!'
    Þe Niȝtingale at þisse worde
Was wel neȝ ut of rede iworþe,   660
An þoȝte ȝorne on hire mode
Ȝif ho oȝt elles understode,
Ȝif ho kuþe oȝt bute singe,
Þat miȝte helpe to oþer þinge.
Herto ho moste andswere vinde,   665
Oþer mid alle bon bihinde:
An hit is suþe strong to fiȝte
Aȝen soþ and aȝen riȝte.
He mot gon to al mid ginne,
Þan þe horte boþ on winne;   670
An þe man mot onoþer segge,
He mot bihemmen and bilegge,
Ȝif muþ wiþute mai biwro
Þat me þe horte noȝt niso.
An sone mai a word misreke   675
Þar muþ shal aȝen horte speke;
An sone mai a word misstorte
Þar muþ shal speken aȝen horte.
Ac noþeles ȝut upe þon,
Her is to red wo hine kon: 680
Vor never nis wit so kene
So wane red him is a wene.
Þanne erest kumed his ȝephede
Wone hit is alre mest on drede.
For Alvered seide of olde quide,   685
An ȝut hit nis of horte islide:
'Wone þe bale is alre hecst,

649 example; bowers. **650** following. **651** alternatives. **652** toilet. **653** will not; too far. **655** chatterbox. **656** secured; faster. **658** can. **660** good ideas. **661** eagerly; mind. **662** anything. **663** knew how to do; except. **664** for anything else. **666** be. **667** difficult. **668** Against. **669** at; cunning. **670** When the heart is troubled. **671** something different. **672** hem round; explain away. **673** outwardly; conceal. **674** cannot see. **675** go astray. **677** misstart. **680** a sound plan; for those who know it. **681** sharp. **682** plan; in doubt. **683** first; comes; astuteness. **684** most of all; jeopardy. **685** saying. **686** mind; slipped. **687** calamity; highest of all.

Þonne is þe bote alre necst.'
Vor wit west among his sore,
An for his sore hit is þe more.   690
Vorþi nis nevere mon redles
Ar his horte bo witles;
Ac ȝif þat he forlost his wit,
Þonne is his redpurs al toslit;
Ȝif he ne kon his wit atholde,   695
Ne vint he red in one volde.
Vor Alvred seide, þat wel kuþe
(Evre he spac mid soþe muþe):
'Wone þe bale is alre hecst,
Þanne is þe bote alre nest.'   700
  Þe Niȝtingale al hire hoȝe
Mid rede hadde wel bitoȝe;
Among þe harde, among þe toȝte,
Ful wel mid rede hire biþoȝte,
An hadde andsuere gode ifunde   705
Among al hire harde stunde.
  'Hule, þu axest me,' ho seide,
'Ȝif Ich kon eni oþer dede
Bute singen in sume tide,
An bringe blisse for and wide.   710
Wi axestu of craftes mine?
Betere is min on þan alle þine,
Betere is o song of mine muþe
Þan al þat evre þi kun kuþe.
An lust? Ich telle þe warevore.   715
Wostu to wan man was ibore?
To þare blisse of hovene riche,
Þar ever is song and murȝþe iliche.
Þider fundeþ evrich man
Þat eni þing of gode kan.   720
Vorþi me singþ in holi chirche,
An clerkes ginneþ songes wirche,
Þat man iþenche bi þe songe
Wider he shal, and þar bon longe:
Þat he þe murȝþe ne vorȝete,   725
Ac þarof þenche and biȝete,
An nime ȝeme of chirche stevene,
Hu murie is þe blisse of hovene.

688 solution; nearest of all. **689** prospers; trouble. **691** without plan. **692** Until. **694** bag of good ideas; split. **695** retain. **696** ideas; fold. **697** was skilled. **701** mind. **702** employed. **703** strained circumstances. **706** moments. **710** far. **712** single one. **714** kind; could do. **715** what for. **716** Do you know; for what. **717** the heavenly kingdom. **719** sets out. **721** people. **722** begin; compose. **723** should consider. **724** shall go. **725** forget. **726** obtain. **727** take note; voice.

Clerkes, munekes, and kanunes,
Þar boþ þos gode wicketunes,   730
Ariseþ up to midelniȝte,
An singeþ of þe hovene liȝte;
An prostes upe londe singeþ,
Wane þe liȝt of daie springeþ.
An Ich hom helpe wat I mai,   735
Ich singe mid hom niȝt and dai,
An ho boþ alle for me þe gladdere,
An to þe songe boþ þe raddere.
    Ich warni men to hore gode
Þat hi bon bliþe on hore mode,   740
An bidde þat hi moten iseche
Þan ilke song þat ever is eche.
Nu þu miȝt, Hule, sitte and clinge;
Her among nis no chateringe.
Ich graunti þat we go to dome   745
Tofore þe sulfe þe Pope of Rome.
Ac abid ȝete, noþeles,
Þu shalt ihere anoþer þes;
Ne shaltu, for Engelonde,
At þisse worde me atstonde.   750
Wi atuitestu me mine unstrengþe,
An mine ungrete and mine unlengþe,
An seist þat Ich nam noȝt strong,
Vor Ich nam noþer gret ne long?
Ac þu nost never wat þu menst,   755
Bute lese wordes þu me lenst:
For Ich kan craft and Ich kan liste,
An þarevore Ich am þus þriste.
Ich kan wit and song mani eine,
Ne triste Ich to non oþer maine;   760
Vor soþ hit is þat seide Alvred:
"Ne mai no strengþe aȝen red."
Oft spet wel a lute liste
Þar muche strengþe sholde miste;
Mid lutle strengþe, þurȝ ginne,   765
Castel and burȝ me mai iwinne;
Mid liste me mai walles felle,
An worpe of horsse kniȝtes snelle.
Uvel strengþe is lutel wurþ,

729 canons. 730 dwelling places. 732 heavenly light. 733 in the country. 737 are.
738 comes the quicker. 739 their. 740 should be; mind. 741 entreat; must seek. 742 same;
eternal. 746 self-same. 748 thing. 750 withstand. 751 do you twit on about. 752 small size.
755 do not know; mean. 756 Only false; proffer. 757 skill; shrewdness. 758 bold. 759 many a
one. 760 trust; strength. 762 good advice. 763 speeds; little. 764 Where; fail. 765 ingenuity.
766 can be won. 768 throw; bold. 769 Force of.

Ac wisdom ne wurþ never unwurþ.   770
Þu myht iseo þurh alle þing
Þat wisdom naveþ non evening.
An hors is strengur þan a mon;
Ac, for hit non iwit ne kon,
Hit berþ on rugge grete semes,   775
An draȝþ bivore grete temes,
An þoleþ boþe ȝerd and spure,
An stont iteid at mulne dure.
An hit deþ þat mon hit hot:
An forþan þat hit no wit not,   780
Ne mai his strenþe hit ishilde
Þat hit nabuȝþ þe lutle childe.
Mon deþ mid strengþe and mid witte
Þat oþer þing nis non his fitte.
Þeȝ alle strengþe at one were,   785
Monnes wit ȝet more were;
Vorþe mon mid his crafte,
Overkumeþ al orþliche shafte.
Also Ich do mid mine one songe
Bet þan þu al þe ȝer longe: 790
Vor mine crafte men me luvieþ,
Vor þine strengþe men þe shunieþ.
Telstu bi me þe wurs forþan
Þat Ich bute anne craft ne kan?
Ȝif tueie men goþ to wraslinge,   795
An eiþer oþer faste þringe,
An þe on can swenges suþe fele,
An kan his wrenches wel forhele,
An þe oþer ne can sweng but anne,
An þe is god wiþ eche manne,   800
An mid þon one leiþ to grunde
Anne after oþer a lutle stunde,
Wat þarf he recche of a mo swenge,
Þone þe on him is swo genge?
Þu seist þat þu canst fele wike,   805
Ac ever Ich am þin unilike.
Do þinc craftes alle togadere,
Ȝet is min on horte betere.
Oft þan hundes foxes driveþ
Þe kat ful wel himsulve liveþ,   810

---

770 is never. 772 equal. 774 has no understanding. 775 back; burdens. 776 before it.
777 suffers; stick. 778 mill door. 779 does what; commands. 781 prevent. 782 yield to.
784 That no other thing equals him. 785 as one. 787 And so. 788 earthly creatures.
790 year. 793 Do you account me. 795 two. 796 presses against. 797 knows many holds.
798 tricks; hide. 799 one hold. 800 a good one against. 802 within a short time. 803 need he
care about. 804 one of his; effective. 805 services. 806 dissimilar. 808 one essentially.

Þeȝ he ne kunne wrench bute anne;
Þe fox so godne ne can nanne,
Þeȝ he kunne so vele wrenche,
Þat he wenþ eche hunde atprenche.
Vor he can paþes riȝte and woȝe,   815
An he kan hongi bi þe boȝe,
An so forlost þe hund his fore,
An turnþ aȝen eft to þan more.
Þe vox kan crope bi þe heie,
An turne ut from his forme weie,   820
An eft sone kume þarto;
Þonne is þe hundes smel fordo:
He not, þurȝ þe imeinde smak,
Weþer he shal avorþ þe abak.
Ȝif þe vox mist of al þis dwole,   825
At þan ende he cropþ to hole;
Ac naþeles mid alle his wrenche,
Ne kan he hine so biþenche,
Þeȝ he bo ȝep an suþe snel,
Þat he ne lost his rede vel.   830
Þe cat ne kan wrench bute anne
Noþer bi dune ne bi venne:
Bute he kan climbe suþe wel,
Þarmid he wereþ his greie vel.
Also Ich segge bi mi solve,   835
Betere is min on þan þine twelve.'
    'Abid! Abid!' Þe Ule seide,
'Þu gest al to mid swikelede:
Alle þine wordes þu bileist
Þat hit þincþ soþ al þat þu seist;   840
Alle þine wordes boþ isliked,
An so bisemed an biliked,
Þat alle þo þat hi avoþ,
Hi weneþ þat þu segge soþ.
Abid! Abid! Me shal þe ȝene.   845
Nu hit shal wurþe wel isene
Þat þu havest muchel iloȝe,
Wone þi lesing boþ unwroȝe.
Þu seist þat þu singist mankunne,
And techest hom þat hi fundieþ honne   850

---

812 does not know any as good. 814 hopes; to elude. 815 straight and crooked. 816 bough.
817 scent. 818 returns; moor. 819 creep; hedge. 823 knows not; variety of smells.
825 escapes; trickery. 826 creeps. 828 arrange it. 829 is clever; quick. 830 pelt. 832 both
by hill; fen. 834 keeps wearing. 835 about. 836 one skill. 838 deceit. 389 explain away.
840 seems true. 841 slick. 842 seem likely and possible. 843 those that hear them.
845 respond. 847 lied. 848 falsehoods; uncovered. 850 should seek to go forward.

Up to þe songe þat evre ilest:
Ac hit is alre wunder mest
Þat þu darst liȝe so opeliche.
Wenest þu hi bringe so liȝtliche
To Godes riche al singinge?   855
Nai, nai, hi shulle wel avinde
Þat hi mid longe wope mote
Of hore sunnen bidde bote,
Ar hi mote ever kume þare.
Ich rede þi þat men bo ȝare,   860
An more wepe þane singe,
Þat fundeþ to þan Hoven-kinge;
Vor nis no man witute sunne.
Vorþi he mot, ar he wende honne,
Mid teres an mid wope bete,   865
Þat him bo sur þat er was swete.
Þarto Ich helpe, God hit wot!
Ne singe Ich hom no foliot:
For al me song is of longinge,
An imend sumdel mid woninge,   870
Þat mon bi me hine biþenche
Þat he groni for his unwrenche.
Mid mine songe Ich hine pulte,
Þat he groni for his gulte.
Ȝif þu gest herof to disputinge,   875
Ich wepe bet þane þu singe.
Ȝif riȝt goþ forþ, and abak wrong,
Betere is mi wop þane þi song.
Þeȝ sume men bo þurȝut gode,
An þurȝut clene on hore mode,   880
Hon longeþ honne noþeles.
Þat boþ her, wo is hom þes,
Vor þeȝ hi bon homsolve iborȝe,
Hi ne soþ her nowiȝt bote sorwe;
Vor oþer men hi wepeþ sore,   885
An for hom biddeþ Cristes ore.
Ich helpe monne on eiþer halve,
Mi muþ haveþ tweire kunne salve:
Þan gode Ich fulste to longinge,
Vor þan hin longeþ, Ich him singe: 890
An þan sunfulle Ich helpe alswo,
Vor Ich him teche þare is wo.

---

851 lasts. **855** kingdom. **857** weeping must. **858** Pray for a remedy for their sins. **860** counsel; prepared. **865** make amends. **866** sour; previously. **868** to them; of any foolishness. **870** partly mixed; lamentation. **872** faults. **873** assail. **874** guilt. **875** go about. **879** thoroughly. **881** to go from here. **882** thus. **883** are themselves saved. **884** see nothing here. **886** mercy. **887** both sides. **888** two kinds saved. **889** help.

3et Ich þe 3ene in oþer wise:
Vor þane þu sittest on þine rise,
Þu dra3st men to fleses luste,   895
Þat wulleþ þine songes luste;
Al þu forlost þe mur3þe of hovene,
For þarto nevestu none stevene.
Al þat þu singst is of golnesse,
For nis on þe non holinesse,   900
Ne wened na man for þi pipinge
Þat eni preost in chircce singe.
3et I þe wulle anoder segge,
3if þu hit const ariht bilegge:
Wi nultu singe anoder þeode,   905
Þar hit is muchele more neode?
Þu neaver ne singst in Irlonde,
Ne þu ne cumest no3t in Scotlonde.
Hwi nultu fare to Noreweie,
An singin men of Galeweie?   910
Þar beoð men þat lutel kunne
Of songe þat is bineoð þe sunne.
Wi nultu þare preoste singe,
An teche of þire writelinge,
An wisi hom mid þire stevene   915
Hu engeles singeð ine heovene?
Þu farest so doð an ydel wel
Þar springeþ bi burne þar is snel,
An let fordrue þe dune,
And flohþ on idel þar adune.   920
Ac Ich fare boþe norþ and suþ:
In eavereuch londe Ich am cuuþ;
East and west, feor and neor,
I do wel faire mi meoster,
An warni men mid mine bere,   925
Þat þi dweole song heo ne forlere.
Ich wisse men mid mine songe,
Þat hi ne sunegi nowiht longe.
I bidde hom þat heo iswike,
Þat heomseolve ne biswike: 930
For betere is þat heo wepen here
Þan elleshwar to beon deovlene fere.'
    Þe Ni3tingale was igremet,
An ek heo was sumdel ofchamed,

---

893 counter you; ways. **894** branch. **895** desires of the flesh. **896** listen to. **898** voice.
899 lust. **901** thinks. **903** another thing. **904** explain. **905** people. **910** Galloway. **913** to
the priests. **914** by your chirping. **915** instruct. **917** idle. **918** by a stream. **919** the hill dry up.
924 follow my calling. **925** behaviour. **926** heretical; does not misguide. **928** do not sin.
929 abandon. **930** betray. **932** elsewhere; devils' companions. **933** furious. **934** ashamed.

For þe Hule hire atwiten hadde   935
In hwucche stude he sat an gradde,
Bihinde þe bure, among þe wede,
Þar men goð to here neode;
An sat sumdel, and heo biþohte,
An wiste wel on hire þohte   940
Þe wraþþe binimeþ monnes red.
For hit seide þe King Alfred:
'Selde endeð wel þe loþe,
An selde plaideð wel þe wroþe.'
For wraþþe meinþ þe horte blod   945
Þat hit floweþ so wilde flod,
An al þe heorte overgeþ,
Þat heo naveþ noþing bute breþ,
An so forleost al hire liht,
Þat heo ne siþ soþ ne riht.   950
Þe Niʒtingale hi understod,
An overgan lette hire mod.
He mihte bet speken a sele
Þan mid wraþþe wordes deale.
        'Hule,' heo seide 'lust nu hider: 955
Þu schalt falle, þe wei is slider.
Þu sciʒt Ich fleo bihinde bure:
Hit is riht, þe bur is ure.
Þar laverd liggeþ and lavedi
Ich schal heom singe and sitte bi.   960
Wenstu þat uise men forlete,
For fule venne, þe riʒtte strete?
Ne sunne þe later shine,
Þeʒ hit bo ful ine nest þine?
Sholde Ich, for one hole brede,   965
Forlete mine riʒte stede,
Þat Ich ne singe bi þe bedde
Þar loverd haveþ his love ibedde?
Hit is mi riʒt, hit is mi laʒe,
Þar to þe hexst Ich me draʒe;   970
Ac ʒet þu ʒelpst of þine songe
Þat þu canst ʒolle wroþe and stronge,
An seist þu visest mankunne,
Þat hi biwepen hore sunne.
Solde euch mon wonie and grede   975
Riʒt suich hi weren unlede,

---

935 reproached. 936 place; cried. 937 chamber. 938 when necessity calls. 941 deprives; judgement. 943 hated person. 944 angry. 946 like a. 947 overwhelms. 950 does not see. 952 allowed her mood to pass. 953 in a happy mood. 956 slippery. 958 ours. 959 where; lie. 962 mud. 968 as a bed-fellow. 970 highest. 974 bewail; sins. 975 lament; cry out. 976 miserable.

Solde hi ȝollen also þu dest,
Hi miȝte oferen here prost.
Man schal bo stille and noȝt grede,
He mot biwepe his misdede;   980
Ac þar is Cristes heriinge,
Þar me shal grede and lude singe:
Nis noþer to lud ne to long,
At riȝte time chirche-song.
Þu ȝolst and wones, and Ich singe: 985
Þi stevene is wop, and min skentinge.
Ever mote þu ȝolle and wepen
Þat þu þi lif mote forleten,
An ȝollen more þu so heȝe
Þat ut berste bo þin eȝe.   990
Weþer is betere of twere twom:
Þat mon bo bliþe oþer grom?
So bo hit ever in unker siþe,
Þat þu bo sori and Ich bliþe.
   Ȝut þu aisheist wi Ich ne fare   995
Into oþer londe and singe þare?
No! Wat sholde Ich among hom do
Þar never blisse ne com to?
Þat lond nis god, ne hit nis este,
Ac wildernisse hit is and weste: 1000
Knarres and cludes hoventinge,
Snou and haȝel hom is genge.
Þat lond is grislich and unvele,
Þe men boþ wilde and unisele,
Hi nabbeþ noþer griþ ne sibbe: 1005
Hi ne reccheþ hu hi libbe.
Hi eteþ fihs an flehs unsode,
Suich wulves hit hadde tobrode:
Hi drinkeþ milc and wei þarto,
Hi nute elles þat hi do;   1010
Hi nabbeþ noþer win ne bor,
Ac libbeþ also wilde dor;
Hi goþ bitiȝt mid ruȝe velle,
Riȝt suich hi comen ut of helle.
Þeȝ eni god man to hom come,   1015
So wile dude sum from Rome,

977 as. 978 frighten; priest. 980 must. 981 praise. 982 a person. 983 neither. 985 weep.
986 lamentation; entertainment. 988 must forsake. 990 both. 991 the two. 992 angry.
993 our case. 995 journey. 997 them. 999 pleasant. 1001 Crags and rocky hills reaching the
skies. 1002 hail; common. 1003 ghastly and wretched. 1004 unhappy. 1005 peace nor truce.
1006 care. 1007 uncooked fish and meat. 1008 As if; ripped apart. 1010 know not any other
way. 1011 beer. 1012 live like; animals. 1013 clothed; rough pelts. 1016 on one occasion; a
certain one.

For hom to lere gode þewes,
An for to leten hore unþewes,
He miʒte bet sitte stille,
Vor al his wile he sholde spille: 1020
He miʒte bet teche ane bore
To weʒe boþe sheld and spere,
Þan me þat wilde folc ibringe
Þat hi me wolde ihere singe.
Wat sol Ich þar mid mine songe?   1025
Ne sunge Ich hom never so longe,
Mi song were ispild ech del:
For hom ne mai halter ne bridel
Bringe vrom hore wude wise,
Ne mon mid stele ne mid ire.   1030
   Ac war lond is boþe este and god,
An þar men habbeþ milde mod,
Ich noti mid hom mine þrote,
Vor Ich mai do þar gode note,
An bringe hom love tiþinge,   1035
Vor Ich of chirche songe singe.
Hit was iseid in olde laʒe,
An ʒet ilast þilke soþsaʒe,
Þat man shal erien an sowe,
Þar he wenþ after sum god mowe: 1040
For he is wod þat soweþ his sed
Þar never gras ne sprinþ ne bled.'
   Þe Hule was wroþ, to cheste rad,
Mid þisse worde hire eʒen abrad:
'Þu seist þu witest manne bures,   1045
Þar leves boþ and faire flores,
Þar two ilove in one bedde
Liggeþ biclopt and wel bihedde.
Enes þu sunge, Ic wod wel ware,
Bi one bure, and woldest lere   1050
Þe lefdi to an uvel luve,
An sunge boþe loʒe and buve,
An lerdest hi to don shome
An unriʒt of hire licome.
Þe loverd þat sone underʒat,   1055
Liim and grine and wel eiwat,

1017 teach; habits. 1018 abandon; vices. 1020 time; waste. 1021 bear. 1022 carry.
1025 would I do. 1027 entirely. 1029 Dissuade; mad ways. 1030 iron. 1031 pleasant.
1033 use. 1034 service. 1035 welcome tidings. 1038 that same true saying. 1039 plough.
1040 hopes; reap. 1041 mad. 1042 blossoms. 1043 eager for strife. 1044 widened.
1045 protect men's. 1047 lovers. 1048 embraced; watched over. 1049 Once; know.
1050 teach. 1051 lady. 1052 low and high. 1054 do wrong with her body. 1055 soon
perceived. 1056 Bird-lime; snares; all manner of things.

Sette and ledde þe for to lacche.
Þu come sone to þan hacche,
Þu were inume in one grine,
Al hit aboȝte þine shine: 1060
Þu naddest non oþer dom ne laȝe,
Bute mid wilde horse were todraȝe.
Vonde ȝif þu miȝt eft misrede,
Waþer þu wult, wif þe maide:
Þi song mai bo so longe genge   1065
Þat þu shalt wippen on a sprenge.'
    Þe Niȝtingale at þisse worde
Mid sworde an mid speres orde,
Ȝif ho mon were, wolde fiȝte:
Ac þo ho bet do ne miȝte   1070
Ho vaȝt mid hire wise tunge:
'Wel fiȝt þat wel specþ', seiþ in þe songe.
Of hire tunge ho nom red:
'Wel fiȝt þat wel specþ', seide Alvred.
    'Wat! Seistu þis for mine shome   1075
Þe loverd hadde herof grame?
He was so gelus of his wive,
Þat he ne miȝte for his live
Iso þat man wiþ hire speke,
Þat his horte nolde breke.   1080
He hire bileck in one bure,
Þat hire was boþe stronge and sure:
Ich hadde of hire milse an ore,
An sori was for hire sore,
An skente hi mid mine songe   1085
Al þat Ich miȝte, raþe an longe.
Vorþan þe kniȝt was wiþ me wroþ,
Vor riȝte niþe Ich was him loþ.
He dude me his oȝene shome,
Ac al him turnde it to grome.   1090
Þat underyat þe king Henri:
Jesus his soule do merci!
He let forbonne þene kniȝt,
Þat hadde idon so muchel unriȝt
Ine so gode kinges londe;   1095
Vor riȝte niþe and for fule onde

1057 laid; you; catch. 1058 casement. 1059 trapped. 1060 paid for; shins. 1061 judgement;
law. 1062 drawn. 1063 Try; again lead astray. 1064 Whichever. 1065 effective. 1066 dangle;
snare. 1068 point. 1069 a man. 1070 because. 1071 fought. 1073 took advice. 1076 suf-
fered from this. 1079 Sees. 1081 locked. 1082 for her. 1083 mercy and pity. 1085 amused.
1086 quickly and lengthily. 1087 Therefore. 1088 downright malice; loathsome. 1089 placed
on. 1090 grief. 1091 perceived. 1093 ordered to be outlawed. 1096 ill-will.

Let þane lutle fuȝel nime
An him fordeme lif an lime.
Hit was wurþsipe al mine kunne,
Forþon þe kniȝt forles his wunne,   1100
An ȝaf for me an hundred punde;
An mine briddes seten isunde,
An hadde soþþe blisse and hiȝte,
An were bliþe, and wel miȝte.
Vorþon Ich was so wel awreke,   1105
Ever eft Ich dar þe bet speke:
Vor hit bitidde ene swo,
Ich am þe bliþur ever mo.
Nu Ich mai singe war Ich wulle,
Ne dar me never eft mon agrulle.   1110
   Ac þu, ereming! Þu wrecche gost!
Þu ne canst finde, ne þu nost,
An holȝ stok þar þu þe miȝt hude,
Þat me ne twengeþ þine hude.
Vor children, gromes, heme and hine,   1115
Hi þencheþ alle of þire pine:
Ȝif hi muȝe iso þe sitte,
Stones hi doþ in hore slitte,
An þe totorved and toheneþ,
An þine fule bon tosheneþ.   1120
Ȝif þu art iworpe oþer ishote,
Þanne þu miȝt erest to note;
Vor me þe hoþ in one rodde,
An þu, mid þine fule codde,
An mid þine ateliche swore,   1125
Biwerest manne corn vrom dore.
Nis noþer noȝt, þi lif ne þi blod:
Ac þu art shueles suþe god.
Þar nowe sedes boþe isowe,
Pinnuc, golfinc, rok, ne crowe   1130
Ne dar þar never cumen ihende,
Ȝif þi buc hongeþ at þan ende;
Þar tron shulle a ȝere blowe,
An ȝunge sedes springe and growe,
Ne dar no fuȝel þarto vonge,   1135

1097 To allow the little bird to be taken. 1098 condemned it in life and limb. 1099 came back to the honour of. 1100 Because of this; lost; joys. 1102 soundly. 1103 joy. 1105 avenged. 1106 more easily. 1107 happened; once; like this. 1110 annoy. 1111 wretch. 1112 know not. 1113 stump; hide. 1114 pinch; skin. 1116 torment. 1118 place; pockets. 1119 pelt and stone to pieces. 1120 break. 1121 hit or shot. 1122 at last be useful. 1123 people hang you on a rod. 1124 belly. 1125 horrible neck. 1126 Guard men's corn against animals. 1128 scarecrow. 1129 new; are. 1130 Sparrow, goldfish. 1131 near. 1132 carcass. 1133 trees; every year. 1135 ravage them.

3if þu art þarover ihonge.
Þi lif is evre luþer and qued,
Þu nard no3t bute ded.
Nu þu mi3t wite sikerliche
Þat þine leches boþ grisliche   1140
Þe wile þu art on lifda3e;
Vor wane þu hongest isla3e,
3ut hi boþ of þe ofdradde,
Þe fu3eles þat þe er bigradde.
Mid ri3te men boþ wiþ þe wroþe,   1145
For þu singist ever of hore loþe:
Al þat þu singst, raþe oþer late,
Hit is ever of manne unwate.
Wane þu havest ani3t igrad
Men boþ of þe wel sore ofdrad.   1150
Þu singst þar sum man shal be ded:
Ever þu bodest sumne qued.
Þu singst a3en ei3te lure,
Oþer of summe frondes rure,
Oþer þu bodes huses brune,   1155
Oþer ferde of manne, oþer þoves rune;
Oþer þu bodest cualm of oreve,
Oþer þat londfolc wurþ idorve,
Oþer þat wif lost hire make,
Oþer þu bodest cheste an sake.   1160
Ever þu singist of manne hareme,
Þur3 þe hi boþ sori and areme;
Þu ne singst never one siþe
Þat hit nis for sum unsiþe.
Hervore hit is þat me þe shuneþ,   1165
An þe totorveþ and tobuneþ
Mid stave, and stoone, and turf, and clute,
Þat þu ne mi3t nowar atrute.
Dahet ever suich budel in tune
Þat ever bodeþ unwreste rune,   1170
An ever bringeþ uvele tiþinge,
An þat ever specþ of uvele þinge!
God Almi3ti wurþe him wroþ,
An al þat werieþ linnene cloþ!'
    Þe Hule ne abod no3t swiþ longe,   1175

1137 worthless and wicked. 1138 are worthless unless. 1139 truly. 1140 looks. 1142 slaugh-
tered. 1143 frightened. 1144 cried out at before. 1146 troubles. 1147 early. 1148 ill luck.
1149 at night. 1152 prophesy; misfortune. 1154 friend's ruin. 1155 burning. 1156 invasion;
the hue and cry for a thief. 1157 plague of cattle. 1158 will become stricken. 1159 will lose her
mate. 1160 conflict and strife. 1161 harm. 1162 wretched. 1163 time. 1164 mishap.
1166 beat severely. 1167 clods. 1168 escape. 1169 Cursed be; town-crier. 1170 bad news.
1173 be angry with him. 1174 linen clothes. 1175 did not wait.

Ah ʒef ondsware starke and stronge:
'Wat,' quaþ ho, 'hartu ihoded?
Oþer þu kursest al unihoded?
For prestes wike Ich wat þu dest;
Ich not ʒef þu were ʒavre prest,   1180
Ich not ʒef þu canst masse singe:
Inoh þu canst of mansinge.
Ah hit is for þine alde niþe,
Þat þu me akursedest oþer siðe.
Ah þarto is lihtlich ondsware: 1185
"Drah to þe!" cwað þe cartare.
Wi attwitestu me mine insihte,
An min iwit and mine miʒte?
For Ich am witi, ful iwis,
An wod al þat to kumen is: 1190
Ich wot of hunger, of hergonge,
Ich wot ʒef men schule libbe longe,
Ich wat ʒef wif luste hire make,
Ich wat þar schal beo niþ and wrake,
Ich wot hwo schal beon anhonge,   1195
Oþer elles fulne deþ afonge.
ʒef men habbeþ bataile inume,
Ich wat hwaþer schal beon overkume.
Ich wat ʒif cwalm scal comen on orfe,
An ʒif dor schul ligge astorve;   1200
Ich wot ʒef treon schule blowe,
Ich wat ʒef cornes schule growe,
Ich wot ʒef huses schule berne,
Ich wot ʒef men schule eorne oþer erne,
Ich wot ʒef sea schal schipes drenche,   1205
Ich wot ʒef smiþes schal uvele clenche.
An ʒet Ich con muchel more:
Ich con inoh in bokes lore,
An eke Ich can of þe goddspelle
More þan Ich nule þe telle;   1210
For Ich at chirche come ilome,
An muche leorni of wisdome.
Ich wat al of þe tacninge,
An of oþer feole þinge.
ʒef eni mon schal rem abide,   1215

1179 functions; perform. 1180 did not know; previously. 1182 Enough; know; excommunication. 1183 ancient malice. 1184 a second time. 1185 easy. 1186 Slow down; carter. 1187 insight. 1188 wisdom. 1189 wise, certainly. 1190 know. 1191 invasions. 1193 will lose. 1194 vengeance. 1196 receive. 1197 undertaken judicial combat. 1198 defeated. 1199 plague; cattle. 1200 wild animals; dead. 1204 run or ride. 1205 cause to founder. 1206 poorly rivet. 1207 know. 1208 scholarship. 1211 often. 1213 divining the future. 1214 many. 1215 raise a hue and cry.

Al Ich hit wot ear hit itide.
Ofte, for mine muchele iwitte,
Wel sorimod and worþ Ich sitte:
Wan Ich iseo þat sum wrechede
Is manne neh, innoh Ich grede;   1220
Ich bidde þat men beon iwarre,
An habbe gode reades ȝarre.
For Alfred seide a wis word,
Euch mon hit schulde legge on hord:
"ȝef þu isihst er he beo icume,   1225
His strencþe is him wel neh binume."
An grete duntes beoþ þe lasse,
ȝef me ikepþ mid iwarnesse,
An fleo schal toward misȝenge,
ȝef þu isihst hu fleo of strenge;   1230
For þu miȝt blenche wel and fleo,
ȝif þu isihst heo to þe teo.
Þat eni man beo falle in odwite,
Wi schal he me his sor atwite?
Þah Ich iseo his harm bivore,   1235
Ne comeþ hit noȝt of me þarvare.
Þah þu iseo þat sum blind mon,
Þat nanne rihtne wei ne con,
To þare diche his dweole fulied,
An falleþ, and þarone sulied,   1240
Wenest þu, þah Ich al iseo,
Þat hit for me þe raþere beo?
   Alswo hit fareþ bi mine witte:
Hwanne Ich on mine bowe sitte,
Ich wot and iseo swiþe brihte   1245
An summe men kumed harm þarrihte.
Schal he, þat þerof noþing not,
Hit wite me for Ich hit wot?
Schal he his mishap wite me,
For Ich am wisure þane he?   1250
Hwanne Ich iseo þat sum wrechede
Is manne neh, inoh Ich grede,
An bidde inoh þat hi heom schilde,
For toward heom is harm unmylde.
Ah þah Ich grede lude an stille,   1255

1216 before it happens. 1218 sad at heart; angry. 1219 grief. 1220 near; cry out. 1221 beseech; aware. 1222 counsels prepared. 1224 store up as treasure. 1225 see before it (grief). 1226 taken from. 1227 blows. 1228 take heed by being aware. 1229 arrow; miss its mark. 1230 it flew from the string. 1231 dodge; flee. 1232 it proceeding towards you. 1233 Though; shame. 1234 sorrow; blame. 1236 derives; therefore. 1238 does not know. 1239 error follows. 1240 is made dirty by it. 1242 because of me happened quicker. 1243 Likewise. 1245 clearly. 1246 To; straight away. 1247 knows. 1248 blame. 1254 harsh.

Al hit itid þurþ Godes wille.
Hwi wulleþ men of me hi mene,
Þah Ich mid soþe heo awene?
Þah Ich hi warni al þat ʒer,
Nis heom þerfore harem no þe ner.   1260
Ah Ich heom singe for Ich wolde
Þat hi wel understonde schulde
Þat sum unselþe heom is ihende,
Hwan Ich min huing to heom sende.
Naveþ no man none sikerhede   1265
Þat he ne mai wene and adrede
Þat sum unhwate neþ him beo,
Þah he ne conne hit iseo.
Forþi seide Alfred swiþe wel,
And his worde was goddspel,   1270
Þat evereuch man, þe bet him beo,
Eaver þe bet he hine beseo;
Ne truste no mon to his weole
To swiþe, þah he habbe veole:
"Nis nout so hot þat hit nacoleþ,   1275
Ne noʒt so hwit þat hit ne soleþ,
Ne noʒt so leof þat hit ne aloþeþ,
Ne noʒt so glad þat hit ne awroþeþ;
Ac evereuch þing þat eche nis,
Agon schal, and al þis worldes blis."   1280
      Nu þu miʒt wite readliche
Þat eavere þu spekest gideliche,
For al þat þu me seist for schame,
Ever þe seolve hit turneþ to grome.
Go so hit go, at eche fenge   1285
Þu fallest mid þine ahene swenge;
Al þat þu seist for me to schende,
Hit is mi wurschipe at þan ende.
Bute þu wille bet aginne,
Ne shaltu bute schame iwinne.'   1290
      Þe Niʒtingale sat and siʒte,
And hohful was, and ful wel miʒte,
For þe Hule swo ispeke hadde,
An hire speche swo iladde.
Heo was hoþful, and erede   1295

1256 through. **1257** complain. **1258** vex them. **1260** the nearer. **1263** misfortune; near. **1264** hooting. **1265** certainty. **1266** expect. **1267** calamity. **1271** better he may be. **1272** should look to himself. **1273** wealth. **1274** a great deal. **1275** cool. **1276** soil. **1277** beloved; become hateful. **1278** become angry. **1279** is not eternal. **1280** Shall pass away. **1281** know. **1282** foolishly. **1284** to your own harm. **1285** round of the fight. **1286** swing. **1287** revile. **1289** go about things. **1291** sighed. **1292** thoughtful. **1294** conducted. **1295** unsure.

Hwat heo þarafter hire sede:
Ah neoþeles heo hire understod.
'Wat!' heo seide, 'Hule, artu wod?
Þu ȝeolpest of seolliche wisdome,
Þu nustest wanene he þe come,   1300
Bute hit of wicchecrefte were.
Þarof þu, wrecche, moste þe skere
ȝif þu wult among manne beo,
Oþer þu most of londe fleo,
For alle þeo þat þerof cuþe,   1305
Heo were ifurn of prestes muþe
Amanset: swuch þu art ȝette,
Þu wiecchecrafte neaver ne lete.
Ich þe seide nu lutel ere,
An þu askedest ȝef Ich were   1310
A bisemere to preost ihoded:
Ah þe mansing is so ibroded,
Þah no preost a londe nere,
A wrecche neoþeles þu were,
For eavereuch child þe cleopeþ fule,   1315
An evereuch man a wrecche hule.
Ich habbe iherd, and soþ hit is,
Þe mon mot beo wel storrewis,
And wite innoþ of wucche þinge kume,
So þu seist þe is iwune.   1320
Hwat canstu, wrecche þing, of storre,
Bute þat þu bihalst hi feorre?
Alswo deþ mani dor and man,
Þeo of swucche nawiht ne con.
On ape mai a boc bihalde,   1325
An leves wenden and eft folde;
Ac he ne con þe bet þarvore
Of clerkes lore top ne more.
Þah þu iseo þe steorre alswa,
Nartu þe wisure neaver þe mo.   1330
Ah ȝet þu, fule þing, me chist
An wel grimliche me atwist
Þat Ich singe bi manne huse,
An teache wif breke spuse.
Þu liest iwis, þu fule þing,   1335

1297 understood (the Owl's words). 1299 boast; strange. 1302 must clear your name. 1304 flee into exile. 1305 those that are familiar with it. 1306 previously. 1307 Excommunicated; still. 1308 abandoned. 1309 a little while before. 1311 mockery. 1312 excommunication; widespread. 1313 were in the land. 1315 calls foul. 1318 star-wise. 1319 enough of what things might happen. 1320 customary. 1321 do you know; of the stars. 1322 Except; look on them; far off. 1324 such things; know nothing. 1326 turn; close. 1328 from beginning to end. 1331 chide. 1332 reproach. 1334 marriage vows.

Þurh me nas neaver ischend spusing.
Ah soþ hit is, Ich singe and grede
Þar lavedies beoþ and faire maide;
And soþ hit is of luve Ich singe,
For god wif mai i spusing   1340
Bet luvien hire oӡene were,
Þane awer hire copenere;
An maide mai luve cheose
Þat hire wurþschipe ne forleose,
An luvie mid rihte luve   1345
Þane þe schal beon hire buve.
Swiche luve Ich itache and lere,
Þerof beoþ al mine ibere.
Þah sum wif beo of nesche mode,
For wummon beoþ of softe blode,   1350
Þat heo, for sume sottes lore
Þe ӡeorne bit and sikeþ sore,
Misrempe and misdo sume stunde,
Schal Ich þarvore beon ibunde?
Ӡif wimmen luvieþ unrede,   1355
Hwitistu me hore misdede?
Ӡef wimmon þencheþ luvie derne,
Ne ne mai Ich mine songes werne.
Wummon mai pleie under cloþe,
Weþer heo wile, wel þe wroþe: 1360
And heo mai do bi mine songe
Hwaþer heo wule, wel þe wronge.
For nis a worlde þing so god
Þat ne mai do sum ungod
Ӡif me hit wule turne amis.   1365
For gold and seolver, god hit is:
An noþeles þarmid þu miӡt
Spusbruche buggen and unriӡt.
Wepne beoþ gode griþ to halde,
Ah neoþeles þarmide beoþ men acwalde   1370
Aӡeines riht an fale londe,
Þar þeoves hi bereð an honde.
Alswa hit is bi mine songe,
Þah heo beo god, me hine mai misfonge
An drahe hine to sothede,   1375
An to oþre uvele dede.

1336 a marriage broken. **1341** man. **1342** anywhere else; lover. **1344** honour; abandon. **1346** The one (Christ); above. **1348** cries. **1349** tender. **1351** fool's teaching. **1352** eagerly beseeches; sighs. **1353** Go astray; on occasion. **1354** made responsible. **1355** ill-advisedly. **1356** Why blame me. **1357** intend; secretly. **1358** Not at all; deny. **1360** honestly or dishonestly. **1364** evil. **1365** a person. **1368** Buy adultery. **1369** Weapons; peace. **1370** killed. **1371** Against the law in many lands. **1374** it; misuse. **1375** convert it to folly.

Ah schaltu wrecch, luve tele?
Bo wuch ho bo, uich luve is fele
Bitweone wepmon and wimmane;
Ah ȝef heo is atbroide, þenne   1380
He is unfele and forbrode.
Wroþ wurþe heom þe holi rode,
Þe rihte ikunde swo forbreideþ!
Wunder hit is þat heo nawedeþ:
An swo heo doþ, for heo beoþ wode   1385
Þe bute nest goþ to brode.
Wummon is of nesche flesche,
An flesches lustes is strong to cwesse;
Nis wunder nan þah he abide,
For flesches lustes hi makeþ slide.   1390
Ne beoþ heo noþt alle forlore,
Þat stumpeþ at þe flesches more,
For moni wummon haveþ misdo
Þat aris op of þe slo.
Ne beoþ noþt ones alle sunne,   1395
Forþan hi beoþ tweire kunne:
Sun arist of þe flesches luste,
An sum of þe gostes custe.
Þar flesch draheþ men to drunnesse,
An to wrovehede and to golnesse,   1400
Þe gost misdeþ þurch niþe an onde,
And seoþþe mid murhþe of monne shonde,
An ȝeoneþ after more and more,
An lutel rehþ of milce and ore;
An stiȝþ on heþ þurþ modinesse,   1405
An overhoheð þanne lasse.
Sei me sooþ, ȝef þu hit wost,
Hweþer deþ wurse, flesch þe gost?
Þu miȝt segge, ȝef þu wult,
Þat lasse is þe flesches gult: 1410
Moni man is of his flesche clene,
Þat is mid mode deovel imene.
Ne schal non mon wimman bigrede,
An flesches lustes hire upbreide;

1377 blame. 1378 Be as it may be, each love is good. 1380 snatched away. 1381 improper and perverted. 1382 May the holy Cross be angry with those. 1383 Who pervert proper nature like this. 1384 do not go mad. 1386 Who go and breed without a nest. 1387 tender. 1388 suppress. 1389 he persists. 1390 will make her yield. 1392 stumbles over; root. 1394 mire. 1395 of one kind; sins. 1396 types. 1398 spirit's character. 1399 drunkenness. 1400 perverseness; lechery. 1401 malice and envy. 1402 after; joy in man's shame. 1403 longs with open mouth for. 1404 cares about mercy and pity. 1405 ascends; pride. 1406 derides; humble man. 1407 know. 1412 in mind, a companion of the devil. 1413 speak out against. 1414 reproach.

Swuch he may tellen of golnesse 1415
Þat sunegeþ wurse i modinesse.
Hwet ȝif Ich schulde a luve bringe
Wif oþer maide hwanne Ich singe?
Ich wolde wiþ þe maide holde,
ȝif þu hit const ariht atholde. 1420
Lust nu, Ich segge þe hwarvore,
Up to þe toppe from þe more:
ȝef maide luveþ dernliche
Heo stumpeþ and falþ icundeliche;
For þah heo sum hwile pleie, 1425
Heo nis nout feor ut of þe weie;
Heo mai hire guld atwende
A rihte weie þurþ chirche bende,
An mai eft habbe to make
Hire leofmon wiþute sake, 1430
An go to him bi daies lihte
Þat er stal to bi þeostre nihte.
An ȝunling not hwat swuch þing is,
His ȝunge blod hit draȝeþ amis,
An sum sot mon hit tihþ þarto 1435
Mid alle þan þat he mai do:
He comeþ and fareþ and beod and bid,
An heo bistant and oversid,
An bisehþ ilome and longe.
Hwat mai þat chil þah hit misfonge? 1440
Hit nuste neaver hwat hit was;
Forþi hit þohte fondi þas,
An wite iwis hwuch beo þe gome
Þat of so wilde makeþ tome.
Ne mai Ich for reoþe lete, 1445
Wanne Ich iseo þe tohte ilete
Þe luve bring on þe ȝunglinge,
Þat Ich of murȝþe him ne singe.
Ich teache heom bi mine songe
Þat swucch luve ne lest noȝt longe; 1450
For mi song lutle hwile ilest,
An luve ne deþ noȝt bute rest
On swuch childre, and sone ageþ,
An falþ adun þe hote breþ.

1415 reprove; lechery. **1416** sins; through pride. **1417** to love. **1419** side. **1420** understand. **1422** bottom. **1423** secretly. **1424** by natural instinct. **1427** guilt; escape from. **1428** In the; bonds. **1430** sweetheart; blame. **1432** stole away to; dark. **1435** foolish; leads. **1437** commands and beseeches. **1438** harrasses; neglects. **1439** pleads; often. **1440** child do, though it is wrong. **1442** Thus she thought to try it. **1443** for certain what the game is. **1444** a tame one. **1445** pity refrain. **1446** strained face. **1448** for pleasure for her. **1450** lasts. **1452** rest for a moment. **1453** departs. **1454** declines; passion.

Ich singe mid heom one þroȝe,   1455
Biginne on heh and endi laȝe,
An lete mine songes falle
An lutle wile adun mid alle.
Þat maide wot, hwanne Ich swike,
Þat luve is mine songes iliche;   1460
For hit nis bute a lutel breþ
Þat sone kumeþ, and sone geþ.
Þat child bi me hit understond,
An his unred to red wend,
An iseȝþ wel, bi mine songe,   1465
Þat dusi luve ne last noȝt longe.
Ah wel Ich wule þat þu hit wite:
Loþ me beoþ wives utschute;
Ah wif mai of me nime ȝeme,
Ich ne singe naþt hwan Ich teme.   1470
An wif ah lete sottes lore,
Þah spusingbendes þuncheþ sore.
Wundere me þungþ wel starc and stor,
Hu eni mon so eavar for
Þat he his heorte miȝte drive   1475
An do hit to oþers mannes wive:
For oþer hit is of twam þinge,
Ne mai þat þridde no man bringe;
Oþar þe laverd is wel aht,
Oþer aswunde, and nis naht.   1480
Ȝef he is wurþful and aht man,
Nele no man, þat wisdon can,
Hure of is wive do him schame:
For he mai him adrede grame,
An þat he forleose þat þer hongeþ,   1485
Þat him eft þarto noȝt ne longeþ.
An þah he þat noȝt ne adrede,
Hit is unriȝt and gret sothede
An misdon one gode manne,
An his ibedde from him spanne.   1490
Ȝef hire laverd is forwurde,
An unorne at bedde and at borde,
Hu miȝte þar beo eni luve

1455 for a while. 1457 allow; to fall away. 1458 completely. 1459 stop. 1462 goes. 1463 by my example. 1464 her foolishness; turns to good sense. 1465 she sees. 1466 foolish. 1468 Hateful; immoderation. 1469 take example. 1470 mate. 1471 ought to abandon a fool's teaching. 1472 marriage ties; seem. 1473 It seems to me a wonder; severe. 1474 behaved. 1476 another. 1479 able. 1480 feeble. 1481 honourable and valiant. 1482 no one that is wise will want to. 1483 bring shame on him through his wife. 1484 be fearful of harm. 1485 lose; depends on that. 1486 long for. 1489 do wrong to. 1490 bed-fellow; urge. 1491 enfeebled. 1492 useless.

Wanne a swuch cheorles buc hire ley buve?
Hu mai þar eni luve beo   1495
Þar swuch man gropeþ hire þeo?
Herbi þu miȝt wel understonde
Þat on is aren, þat oþer schonde,
To stele to oþres mannes bedde;
For ȝif aht man is hire bedde,   1500
Þu miȝt wene þat þe mistide,
Wanne þu list bi hire side.
An ȝef þe laverd is a wrecche,
Hwuch este miȝtistu þar vecche?
Ȝif þu biþenchest hwo hire ofligge,   1505
Þu miȝt mid wlate þe este bugge.
Ich not hu mai eni freoman
For hire sechen after þan.
Ȝef he biþencþ bi hwan he lai,
Al mai þe luve gan awai.'   1510
    Þe Hule was glad of swuche tale;
Heo þoȝte þatte Nihtegale,
Þah heo wel speke atte frume,
Hadde at þen ende misnume,
An seide: 'Nu Ich habbe ifunde   1515
Þat maidenes beoþ of þine imunde:
Mid heom þu holdest, and heom biwerest,
An overswiþe þu hi herest.
Þe lavedies beoþ to me iwend,
To me heo hire mode send.   1520
For hit itit ofte and ilome
Þat wif and were beoþ unisome;
And þerfore þe were gulte,
Þat leof is over wummon to pulte,
An speneþ on þare al þat he haveþ,   1525
An siveþ þare þat no riht naveþ,
An haveþ attom his riȝte spuse,
Wowes weste, and lere huse,
Wel þunne ischrud and ived wroþe,
An let heo bute mete and cloþe.   1530
Wan he comeþ ham eft to his wive,
Ne dar heo noȝt a word ischire;
He chid and gred swuch he beo wod,

1494 churl's body lies above her. **1496** thigh. **1498** harm; shame. **1500** able; bed-fellow. **1501** anticipate; it may get bad results. **1502** lie. **1503** wretch. **1504** pleasure; get. **1505** may have lain with her. **1506** disgust; buy. **1507** man of standing. **1509** whom. **1513** the beginning. **1514** gone wrong. **1516** concern. **1517** protect. **1518** immoderately; praise. **1519** turned. **1521** happens; frequently. **1522** at odds. **1523** is guilty. **1524** Who likes; to assail. **1525** her. **1526** follows. **1527** at home. **1528** Desolate walls and empty. **1529** scantily clothed and fed badly. **1530** abandons her without. **1532** utter. **1533** mad.

An ne bringþ hom non oþer god.
Al þat heo deþ him is unwille,   1535
Al þat heo spekeþ hit is him ille;
An oft hwan heo noȝt ne misdeþ,
Heo haveþ þe fust in hire teþ.
Nis nan mon þat ne mai ibringe
His wif amis mid swucche þinge: 1540
Me hire mai so ofte misbeode
Þat heo do wule hire ahene neode.
La, Godd hit wot, heo nah iweld,
Þa heo hine makie kukeweld.
For hit itit lome and ofte,   1545
Þat his wif is wel nesche and softe,
Of faire bleo and wel idiht:
Wi, hit is þe more unriht
Þat he his luve spene on þare
Þat nis wurþ one of hire heare.   1550
An swucche men beoþ wel manifolde,
Þat wif ne kunne noþt ariȝt holde.
Ne mot non mon wiþ hire speke;
He ueneð heo wule anon tobreke
Hire spusing, ȝef heo lokeþ   1555
Oþer wiþ manne faire spekeþ.
He hire biluþ mid keie and loke:
Þarþurh is spusing ofte tobroke;
For ȝef heo is þarto ibroht,
He deþ þat heo nadde ear iþoht.   1560
Dahet þat to swuþe hit bispeke,
Þah swucche wives heom awreke!
Herof þe lavedies to me meneþ
An wel sore me ahweneþ;
Wel neh min heorte wule tochine,   1565
Hwon Ich biholde hire pine.
Mid heom Ich wepe swiþe sore,
An for heom bidde Cristis ore,
Þat þe lavedi sone aredde
An hire sende betere ibedde.   1570
    Anoþer þing Ich mai þe telle,
Þat þu ne schald, for þine felle,
Ondswere none þarto finde;

1535 displeasing to. 1537 does no wrong. 1538 his fist. 1539 send. 1540 astray. 1541 mis-
treated. 1542 attend to her own needs. 1543 is not responsible. 1544 a cuckold. 1546 tender.
1547 complexion; shaped. 1550 hairs. 1551 numerous. 1554 thinks; immediately break.
1557 locks up. 1558 marriage. 1559 brought to that. 1560 what she had not thought of
previously. 1561 Cursed be; speaks about. 1562 avenge themselves. 1563 lament. 1564 they
grieve. 1565 break asunder. 1566 torment. 1568 pity. 1569 may rescue. 1572 shall; skin.

Al þi sputing schal aswinde.
Moni chapmon and moni cniht   1575
Luveþ and hald his wif ariht,
An swa deþ moni bondeman.
Þat gode wif deþ after þan,
An serveþ him to bedde and to borde
Mid faire dede and faire worde,   1580
An ȝeorne fondeþ hu heo muhe
Do þing þat him beo iduȝe.
Þe laverd into þare þeode
Fareþ ut on þare beire nede,
An is þat gode wif unbliþe   1585
For hire laverdes houdsiþe,
An sit and sihð wel sore oflonged,
An hire sore an horte ongred;
Al for hire loverdes sake
Haveþ daies kare and niȝtes wake,   1590
An swuþc longe hire is þe hwile,
An euch steape hire þunþ a mile.
Hwanne oþre slepeþ hire abute,
Ich one lust þar wiðþute,
An wot of hire sore mode,   1595
An singe a niȝt for hire gode:
An mine gode song, for hire þinge,
Ich turne sundel to murnige.
Of hure seorhe Ich bere sume,
Forþan Ich am hire wel welcume: 1600
Ich hire helpe hwat I mai,
For hoȝeþ þane rehte wai.
Ah þu me havest sore igramed
Þat min heorte is wel neh alamed,
Þat Ich mai unneaþe speke;   1605
Ah ȝet Ich wule forþure reke.
Þu seist þat Ich am manne loð,
An evereuch man is wið me wroð,
An me mid stone and lugge þreteþ,
An me tobusteþ and tobeteþ,   1610
An hwanne heo habeþ me ofslahe,
Heo hongeþ me on heore hahe,
Þar Ich aschewele pie an crowe
Fron þan þe þar is isowe.

1574 contention; fail. 1575 merchants. 1577 peasants. 1578 acts in response to that.
1579 in. 1581 eagerly; tries; might. 1582 may do him good. 1584 both of their needs.
1585 unhappy. 1586 departure. 1587 in longing. 1588 grieves. 1591 to her. 1592 seems.
1594 alone. 1598 in part; mourning. 1599 sorrow. 1602 Being mindful of. 1603 annoyed.
1604 paralysed. 1605 Such that; uneasily. 1606 proceed further. 1609 sticks. 1611 killed:
1612 hedge. 1613 scare away the magpie. 1614 that which there is sown.

Þah hit beo soþ, Ich do heom god,   1615
An for heom Ich chadde mi blod.
Ich do heom god mid mine deaþe,
Warvore þe is wel unneaþe.
For þah þu ligge dead and clinge,
Þi deþ nis naþt to none þinge: 1620
Ich not neaver to hwan þu miȝt,
For þu nart bute a wrecche wiȝt.
Ah þah mi lif me beo atschote,
Þe ȝet Ich mai do gode note:
Me mai up one smale sticke   1625
Me sette a wude ine þe þicke,
An swa mai mon tolli him to
Lutle briddes and ivo,
An swa me mai mid me biȝete
Wel gode brede to his mete.   1630
Ah þu nevre mon to gode
Lives ne deaþes stal ne stode:
Ich not to hwan þu breist þi brod,
Lives ne deaþes ne deþ hit god.'
        Þe Nihtegale iherde þis,   1635
An hupte uppon on blowe ris,
An herre sat þan heo dude ear:
        'Hule,' heo seide, 'beo nu wear,
Nulle Ich wiþ þe plaidi na more,
For her þe mist þi rihte lore: 1640
Þu ȝulpest þat þu art manne loþ,
An evereuch wiht is wið þe wroþ;
An mid ȝulinge and mid igrede
Þu wanst wel þat þu art unlede.
Þu seist þat gromes þe ifoð,   1645
An heie on rodde þe anhoð,
An þe totwichet and toschakeð,
An summe of þe schawles makeð.
Me þunch þat þu forleost þat game,
Þu ȝulpest of þire oȝe schame;   1650
Me þunch þat þu me gest an honde,
Þu ȝulpest of þire oȝene schome.'
        Þo heo hadde þeos word icwede,
Heo sat in one faire stude,

1616 shed. 1619 shrivel up. 1620 nothing. 1621 I don't know what you are useful for.
1622 are nothing; creature. 1623 shot out of. 1624 service. 1626 thicket. 1627 attract.
1628 trap them. 1629 one can get with me. 1630 roast meat for his food. 1632 In life or
death you were no use. 1633 for what reason; breed. 1636 hopped; blossoming branch.
1637 higher; earlier. 1639 debate. 1640 fails; skill. 1641 boast. 1643 yelling; crying out.
1644 know; vile. 1645 boys; catch. 1646 rod; hang. 1647 pluck and shake to pieces.
1648 a scarecrow. 1651 you are submitting to me. 1654 place.

An þarafter hire stevene dihte,   1655
An song so schille and so brihte,
Þat feor and ner me hit iherde.
Þarvore anan to hire cherde
Þrusche and þrostle and wudewale,
An fuheles boþe grete and smale;   1660
Forþan heom þuhte þat heo hadde
Þe Houle overcome, vorþan heo gradde
An sungen alswa vale wise;
An blisse was among þe rise.
Riȝt swa me gred þe manne a schame   1665
Þat taveleþ and forleost þat gome.
    Þeos Hule, þo heo þis iherde,
'Havestu,' heo seide, 'ibanned ferde?
An wultu, wreche, wið me fiȝte?
Nai! Nai! Navestu none miȝte!   1670
Hwat gredeþ þeo þat hider come?
Me þuncþ þu ledest ferde to me.
Ȝe schule wite, ar ȝe fleo heonne,
Hwuch is þe strenþe of mine kunne;
For þeo þe haveþ bile ihoked,   1675
An clivres charpe and wel icroked,
Alle heo beoþ of mine kunrede,
An walde come ȝif Ich bede.
Þe seolfe coc, þat wel can fiȝte,
He mot mid me holde mid riȝte,   1680
For boþe we habbeþ stevene briȝte,
An sitteþ under weolkne bi niȝte.
Schille Ich an utest uppen ow grede,
Ich schal swo stronge ferde lede
Þat ower proude schal avalle.   1685
A tort ne ȝive Ich for ow alle!
Ne schal, ar hit beo fulliche eve,
A wreche feþer on ow bileave.
Ah hit was unker voreward,
Þo we come hiderward,   1690
Þat we þarto holde scholde,
Þar riht dom us ȝive wolde.
Wultu nu breke foreward?
Ich wene dom þe þingþ to hard:
For þu ne darst domes abide,   1695

1655 voice attuned. 1656 clearly. 1658 turned. 1659 throstle; woodpecker. 1662 because she cried out. 1663 and likewise, they sang many songs. 1666 gambles. 1668 summoned an army. 1673 should know; from here. 1674 What; kindred. 1675 hooked beaks. 1676 sharp talons. 1678 ask them. 1682 the clouds. 1683 If I shall call a hue and cry on you. 1685 pride; fall. 1686 turd. 1688 leave. 1689 our agreement. 1691 should agree to hold to. 1692 proper judgement given. 1694 I expect; seems to you too hard. 1695 wait for.

Þu wult nu, wreche, fiȝte and chide.
Ȝet Ich ow alle wolde rede,
Ar Ich utheste uppon ow grede,
Þat ower fihtlac leteþ beo,
An ginneþ raþe awei fleo;   1700
For bi þe clivres þat Ich bere,
Ȝef ȝe abideþ mine here,
Ȝe schule on oþer wise singe,
An acursi alle fiȝtinge;
Vor nis of ow non so kene,   1705
Þat durre abide mine onsene.'
   Þeos Hule spac wel baldeliche,
For þah heo nadde swo hwatliche
Ifare after hire here,
Heo walde neoþeles ȝefe answere   1710
Þe Niȝtegale mid swucche worde.
For moni man mid speres orde
Haveþ lutle strencþe, and mid his chelde,
Ah neoþeles in one felde,
Þurh belde worde an mid ilete,   1715
Deþ his ivo for arehþe swete.
   Þe Wranne, for heo cuþe singe,
Þar com in þare moreȝeninge
To helpe þare Niȝtegale;
For þah heo hadde stevene smale,   1720
Heo hadde gode þrote and schille,
An fale manne song a wille.
Þe Wranne was wel wis iholde,
For þeg heo nere ibred a wolde,
Ho was itoȝen among mankenne,   1725
An hire wisdom brohte þenne.
Heo miȝte speke hwar heo walde,
Tovore þe king þah heo scholde.
   'Lusteþ,' heo cwaþ, 'lateþ me speke.
Hwat! Wulle ȝe þis pes tobreke,   1730
An do þanne kinge swuch schame?
Ȝe! Nis he nouþer ded ne lame.
Hunke schal itide harm and schonde,
Ȝef ȝe doþ griþbruche on his londe.
Lateþ beo, and beoþ isome,   1735

1697 counsel. 1698 call out a hue and cry. 1699 your quarrel. 1700 begin quickly. 1702 wait for; army. 1704 curse. 1705 bold. 1706 face. 1708 as quickly. 1709 Gone. 1710 to give an answer to. 1712 point. 1713 or with; shield. 1714 on one battlefield. 1715 bold; behaviour. 1716 Makes his enemy sweat for cowardice. 1717 Wren. 1722 And sang to please many men. 1723 held to be. 1724 though; raised in the forest. 1725 brought up. 1728 Before; she wanted. 1730 peace. 1733 On you both; will arise. 1734 breach of the peace. 1735 united.

An fareþ riht to ower dome,
An lateþ dom þis plaid tobreke,
Alswo hit was erur bispeke.'
　'Ich an wel,' cwað þe Niʒtegale,
'Ah, Wranne, naþt for þire tale,　　　　　　　　　　1740
Ah do for mire lahfulnesse:
Ich nolde þat unrihtfulnesse
Me at þen ende overkome.
Ich nam ofdrad of none dome.
Bihote Ich habbe, soþ hit is,　　　　　　　　　　　1745
Þat Maister Nichole, þat is wis,
Bituxen us deme schule,
An ʒet Ich wene þat he wule.
Ah, war mihte we hine finde?'
　Þe Wranne sat in ore linde;　　　　　　　　　　　1750
'Hwat! Nuste ʒe,' cwaþ heo, 'his hom?
He wuneþ at Porteshom,
At one tune ine Dorsete,
Bi þare see in ore utlete:
Þar he demeþ manie riʒte dom,　　　　　　　　　　1755
An diht and writ mani wisdom,
An þurh his muþe and þurh his honde
Hit is þe betere into Scotlonde.
To seche hine is lihtlich þing,
He naveþ bute one woning.　　　　　　　　　　　　1760
Þat his bischopen muchel schame,
An alle þan þat of his nome
Habbeþ ihert, and of his dede.
Hwi nulleþ hi nimen heom to rede,
Þat he were mid heom ilome　　　　　　　　　　　1765
For teche heom of his wisdome,
An ʒive him rente a vale stude,
Þat he miʒte heom ilome be mide?'
　'Certes,' cwaþ þe Hule, 'þat is soð:
Þeos riche men wel muche misdoð,　　　　　　　　　1770
Þat leteþ þane gode mon,
Þat of so feole þinge con,
An ʒiveþ rente wel misliche,

1736 go straight. 1737 decide this debate. 1738 earlier agreed. 1739 grant that readily.
1740 because of. 1741 I do so; lawfulness. 1742 I should not want unlawfulness. 1744 afraid;
any. 1745 Promised. 1747 Between. 1749 where can we find him. 1750 a linden tree.
1751 Don't you know. 1752 Portesham. 1753 town; Dorset. 1754 Near; inlet. 1756 com-
poses and writes. 1757 because of his. 1758 Things are; as far as. 1759 easy. 1760 dwelling.
1761 is to the bishops. 1762 to all those; name. 1763 heard. 1764 will they not take as advice.
1765 might be; frequently. 1766 In order to. 1767 income from many places. 1768 be with
them. 1772 knows. 1773 income very irregularly.

An of him leteþ wel lihtliche.
Wið heore cunne heo beoþ mildre   1775
An ȝeveþ rente litle childre:
Swo heore wit hi demþ a dwole,
Þat ever abid Maistre Nichole.
Ah ute we þah to him fare,
For þar is unker dom al ȝare.'   1780
    'Do we,' þe Niȝtegale seide;
'Ah wa schal unker speche rede,
An telle tovore unker deme?'
    'Þarof Ich schal þe wel icweme,'
Cwaþ þe Houle, 'for al, ende of orde,   1785
Telle Ich con, word after worde.
An ȝef þe þincþ þat Ich misrempe,
Þu stond aȝein and do me crempe.'
    Mid þisse worde forþ hi ferden,
Al bute here and bute verde,   1790
To Portesham þat heo bicome.
Ah hu heo spedde of heore dome
Ne can Ich eu na more telle:
Her nis na more of þis spelle.

From the Auchinleck Manuscript

Sir Orfeo

We redeþ ofte and findeþ ywrite,
And þis clerkes wele it wite,
Layes þat ben in harping
Ben yfounde of ferli þing.
Sum beþe of wer and sum of wo,   5
And sum of joie and mirþe also,
And sum of trecherie and of gile
Of old aventours þat fel while,
And sum of bourdes and ribaudy,
And mani þer beþ of fairy: 10
Of al þinges þat men seþ
Mest o love for soþ þai beþ.
In Breteyne þis layes were wrouȝt,
First yfounde and forþ ybrouȝt
Of aventours þat fel bi dayes,   15
Wherof Bretouns made her layes.
When kinges miȝt our yhere
Of ani mervailes þat þer were,
Þai token an harp in gle and game,
And maked a lay and ȝaf it name.   20
Now of þis aventours þat weren yfalle
Y can tel sum, ac nouȝt alle.
Ac herkneþ, lordinges þat beþ trewe,
Ichil ȝou telle of Sir Orfewe.
   Orfeo mest of ani þing   25
Loved þe gle of harping;
Siker was everi gode harpour
Of him to have miche honour.
Himself he lerned forto harp
And leyd þeron his wittes scharp;   30
He lerned so, þer noþing was
A better harpour in no plas.

---

2 well; know. **4** composed; marvellous. **5** war. **8** events. **9** jests; ribaldry. **12** of. **13** made. **17** anywhere; hear. **19** revelry. **24** I will. **27** Sure. **28** much. **32** place.

In al þe warld was no man bore
Þat ones Orfeo sat bifore,
And he miȝt of his harping here,   35
Bot he schulde þenche þat he were
In on of þe joies of Paradis,
Swiche melody in his harping is.
　　Orfeo was a king
In Inglond, an heiȝe lording,   40
A stalworþ man and hardi bo,
Large and curteys he was also.
His fader was comen of King Pluto,
And his moder of King Juno,
Þat sumtime were as godes yhold   45
For aventours þat þai dede and told.
Þis king sojournd in Traciens,
Þat was a cité of noble defens:
For Winchester was cleped þo
Traciens, wiþouten no.   50
　　Þe king hadde a quen of priis
Þat was ycleped Dame Herodis,
Þe fairest levedi for þe nones
Þat miȝt gon on bodi and bones,
Ful of love and of godenisse;   55
Ac no man may telle hir fairnise.
　　Bifel so in þe comessing of May,
When miri and hot is þe day,
And oway beþ winter schours,
And everi feld is ful of flours,   60
And blosme breme on everi bouȝ
Overal wexeþ miri anouȝ,
Þis ich quen, Dame Heurodis,
Tok to maidens of priis,
And went in an undrentide   65
To play bi an orchard side,
To se þe floures sprede and spring,
And to here þe foules sing.
Þai sett hem doun all þre
Under a fair ympe-tre,   70
And wel sone þis fair quene
Fel on slepe opon þe grene.
Þe maidens durst hir nouȝt awake,
Bot lete hir ligge and rest take.
So sche slepe til after none,   75

---

33 born. 41 as well. 42 Generous. 47 lived. 48 fortifications. 49 called; then. 50 denial.
51 precious. 53 lady. 54 walk. 57 beginning. 61 bright. 62 grows; enough. 63 same.
65 late morning. 70 grafted tree. 74 lie.

Þat undertide was al ydone.
Ac as sone as sche gan awake
She crid, and loþli bere gan make:
Sche froted hir honden and hir fet,
And crached hir visage, it bled wete;   80
Hir riche robe hye al torett
And was reveyd out of hir wit.
Þe tuo maidens hir biside
No durst wiþ hir no leng abide,
Bot ourn to þe palays ful riȝt   85
And told boþe squier and kniȝt
Þat her quene awede wold,
And bad hem go and hir at-hold.
Kniȝtes urn, and levedis also –
Damisels sexti and mo.   90
In þe orchard to þe quen hye come,
And her up in her armes nome
And brouȝt hir to bed atte last,
And held hir þere fine fast;
Ac ever sche held in o cri,   95
And wold up and owy.
When Orfeo herd þat tiding,
Never him nas wers for noþing.
He come wiþ kniȝtes tene
To chaumber riȝt bifor þe quene,   100
And biheld, and seyd wiþ grete pité:
'O lef liif, what is te,
Þat ever ȝete hast ben so stille,
And now gredest wonder schille?
Þi bodi þat was so white ycore   105
Wiþ þine nailes is al totore;
Allas, þi rode þat was so red
Is al wan as þou were ded;
And also þine fingres smale
Beþ al blodi and al pale.   110
Allas, þi lovesom eyȝen to
Lokeþ so man doþ on his fo.
A, dame, Ich biseche, merci!
Lete ben al þis reweful cri,
And tel me what þe is, and hou,   115
And what þing may þe help now.'
      Þo lay sche stille atte last

76 gone. 78 loathsome outcry. 79 rubbed. 80 face. 81 tore to pieces. 82 driven. 84 dared.
85 ran; straight. 87 had gone mad. 88 urged; restrain. 91 they. 92 took. 95 persisted.
96 away. 98 worse; nothing (i.e. any reason). 99 ten. 102 dear; is wrong. 104 cries out; shrilly.
105 excellently. 106 torn to pieces. 107 complexion. 108 as if. 111 beautiful. 112 as.
115 how it happened.

And gan to wepe swiþe fast,
And seyd þus þe king to:
'Allas, mi lord Sir Orfeo,   120
Seþþen we first togider were,
Ones wroþ never we nere,
Bot ever Ich have yloved þe
As mi liif, and so þou me;
Ac now we mot delen ato   125
Do þi best, for Y mot go.'
    'Allas!' quaþ he, 'Forlorn Icham!
Whider wiltow go, and to wham?
Whider þou gost Ichil wiþ þe,
And whider Y go þou schalt wiþ me.'   130
    'Nay, nay, sir, þat nouȝt nis;
Ichil þe telle al hou it is.
As Ich lay þis undertide
And slepe under our orchard side,
Þer come to me to faire kniȝtes   135
Wele yarmed al to riȝtes,
And bad me comen an heiȝing
And speke wiþ her lord þe king;
And Ich answerd at wordes bold,
Y no durst nouȝt, no Y nold.   140
Þai pricked oȝain as þai miȝt drive.
Þo com her king also blive
Wiþ an hundred kniȝtes and mo,
And damisels an hundred also,
Al on snowe-white stedes;   145
As white as milke were her wedes.
Y no seiȝe never ȝete bifore
So faire creatours ycore.
Þe king hadde a croun on hed,
It nas of silver no of gold red,   150
Ac it was of a precious ston;
As briȝt as þe sonne it schon.
And as son as he to me cam,
Wold Ich, nold Ich, he me nam,
And made me wiþ him ride   155
Opon a palfray bi his side;
And brouȝt me to his palays,
Wele atird in ich ways,

---

118 very. **121** Since. **122** were not. **125** must be split apart. **127** I am. **128** will you; whom. **129** I will. **131** cannot be. **136** properly. **137** in haste. **138** their. **139** with. **140** dared not; would not. **141** They rode again as fast as they could. **142** immediately. **146** clothes. **147** saw. **148** excellent. **150** was not. **153** soon. **154** Whether I wanted to or not, he took me. **158** adorned; each.

And shewed me castels and tours,
Rivers, forestes, friþ wiþ flours,   160
And his riche stedes ichon,
And seþþen me brouȝt oȝain hom
Into our owhen orchard,
And said to me þus afterward:
"Loke, dame, tomorwe þatow be   165
Riȝt here under þis ympe-tre,
And þan þou schalt wiþ ous go
And live wiþ ous evermo;
And ȝif þou makest ous ylet,
Whar þou be, þou worst yfet,   170
And totore þine limes al,
Þat noþing help þe no schal;
And þei þou best so totorn,
Ȝete þou worst wiþ ous yborn." '
    When King Orfeo herd þis cas,   175
'O we!' quaþ he, 'Allas, allas!
Lever me were to lete mi liif
Þan þus to lese þe quen mi wiif.'
He asked conseyl at ich man,
Ac no man him help no can.   180
Amorwe þe undertide is come
And Orfeo haþ his armes ynome
And wele ten hundred kniȝtes wiþ him,
Ich yarmed stout and grim,
And wiþ þe quen wenten he   185
Riȝt unto þat ympetre.
Þai made scheltrom in ich a side,
And sayd þai wold þere abide
And dye þer everichon,
Er þe quen schuld fram hem gon;   190
Ac ȝete amiddes hem ful riȝt
Þe quen was oway ytuiȝt,
Wiþ fairi forþ ynome:
Men wist never wher sche was bicome.
    Þo was þer criing, wepe and wo;   195
Þe king into his chaumber is go,
And oft swoned opon þe ston,
And made swiche diol and swiche mon
Þat neiȝe his liif was yspent.
Þer was non amendement.   200

---

160 woodland. **161** estates; each one. **162** then. **163** own. **165** that you. **166** grafted tree.
169 cause; hindrance. **170** Wherever; will; be fetched. **171** limbs. **173** even though; will be.
174 will be; carried. **175** event. **176** woe. **177** Rather; lose. **181** On the next day. **182** taken.
184 Each. **186** grafted tree. **187** shield wall. **191** straight away. **192** snatched. **194** knew;
disappeared. **197** stone floor. **198** sorrow; lamentation. **200** remedy.

He cleped togider his barouns,
Erls, lordes of renouns;
And when þai al ycomen were,
'Lordinges,' he said, 'bifor ȝou here
Ich ordainy min heiȝe steward   205
To wite mi kingdom afterward.
In mi stede ben he schal
To kepe mi londes over al;
For now Ichave mi quen ylore,
Þe fairest levedi þat ever was bore,   210
Never eft Y nil no woman se.
Into wildernes Ichil te
And live þer evermore
Wiþ wilde bestes in holtes hore.
And when ȝe understond þat Y be spent,   215
Make ȝou þan a parlement
And chese ȝou a newe king.
Now doþ ȝour best wiþ al mi þing.'
    Þo was þer wepeing in þe halle,
And grete cri among hem alle;   220
Unneþe miȝt old or ȝong
For wepeing speke a word wiþ tong.
Þai kneled adoun al yfere
And praid him, ȝif his wille were,
Þat he no schuld nouȝt fram hem go.   225
'Do way!' quaþ he, 'It schal be so!'
Al his kingdom he forsoke,
Bot a sclavin on him he toke:
He no hadde kirtel no hode,
No schert, no noþer gode;   230
Bot his harp he tok algate
And dede him barfot out atte ȝate;
No man most wiþ him go.
    O, way! What þer was wepe and wo
When he þat hadde ben king wiþ croun   235
Went so poverlich out of toun.
Þurth wode and over heþ
Into þe wildernes he geþ.
Noþing he fint þat him is ays,
Bot ever he liveþ in gret malais.   240
He þat hadde ywerd þe fowe and griis,

---

201 called. **205** appoint. **206** rule. **207** place. **209** I have; lost. **211** again. **212** I will; go. **214** grey woods. **215** dead. **217** choose. **218** goods. **221** Scarcely. **223** together. **226** Enough. **228** Only; pilgrim's mantle. **229** short coat. **230** other. **231** at any rate. **232** went (word-play on 'dead'?); gate. **234** alas. **236** in poverty. **237** Through. **238** goes. **239** finds; comfort. **240** discomfort. **241** worn; patterned fur; grey fur.

And on bed þe purper biis,
Now on hard heþe he liþ,
Wiþ leves and gresse he him wriþ.
He þat hadde had castels and tours,   245
River, forest, friþ wiþ flours,
Now, þei it comenci to snewe and frese,
Þis king mot make his bed in mese.
He þat had yhad kniȝtes of priis
Bifor him kneland, and levedis,   250
Now seþ he noþing þat him likeþ,
Bot wilde wormes bi him strikeþ.
He þat had yhad plenté
Of mete and drink, of ich deynté,
Now may he al day digge and wrote   255
Er he finde his fille of rote.
In somer he liveþ bi wild frut,
And berien bot gode lite;
In winter may he noþing finde
Bot rote, grases and þe rinde.   260
Al his bodi was oway duine
For missays, and al tochine.
Lord, who may telle þe sore
Þis king sufferd ten ȝere and more?
His here of his berd, blac and rowe,   265
To his girdelstede was growe.
His harp, whereon was al his gle
He hidde in an holwe tre,
And when þe weder was clere and briȝt
He toke his harp to him wel riȝt,   270
And harped at his owhen wille.
Into alle þe wode þe soun gan schille,
Þat alle þe wilde bestes þat þer beþ
For joie abouten him þai teþ,
And alle þe foules þat þer were   275
Come and sete on ich a brere
To here his harping afine –
So miche melody was þerin;
And when he his harping lete wold,
No best bi him abide nold.   280
    He miȝt se him bisides,
Oft in hot undertides,

242 purple; fine linen. 244 covers. 246 woodland. 247 though; begins. 248 moss.
250 kneeling. 252 snakes; glide. 255 root around. 256 root. 258 And berries of only little
good. 260 bark. 261 wasted away. 262 hardship; scarred. 263 sorrow. 265 unkempt.
266 waist. 267 revelry. 270 straight away. 272 to resound. 274 approach. 275 may be.
276 branch. 278 much. 279 stop. 280 stay. 281 moreover.

Þe king o fairy wiþ his rout
Com to hunt him al about
Wiþ dim cri and bloweing,   285
And houndes also wiþ him berking;
Ac no best þai no nome,
No never he nist whider þai bicome.
And oþerwhile he miȝt him se
As a gret ost bi him te,   290
Wele atourned, ten hundred kniȝtes,
Ich yarmed to his riȝtes,
Of cuntenaunce stout and fers,
Wiþ mani desplaid baners,
And ich his swerd ydrawe hold;   295
Ac never he nist whider þai wold.
And oþerwhile he seiȝe oþer þing:
Kniȝtes and levedis com daunceing
In queynt atire, gisely,
Queynt pas and softly.   300
Tabours and trunpes ȝede hem bi,
And al maner menstraci.
    And on a day he seiȝe him biside
Sexti levedis on hors ride,
Gentil and jolif as brid on ris.   305
Nouȝt o man amonges hem þer nis;
And ich a faucon on hond bere,
And riden on haukin bi o rivere.
Of game þai founde wel gode haunt,
Maulardes, hayroun and cormeraunt.   310
Þe foules of þe water ariseþ;
Þe faucouns hem wele deviseþ;
Ich faucoun his pray slouȝ.
Þat seiȝe Orfeo and louȝ.
'Parfay!' quaþ he, 'þer is fair game;   315
Þider Ichil, bi Godes name:
Ich was ywon swiche werk to se.'
    He aros and þider gan te.
To a levedi he was ycome,
Biheld and haþ wele undernome,   320
And seþ bi al þing þat it is
His owhen quen, Dam Heurodis.

---

283 company. **285** faint. **287** caught. **288** where; went. **289** sometimes. **290** What seemed
to be a great army go by him. **291** equipped. **292** properly. **293** fierce. **296** were going.
299 elegant; skilfully. **300** pace. **301** trumpets. **302** revelry. **303** moreover. **305** Charming
and cheerful as a bird on a twig. **307** falcon. **308** hawking. **309** abundance. **310** Mallards.
312 aim at. **313** killed. **314** laughed. **315** Indeed. **316** There I will (go). **317** accustomed.
318 went. **320** recognized. **322** own.

ȝern he biheld hir, and sche him eke,
Ac noiþer to oþer a word no speke.
For messais þat sche on him seiȝe,   325
Þat had ben so riche and so heiȝe,
Þe teres fel out of her eiȝe.
Þe oþer levedis þis yseiȝe
And maked hir oway to ride;
Sche most wiþ him no lenger abide.   330
'Allas,' quaþ he, 'now me is wo.
Whi nil deþ now me slo?
Allas, wroche, þat Y no miȝt
Dye now after þis siȝt.
Allas, to long last mi liif,   335
When Y no dar nouȝt wiþ mi wiif,
No hye to me, o word speke.
Allas, whi nil min hert breke?
Parfay,' quaþ he, 'tide wat bitide,
Whider so þis levedis ride,   340
Þe selve way Ichil streche –
Of liif no deþ me no reche.'
   His sclavain he dede on also spac
And henge his harp opon his bac,
And had wel gode wil to gon;   345
He no spard noiþer stub no ston.
In at a roche þe levedis rideþ
And he after, and nouȝt abideþ.
When he was in þe roche ygo
Wele þre mile oþer mo,   350
He com into a fair cuntray
As briȝt so sonne on somers day,
Smoþe and plain and al grene,
Hille no dale nas þer non ysene.
Amidde þe lond a castel he siȝe,   355
Riche and real and wonder heiȝe.
Al þe utmast wal
Was clere and schine as cristal;
An hundred tours þer were about,
Degiselich and bataild stout;   360
Þe butras com out of þe diche
Of rede gold yarched riche;
Þe vousour was avowed al
Of ich maner divers aumal.

323 Eagerly; also. **325** discomfort; saw. **330** could. **332** kill. **333** wretch. **334** sight. **339** Let whatever may happen happen. **341** same; go. **342** care. **343** put; at once. **346** stopped for; tree trunk. **347** rock. **353** flat. **355** saw. **356** royal. **360** Wonderful; crenellated. **361** buttress; moat. **363** vaulting; decorated. **364** enamel.

Wiþin þer wer wide wones   365
Al of precious stones;
Þe werst piler on to biholde
Was al of burnist gold.
Al þat lond was ever liȝt,
For when it schuld be þerk and niȝt,   370
Þe riche stones liȝt gonne
As briȝt as doþ at none þe sonne.
No man may telle no þenche in þouȝt
Þe riche werk þat þer was wrouȝt.
Bi al þing him þink þat it is   375
Þe proude court of Paradis.
In þis castel þe levedis aliȝt;
He wold in after ȝif he miȝt.
     Orfeo knokkeþ atte gate;
Þe porter was redi þerate   380
And asked what he wold have ydo.
'Parfay,' quaþ he, 'Ich am a minstrel, lo!
To solas þi lord wiþ mi gle,
Ȝif his swete wille be.'
Þe porter undede þe ȝate anon   385
And lete him in to þe castel gon.
     Þan he gan bihold about al,
And seiȝe liggeand wiþin þe wal
Of folk þat were þider ybrouȝt,
And þouȝt dede and nare nouȝt.   390
Sum stode wiþouten hade,
And sum non armes nade,
And sum þurth þe bodi hadde wounde,
And sum lay wode ybounde,
And sum armed on hors sete,   395
And sum astrangled as þai ete,
And sum were in water adreynt,
And sum wiþ fire al forschreynt.
Wives þer lay on child-bedde,
Sum ded and sum awedde,   400
And wonder fele þer lay bisides
Riȝt as þai slepe her undertides.
Eche was þus in þis warld ynome,
Wiþ fairi þider ycome.
Þer he seiȝe his owhen wiif,   405
Dame Heurodis, his lef liif,

365 dwelling-places. 367 pillar. 368 burnished. 370 dark. 371 shone. 372 noon. 373 think.
374 made. 375 it seems to him. 378 he wished (to go). 380 at it. 383 minstrelsy. 385 undid.
388 lying. 390 seemed; were not. 391 head. 394 mad. 395 sat. 396 choked; ate.
397 drowned. 398 shrivelled. 400 gone mad. 401 many. 402 morning nap. 403 taken.
406 dear.

Slepe under an ympe-tre;
Bi her cloþes he knewe þat it was he.
  And when he hadde bihold þis mervails alle
He went in to þe kinges halle;   410
Þan seiȝe he þer a semly siȝt,
A tabernacle blisseful and briȝt,
Þerin her maister king sete,
And her quen, fair and swete.
Her crounes, her cloþes schine so briȝt   415
Þat unneþe bihold he hem miȝt.
When he hadde biholden al þat þing,
He kneled adoun bifor þe king.
'O lord,' he seyd, 'ȝif it þi wille were,
Mi menstraci þou schust yhere.'   420
Þe king answerd: 'What man artow
Þat art hider ycomen now?
Ich, no non þat is wiþ me,
No sent never after þe.
Seþþen þat Ich here regni gan,   425
Y no fond never so folehardi man
Þat hider to ous durst wende
Bot þat Ic him wald ofsende.'
'Lord,' quaþ he, 'trowe ful wel,
Y nam bot a pover menstrel,   430
And, sir, it is þe maner of ous
To seche mani a lordes hous;
Þei we nouȝt welcom no be,
ȝete we mot proferi forþ our gle.'
  Bifor þe king he sat adoun   435
And tok his harp so miri of soun,
And tempreþ his harp as he wele can,
And blisseful notes he þer gan,
Þat al þat in þe palays were
Com to him forto here,   440
And liggeþ adoun to his fete,
Hem þenkeþ his melody so swete.
Þe king herkneþ and sitt ful stille,
To here his gle he haþ gode wille.
Gode bourde he hadde of his gle,   445
Þe riche quen also hadde he.
When he hadde stint his harping
Þan seyd to him þe king:
'Menstrel, me likeþ wele þi gle.

407 grafted tree. 408 she. 409 marvels. 412 canopied dais. 413 lord. 416 scarcely.
420 should. 423 Neither I nor those with me. 425 Since; reign. 427 come. 428 Unless I
desired to send for him. 429 believe. 434 offer. 436 sound. 437 tunes. 441 lie; at. 442 It
seems to them. 443 listens. 445 entertainment. 446 she. 447 stopped.

Now aske of me what it be,   450
Largelich Ichil þe pay.
Now speke and tow miȝt asay.'
    'Sir,' he seyd, 'Ich biseche þe
Þatow woldest ȝive me
Þat ich levedi, briȝt on ble,   455
Þat slepeþ under þe ympe-tre.'
'Nay,' quaþ þe king, 'þat nouȝt nere!
A sori couple of ȝou it were,
For þou art lene, rowe and blac,
And sche is lovesum wiþouten lac.   460
A loþlich þing it were forþi
To sen hir in þi compayni.'
    'O sir,' he seyd, 'gentil king,
Ȝete were it a wele fouler þing
To here a lesing of þi mouþe.   465
So, sir, as ȝe seyd nouþe,
What Ich wold aski have Y schold,
And nedes þou most þi word hold.'
Þe king seyd, 'Seþþen it is so,
Take hir bi þe hond and go.   470
Of hir Ichil þatow be bliþe.'
He kneled adoun and þonked him swiþe.
His wiif he tok bi þe hond
And dede him swiþe out of þat lond.
And went him out of þat þede;   475
Riȝt as he come, þe way he ȝede.
So long he haþ þe way ynome
To Winchester he is ycome
Þat was his owhen cité;
Ac no man knewe þat it was he.   480
No forþer þan þe tounes ende
For knoweleche no durst he wende;
Bot wiþ a begger ybilt ful narwe
Þer he tok his herbarwe
To him and to his owhen wiif,   485
As a minstrel of pover liif,
And asked tidinges of þat lond
And who þe kingdom held in hond.
Þe pover begger in his cote
Told him everich a grot: 490
Hou her quen was stole owy

---

451 Generously. **452** if you can test (me). **455** same; complexion. **457** cannot be. **458** miserable; would be. **459** unkempt. **460** beautiful; blemish. **461** loathsome; therefore. **464** sorrier. **465** falsehood. **466** just now. **467** ask. **468** keep. **471** I hope; happy. **472** greatly. **474** went; quickly. **475** country. **481** further. **482** recognition. **483** lodged; poorly. **484** lodging. **489** cottage. **490** single detail.

Ten зer gon wiþ fairy,
And hou her king en exile зede,
Bot no man nist in wiche þede,
And hou þe steward þe lond gan hold,   495
And oþer mani þinges him told.
    Amorwe, oзain nonetide,
He maked his wiif þer abide;
Þe beggers cloþes he borwed anon
And heng his harp his rigge opon,   500
And went him into þat cité
Þat men miзt him bihold and se.
Erls and barouns bold,
Burjays and levedis him gun bihold.
'Lo,' þai seyd, 'swiche a man!   505
Hou long þe here hongeþ him opan!
Lo, hou his berd hongeþ to his kne!
He is yclongen also a tre!'
And as he зede in þe strete,
Wiþ his steward he gan mete,   510
And loude he sett on him a crie:
'Sir steward,' he seyd, 'merci!
Ich am an harpour of heþenisse;
Help me now in þis destresse.'
Þe steward seyd, 'Com wiþ me, come;   515
Of þat Ichave þou schalt have some.
Everich gode harpour is welcom me to
For mi lordes love, Sir Orfeo.'
    In þe castel þe steward sat atte mete,
And mani lording was bi him sete;   520
Þer were trompours and tabourers,
Harpours fele, and crouders.
Miche melody þai maked alle,
And Orfeo sat stille in þe halle
And herkneþ; when þai ben al stille   525
He toke his harp and tempred schille.
Þe blissefulest notes he harped þere
Þat ever ani man yherd wiþ ere:
Ich man liked wele his gle.
Þe steward biheld and gan yse,   530
And knewe þe harp als blive:
'Menstrel,' he seyd, 'so mot þou þrive,
Where hadcstow þis harp and hou?
Y pray þat þou me telle now.'

---

492 years. **493** went. **494** country. **497** The following day, towards noon. **500** back. **504** Townsmen. **508** shrivelled. **513** foreign parts. **518** For the love of my lord. **519** meal. **521** drummers. **522** many; fiddlers. **526** tuned it clearly. **527** most delightful. **528** ear. **531** immediately.

'Lord,' quaþ he, 'in uncouþe þede,   535
Þurth a wildernes as Y ȝede,
Þer Y founde in a dale
Wiþ lyouns a man totorn smale,
And wolves him frete wiþ teþ so scharp,
Bi him Y fond þis ich harp,   540
Wele ten ȝere it is ygo.'
'O', quaþ þe steward, 'now me is wo!
Þat was mi lord Sir Orfeo.
Allas, wreche, what schal Y do
Þat have swiche a lord ylore?   545
A, way, þat Ich was ybore!
Þat him was so hard grace yȝarked
And so vile deþ ymarked!'
Adoun he fel aswon to grounde.
His barouns him tok up in þat stounde   550
And telleþ him hou it geþ:
It nis no bot of mannes deþ.
    King Orfeo knewe wele bi þan
His steward was a trewe man
And loved him as he auȝt to do,   555
And stont up and seyt þus: 'Lo!
Steward, herkne now þis þing:
Ȝif Ich were Orfeo þe king,
And hadde ysuffred ful ȝore
In wildernisse miche sore,   560
And hadde ywon mi quen owy
Out of þe lond of fairy,
And hadde ybrouȝt þe levedi hende
Riȝt here to þe tounes ende,
And wiþ a begger her in ynome,   565
And were miself hider ycome
Poverlich to þe, þus stille,
Forto asay þi gode wille,
And Ich founde þe þus trewe,
Þou no schust it never rewe.   570
Sikerlich, for love or ay,
Þou schust be king after mi day.
And ȝif þou of mi deþ hadest ben bliþe,
Þou schust have voided also swiþe.'
    Þo al þo þat þerin sete   575
Þat it was King Orfeo underȝete,

535 unknown; land. 538 torn into small pieces. 539 gnawed. 540 same. 545 lost. 546 woe;
born. 547 a fate; appointed. 548 marked out. 549 in a swoon. 550 time. 551 goes.
552 There is no remedy for man's death. 553 this. 555 ought. 556 stands; says. 559 long
ago. 560 sorrow. 563 courteous. 567 In poverty. 568 test. 570 should; regret. 571 Cer-
tainly; fear. 573 happy. 574 been banished; just as quickly. 575 Then; those. 576 perceived.

And þe steward him wele knewe:
Over and over þe bord he þrewe
And fel adoun to his fet;
So dede everich lord þat þer sete, 580
And al þai seyd at o criing:
'3e beþ our lord, sir, and our king!'
Glad þai were of his live.
To chaumber þai ladde him als bilive,
And baþed him, and schaved his berd, 585
And tired him as a king apert.
And seþþen, wiþ gret processioun,
Þai brou3t þe quen in to þe toun
Wiþ al maner menstraci.
Lord, þer was grete melody! 590
For joie þai wepe wiþ her ei3e
Þat hem so sounde ycomen sei3e.
Now King Orfeo newe coround is,
And his quen Dame Heurodis,
And lived long afterward, 595
And seþþen was king þe steward.
Harpours in Bretaine after þan
Herd hou þis mervaile bigan,
And made herof a lay of gode likeing,
And nempned it after þe king. 600
Þat lay 'Orfeo' is yhote –
Gode is þe lay, swete is þe note.
Þus com Sir Orfeo out of his care:
God graunt ous alle wele to fare! Amen.

---

578 table. 581 one. 584 immediately. 586 dressed; without disguise. 587 then. 589 revelry.
592 safe; returned. 593 crowned. 599 delight. 600 named. 601 called. 603 sorrow.

From London, British Library, Harley 2253

Alysoun

Bytuene Mersh ant Averil,
When spray biginneþ to springe,
Þe lutel foul haþ hire wyl
On hyre lud to synge.
Ich libbe in love-longinge   5
For semlokest of alle þynge:
He may me blisse bringe;
Icham in hire baundoun.

An hendy hap Ichabbe yhent,
Ichot from hevene it is me sent;   10
From alle wymmen mi love is lent,
Ant lyht on Alysoun.

On heu hire her is fayr ynoh,
Hire browe broune, hire eȝe blake;
Wiþ lossum chere he on me loh,   15
Wiþ middel smal ant wel ymake.
Bote he me wolle to hire take
Forte buen hire owen make,
Longe to lyven Ichulle forsake
Ant, feye, fallen adoun.   20
An hendy hap etc.

Nihtes when Y wende ant wake,
Forþi myn wonges waxeþ won,
Levedi, al for þine sake,
Longinge is ylent me on.   25
In world nis non so wyter mon
Þat al hire bounte telle con:

2 shoots. 3 desire. 4 song. 5 live. 6 most seemly. 7 She. 8 power. 9 fair fortune; received. 10 I know. 11 gone. 12 alighted. 13 hue; hair. 14 eye brows. 15 lovely; countenance; she; laughed. 17 she. 18 be; mate. 20 fated to die. 22 turn; lie awake. 23 cheeks; grow. 25 arrived. 26 wise. 27 goodness.

Hire swyre is whittore þen þe swon,
Ant feyrest may in toune.
An hendi hap etc.   30

Icham for wowyng al forwake,
Wery so water in wore,
Lest eny reve me my make
Ychabbe yȝyrned ȝore.
Betere is þolien whyle sore   35
Þen mournen evermore.
Geynest under gore,
Herkne to my roun.
An hendi hap etc.

Spring

Lenten ys come wiþ love to toune,
Wiþ blosmen ant wiþ briddes roune,
Þat al þis blisse bryngeþ.
Dayeseȝes in þis dales,
Notes suete of nyhtegales,   5
Uch foul song singeþ.
Þe þrestelcoc him þreteþ oo,
Away is huere winter wo
When woderove springeþ.
Þis foules singeþ ferly fele,   10
Ant wlyteþ on huere wynne wele
Þat al þe wode ryngeþ.

Þe rose rayleþ hire rode,
Þe leves on þe lyhte wode
Waxen al wiþ wille.   15
Þe mone mandeþ hire bleo;
Þe lilie is lossom to seo,
Þe fenyl ant þe fille.
Wowes þis wilde drakes,
Miles murgeþ huere makes   20
Ase strem þat strikeþ stille.
Mody meneþ, so doþ mo;

---

28 neck; swan. 29 maid. 31 wooing; weary with waking. 32 weir. 33 rob. 34 yearned; for a long time. 35 to suffer; sorely. 37 loveliest; clothing (i.e. in body). 38 Listen; song. 1 Spring. 2 song. 4 Daisies. 7 thrush; brawls continuously. 8 their. 9 woodruff. 10 in wonderful profusion. 11 warble; abundant joy. 13 puts on; redness. 15 willingness. 16 sends forth; beams. 17 lovely. 18 chervil. 19 Woo. 20 Animals; delight; mates. 21 flows; softly. 22 Passionate men; complain; many.

Ichot Ycham on of þo
For love þat likes ille.

Þe mone mandeþ hire lyht,   25
So doþ þe semly sonne bryht
When briddes singeþ breme.
Deawes donkeþ þe dounes,
Deores wiþ huere derne rounes
Domes forte deme.   30
Wormes woweþ under cloude,
Wymmen waxeþ wounder proude
So wel hit wol hem seme.
Зef me shal wonte wille of on,
Þis wunne weole Y wole forgon,   35
Ant wyht in wode be fleme.

An Old Man's Prayer

Heзe Loverd, þou here my bone,
Þat madest middelert ant mone
Ant mon of murþes munne.
Trusti kyng ant trewe in trone,
Þat þou be wiþ me sahte sone,   5
Asoyle me of sunne.
Fol Ich wes in folies fayn,
In luthere lastes Y am layn,
Þat makeþ myn þryftes þunne,
Þat semly sawes wes woned to seyn,   10
Nou is marred al my meyn,
Away is al my wunne.

Unwunne haveþ myn wonges wet,
Þat makeþ me rouþes rede;
Ne semy nout þer Y am set,   15
Þer me calleþ me 'fulleflet',
Ant 'waynoun wayteglede'.

Whil Ich wes in wille wolde,
In uch a bour among þe bolde
Yholde wiþ þe heste;   20

23 those. 24 badly. 27 brightly. 28 Dews; soak. 29 Animals; secret. 30 Wishes; declare. 31 clod. 32 wonderfully. 33 suit/befit. 34 lack; my desire; from one of them. 35 wealth of joy; forego. 36 as a creature; banished. 1 High; prayer. 2 earth. 3 joys; to think. 4 throne. 5 reconciled. 6 Absolve; sin. 7 eager. 8 wicked; vices. 9 gains; meagre. 10 speeches; accustomed. 11 virtue. 12 joy. 13 Sadness; cheeks. 14 lamentations; utter. 15 suits me; sat. 16 'floor-filler'. 17 'good-for-nothing; fire-gazer'. 18 pleasure's; power. 19 every; noble. 20 In keeping; highest.

Nou Y may no fynger folde,
Lutel loved ant lasse ytolde,
Yleved wiþ þe leste.
A goute me haþ ygreyþed so,
Ant oþer eveles monye mo,   25
Y not whet bote is beste.
Þat er wes wilde ase þe ro,
Nou Y swyke, Y mei nout so,
Hit siweþ me so faste.
Faste Y wes on horse heh,   30
Ant werede worly wede;
Nou is faren al my feh,
Wiþ serewe þat Ich hit ever seh;
A staf ys nou my stede.

When Y se steden styþe in stalle,   35
Ant Y go haltinde in þe halle,
Myn huerte gynneþ to helde.
Þat er wes wildest inwiþ walle,
Nou is under fote yfalle
Ant mey no fynger felde.   40
Þer Ich wes luef Icham ful loht,
Ant alle myn godes me atgoht,
Myn gomenes waxeþ gelde;
Þat feyre founden me mete ant cloht,
Hue wrieþ awey as hue were wroht;   45
Such is evel ant elde.

Evel ant elde ant oþer wo
Foleweþ me so faste,
Me þunkeþ myn herte brekeþ a-tuo,
Suete God, whi shal hit swo?   50
Hou mai hit lengore laste?

Whil mi lif wes luþer ant lees
Glotonie mi glemon wes,
Wiþ me he wonede a while;
Prude wes my plowe-fere,   55
Lecherie my lavendere,
Wiþ hem is gabbe ant gyle.
Coveytise myn keyes bere,
Niþe ant onde were mi fere,

---

21 bend. **22** less; esteemed. **23** Believed to be; among. **24** gout; grieved. **26** remedy. **27** before; wild; roe. **28** desist. **29** pursues. **31** expensive; clothes. **32** gone; property. **33** sorrow; saw. **34** steed. **35** strong. **36** halting. **37** sink. **38** within. **41** loved; loathed. **42** disappeared. **43** pleasures; barren. **44** Those who kindly; food. **45** turn; angry. **46** evil; old age. **50** so. **52** wicked; false. **53** minstrel. **54** lived. **55** play-fellow. **56** laundress (i.e. mistress). **57** mockery; guile. **58** Covetousness; carried off. **59** Anger; envy; companions.

Þat bueþ folkes fyle;   60
Lyare wes mi latymer,
Sleuthe ant slep mi bedyver,
Þat weneþ me unbewhile.

Umbewhile Y am to whene,
When Y shal murþes meten;   65
Monne mest Y am to mene.
Lord, þat hast me lyf to lene,
Such lotes lef me leten.

Such lyf Ich have lad fol ʒore
Merci, Loverd, Y nul namore,   70
Bowen Ichulle to bete.
Syker hit siweþ me ful sore –
Gabbes, les, ant luþere lore:
Sunnes bueþ unsete.
Godes heste ne huld Y noht,   75
Bote ever aʒeyn is wille Y wroht
Mon lereþ me to lete.
Such serewe haþ myn sides þurhsoht
Þat al Y weolewe away to noht
When Y shal murþes mete.   80

To mete murþes Ich wes wel fous
Ant comely mon ta calle;
Y sugge by oþer ase bi ous,
Alse ys hirmon halt in hous,
Ase heved-hount in halle.   85

Dredful deþ, why wolt þou dare
Bryng þis body þat is so bare
Ant yn bale ybounde?
Careful mon ycast in care,
Y falewe as flour ylet forþfare,   90
Ychabbe myn deþes wounde:
Murþes helpeþ me no more.
Help me, lord, er þen Ich hore,
Ant stunt my lyf a stounde;
Þat ʒokkyn haþ yʒyrned ʒore,   95

---

60 vile. 61 translator. 62 Sloth; sleep; bed-fellows. 63 entertained; from time to time.
64 cheered up. 65 merriment; meet. 66 Of men; most; to be pitied. 67 grant. 68 behaviour;
abandon. 69 led; for a long time. 71 amendment. 72 Truly; pursues. 73 lies; wicked; teaching.
74 Sins; unprofitable. 75 commands; held. 76 did (what). 77 I am taught to leave off.
78 pierced. 79 waste away. 81 eager. 82 And a fine man to be called. 83 I speak about others
just as of us. 84 As a; servant; of high rank. 85 head-hound. 88 misery. 89 Anxious. 90 fade; to
die. 93 grow grey. 94 stop; soon. 95 Who with lustful desire has yearned long since.

Nou hit sereweþ him ful sore
Ant bringeþ him to grounde.

To grounde hit haveþ him ybroht;
Whet ys þe beste bote?
Bote heryen him þat haht us boht,   100
Ure Lord þat al þis world haþ wroht,
Ant fallen him to fote.

Nou Icham to deþe ydyht
Ydon is al my dede,
God us lene of ys lyht,   105
Þat we of sontes habben syht
Ant hevene to mede. Amen.

I Syke when Y Singe

I syke when Y singe
For sorewe þat Y se,
When I wiþ wypinge
Biholde upon þe tre,
Ant se Jhesu, þe suete,   5
Is herte blod forlete
For þe love of me.
Ys woundes waxen wete
Þei wepen stille ant mete –
Marie, reweþ þe.   10

Heȝe upon a doune
Þer al folk hit se may
A mile from uch toune
Aboute þe midday
Þe rode is up arered   15
His frendes aren afered
And clyngeþ so þe clay;
Þe rode stond in stone.
Marie stont hire one
And seiþ 'Weylaway!'   20

When Y þe biholde
Wiþ eyȝen bryhte bo,
Ant þi bodi colde,
Þi ble waxeþ blo,
Þou hengest al of blode   25

99 remedy. 100 But; praise. 102 to his feet. 103 prepared. 105 grant. 106 saints; sight.
107 reward. 1 sigh. 3 weeping. 5 sweet. 6 shed. 8 grow wet. 10 pity. 11 hill. 15 raised.
16 afraid. 17 shrunken; as. 18 cross. 19 stands; alone. 22 both. 24 face; leaden. 25 bloody.

So heȝe upon þe rode,
Bituene þeves tuo –
Who may syke more?
Marie wepeþ sore
Ant siht al þis wo.   30

Þe naylles beþ to stronge,
Þe smyþes are to sleye,
Þou bledest al to longe,
Þe tre is al to heyȝe,
Þe stones beoþ al wete: 35
Alas! Jhesu, þe suete.
For nou frend hast þou non
But Seint Johan mournynde,
Ant Marie wepynde,
For pyne þat þe ys on.   40

Ofte when Y sike
And makie my mon,
Wel ille þah me like,
Wonder is hit non.
When Y se honge heȝe   45
And bittre pynes dreȝe,
Jhesu, mi lemmon,
His wondes sore smerte,
Þe spere al to is herte
Ant þourh is sydes gon.   50

Ofte when Y syke
Wiþ care Y am þourhsoht;
When Y wake Y wyke,
Of serewe is al mi þoht.
Alas, men beþ wode   55
Þat suereþ by þe rode,
Ant selleþ him for noht
Þat bohte us out of synne;
He bryng us to wynne   60
Þat haþ us duere boht.   60

30 sees. 32 skilful. 40 torment; upon. 42 lamentation. 43 not at all; though. 46 torments; suffering. 47 sweetheart. 48 hurting. 50 through; his. 52 pierced through. 53 grow weak. 55 mad. 56 swear. 59 joy. 60 dearly.

Richard Rolle
(c.1290–1349)

Song of Love

Now I write a sang of lufe þat þou sal delyte in when þow ert lovand Jhesu Criste:

My sange es in syhtyng, my lyfe es in langynge,
Til I þe se, my Keyng, so fayre in þi schynyng,
So fayre in þi fayrehede, intil þi lyght me lede,
And in þi lufe me fede, in lufe make me to spede,
Þat þou be ever my mede.   5
When wil þou come, Jhesu my joy, and cover me of kare,
And gyf me þe, þat I may se, lifand evermare?
Al my coveytyng war commen, if I myght til þe fare;
I wil na thyng bot anely þe, þat all my will ware.
Jhesu my savyoure, Jhesu my comfortoure,   10
Of al my fayrnes flowre, my helpe and my sokoure,
When may I se þi towre?
When wil þou me kall? Me langes to þi hall
To se þe þan al; þi luf, lat it nat fal.
My hert payntes þe pall þat steds us in stal.   15
Now wax I pale and wan for luf of my lemman.
Jhesu, bath God and man, þi luf þou lerd me þan
When I to þe fast ran; forþi now I lufe kan.
I sytt and syng of luf langyng þat in my breste es bredde.
Jhesu, Jhesu, Jhesu, when war I to þe ledde?   20
Full wele I wate þou sees my state; in lufe my thoght es stedde;
When I þe se and dwels with þe, þan am I fylde and fedde.
Jhesu, þi lufe es fest, and me to lufe thynk best.
My hert, when may it brest to come to þe, my rest?
Jhesu, Jhesu, Jhesu, til þe it es þat I morne   25
For my lyfe and my lyvyng, when may I hethen torne?
Jhesu, my dere and my drewry, delyte ert þou to syng;
Jhesu, my myrth and melody, when will þou com, my Keyng?
Jhesu, my hele and my hony, my whart and my comfortyng,
Jhesu, I covayte forto dy when it es þi payng.   30
Langyng es in me lent þat my lufe hase me sent;

1 sighing. 5 reward. 6 recover. 11 comfort. 17 taught. 21 placed. 23 secure. 24 burst.
26 from here turn. 27 treasure. 29 health. 30 pleasure.

Al wa es fra me went, sen þat my hert es brent
In Criste lufe sa swete, þat never I wil lete;
Bot ever to luf I hete, for lufe my bale may bete,
And til hys blis me bryng, and gyf me my ӡernyng.   35
Jhesu, my lufe, my swetyng:
Langyng es in me lyght, þat byndes me day and nyght
Til I it hafe in syght, his face sa fayre and bryght.
Jhesu, my hope, my hele, my joy ever ilk a dele,
Þi lufe lat it noght kele þat I þi luf may fele,   40
And won with þe in wele.
Jhesu, with þe I byg and belde; lever me war to dy
Þan al þis worlde to welde and hafe it in maystry.
When wil þou rew on me, Jhesu, þat I myght with þe be,
To lufe and lok on þe?   45
My setell ordayne for me, and sett þou me þarin,
For þen moun we never twyn,
And I þi lufe sal syng thorow syght of þi schynyng,
In heven withowten endyng. Amen.

Explicit tractatus Ricardi heremite de Hampole, scriptus cuidam moniali de ӡedyngham.
[Here ends the treatise by Richard, hermit of Hampole, written for a certain nun of Yedingham.]

32 ardent. 34 sorrow; remedy. 35 desire. 39 in every part. 40 cool so that. 41 dwell; prosperity. 43 control. 44 take pity. 46 seat. 47 may; separated.

Wynnere and Wastoure

Here begynnes a tretys and god schorte refreyte bytwixe Wynnere and Wastoure

Sythen that Bretayne was biggede   and Bruyttus it aughte
Thurgh the takynge of Troye   with tresone withinn,
There hathe selcouthes bene sene   in seere kynges tymes,
Bot never so many as nowe   by the nyne dele.
For nowe alle es witt and wyles   that we with delyn,   5
Wyse wordes and slee   and icheon wryeth othere.
Dare never no westren wy,   while this werlde lasteth,
Send his sone southewarde   to see ne to here
That he ne schall holden byhynde   when he hore eldes.
Forthi sayde was a sawe   of Salomon the wyse,   10
It hyeghte harde appone honde,   hope I no noþer,
When wawes waxen schall wilde   and walles bene doun,
And hares appon herthe-stones   schall hurcle in hire tourme,
And eke boyes of blode   with boste and with pryde
Schall wedde ladyes in londe,   and lede hir at will,   15
Thene dredfull domesdaye   it draweth neghe aftir.
Bot whoso sadly will see   and the sothe telle
Say it newely will neghe   or es neghe here.
Whylome were lordes in londe   þat loved in thaire hertis
To here makers of myrthes   þat matirs couthe fynde;   20
And now es no frenchipe in fere   bot fayntnesse of hert,
Wyse wordes withinn   þat wroghte were never
Ne redde in no romance   þat ever renke herde.
Bot now a childe appon chere   withowtten chyn-wedys
Þat never wroghte thurgh witt   thies wordes togedire,   25
Fro he can jangle als a jaye   and japes telle
He schall be lenede and lovede   and lett of a while
Wele more þan þe man   that made it hymselven.
Bot never þe lattere at the laste   when ledys bene knawen;
Werke wittnesse will bere   who wirche kane beste.   30

---

1 founded; conquered. 3 marvels; various. 4 ninth part. 5 guile; cunning; concerned.
7 western man. 8 hear. 10 saying. 11 comes quickly. 12 waves. 13 cower; lairs. 14 also.
15 marry her. 16 soon. 18 soon; approach. 19 Formerly. 20 writers; matters; compose.
22 felt within; expressed. 23 story; any man. 24 in face; a beard. 25 created. 26 Because;
chatter. 27 listened to; regarded. 29 newcomer; men; known. 30 Poetic work; compose.

Bot I schall tell ȝow a tale   þat me bytyde ones
Als I went in the weste   wandrynge myn one.
Bi a bonke of a bourne   bryghte was the sonne
Undir a worthiliche wodde   by a wale medewe
Fele floures gan folde   ther my fote steppede.   35
I layde myn hede one ane hill   ane hawthorne besyde.
The throstills full throly   they threpen togedire;
Hipped up heghwalles   fro heselis tyll othire;
Bernacles with thayre billes   one barkes þay roungen;
Þe jay janglede one heghe,   jarmede the foles;   40
Þe bourne full bremly rane   þe bankes bytwene.
So ruyde were þe roughe stremys   and raughten so heghe
That it was neghande nyghte   or I nappe myghte
For dyn of the depe watir   and dadillyng of fewllys.
Bot as I laye at the laste   þan lowked myn eghne,   45
And I was swythe in a sweven   sweped belyve.
  Me thoghte I was in the werlde,   I ne wiste in whate ende,
One a loveliche lande   þat was ylike grene,
Þat laye loken by a lawe   the lengthe of a myle.
In aythere holte was ane here   in hawberkes full brighte,   50
Harde hattes appon hedes   and helmys with crestys.
Brayden owte thaire baners   bown forto mete;
Schowen owte of the schawes   in schiltrons þay felle,
And bot the lengthe of a launde   thies lordes bytwene.
And alle prayed for the pese   till the prynce come   55
For he was worthiere in witt   than any wy ells:
For to ridde and to rede   and to rewlyn the wrothe
That aythere here appon hethe   had untill othere.
At the creste of a clyffe   a caban was rerede,
Alle raylede with rede   the rofe and the sydes   60
With Ynglysse besantes full brighte   betyn of golde;
And ichone gayly umbygone   with garters of inde,
And iche a gartare of golde   gerede full riche.
Then were ther wordes in þe webbe   werped of heu,
Payntted of plunket   and poyntes bytwene   65
Þat were fourmed full fayre   appon fresche lettres
And alle was it one sawe   appon Ynglysse tonge:
'Hethyng have the hathell   þat any harme thynkes'.

31 happened. 32 on my own. 33 bank; stream. 34 great; pleasant. 35 Many; unfold; where.
37 vigorously; quarrelled. 38 Hopped; woodpeckers. 39 Wild geese; on; gnawed. 40 chirped;
birds. 41 loudly. 42 violent; reached. 43 nearing; before; sleep. 44 twittering; birds. 45 closed;
eyes. 46 dream; swept; quickly. 47 seemed; part. 48 throughout. 49 enclosed; earthworks.
50 grove; army; mail-coats. 51 helmets. 52 They flourished; ready. 53 Marched; woods; phal-
anxes. 54 only; clearing. 55 peace; ruler. 56 other person. 57 judge; advise; anger. 58 each; for
the other. 59 pavilion; erected. 60 adorned. 61 ornaments. 62 surrounded; indigo. 63 dec-
orated. 64 woven; colour. 65 light blue; dots. 67 saying. 68 Scorn; man.

Now the kyng of this kythe   kepe hym oure Lorde!
   Upon heghe one the holt   ane hathell up stondes   70
Wroghte als a wodwyse   alle in wrethyn lokkes,
With ane helme one his hede,   ane hatte appon lofte,
And one heghe one þe hatte   ane hattfull beste,
A lighte lebarde and a longe   lokande full kene
3arked alle of 3alowe golde   in full 3ape wyse.   75
Bot that þat hillede the helme   byhynde in the nekke
Was casten full clenly   in quarters foure:
Two with flowres of Fraunce   before and behynde,
And two out of Ynglonde   with sex grym bestes,
Thre leberdes one lofte   and thre on lowe undir.   80
At iche a cornere a knoppe   of full clene perle
Tasselde of tuly silke   tuttynge out fayre.
And by þe cabane I knewe   the knyghte that I see
And thoghte to wiete or I went   wondres ynewe.
And als I waytted withinn   I was warre sone   85
Of a comliche kynge,   crowned with golde,
Sett one a silken bynche   with septure in honde,
One of the lovelyeste ledis   whoso loveth hym in hert
That ever segge under sonn   sawe with his eghne.
This kynge was comliche clade   in kirtill and mantill,   90
Bery-brown was his berde   brouderde with fewlys;
Fawkons of fyne golde   flakerande with wynges;
And ichone bare in ble,   blewe als me thoghte
A grete gartare of ynde   gerde full riche.
Full gayly was that grete lorde   girde in the myddis   95
A brighte belte of ble   broudirde with fewles;
With drakes and with dukkes   daderande þam semede
For ferdnes of fawkons fete   lesse fawked þay were.
And ever I sayd to myselfe: 'Full selly me thynke
Bot if this renke to the revere   ryde umbestounde.'   100
   The kyng biddith a beryn   by hym þat stondeth
One of the ferlyeste frekes   þat faylede hym never:
'Thynke I dubbede the knyghte   with dynttis to dele?
Wende wightly thy waye   my willes to kythe.
Go bidd þou 3ondere bolde batell   þat one þe bent hoves   105
That they never neghe   nerre togedirs;
For if thay strike one stroke   stynte þay ne thynken.'

69 country; may protect. 70 soldier. 71 dressed; wild man; curled. 72 cap; on top. 73 wrathful animal. 74 nimble lion; long one. 75 Made; yellow; clever. 76 covered. 77 divided. 79 six fierce. 80 on top; underneath. 81 knob. 82 fine red; spreading. 83 recognized. 84 learn something before. 85 aware. 87 throne. 88 most attractive men. 89 a man; eyes. 90 tunic; mantle. 91 embroidered; birds. 92 Falcons; flapping. 93 colour; seemed. 94 adorned. 95 girded in the middle. 97 trembling. 98 fear; in case seized. 99 marvellous; it seems. 100 man; riverbank; at times. 101 asks; knight. 102 most wonderful; soldiers. 103 blows; fight. 104 Go; boldly; proclaim. 105 on the battlefield; lingers. 106 come close to fight; nearer. 107 cease.

'3is lorde,' said þe lede, 'while my life dures.'
     He dothe hym doun one þe bonke   and dwellys a while
Whils he busked and bown was   one his beste wyse: 110
He laped his legges in yren   to the lawe bones;
With pysayne and with pawnce   polischede full clene;
With brases of broun stele   brauden full thikke;
With plates buklede at þe bakke   þe body to 3eme;
With a jupown full juste   joynede by the sydes;   115
A brod chechun at þe bakke,   þe breste had anoþer,
Thre wynges inwith   wroghte in the kynde
Umbygon with a gold wyre.   When I þat gome knewe –
What! He was 3ongeste of 3eris   and 3apeste of witt
Þat any wy in this werlde   wiste of his age.   120
He brake a braunche in his hande   and caughte it swythe,
Trynes one a grete trotte   and takes his waye
There bothe thies ferdes folke   in the felde hoves.
     Sayd: 'Loo! The kyng of this kyth,   þer kepe hym oure Lorde,
Send his erande by me   als hym beste lyketh,   125
That no beryn be so bolde   one bothe his two eghne
Ones to strike one stroke,   ne stirre none nerre
To lede rowte in his rewme   so ryall to thynke
Pertly with 3oure powers   his pese to disturbe.
For this es the usage here   and ever schall worthe,   130
If any beryn be so bolde   with banere for to ryde
Withinn þe kyngdome riche,   bot the kynge one,
That he schall losse the londe   and his lyfe aftir.
Bot sen 3e knowe noghte this kythe,   ne the kynge ryche,
He will forgiffe 3ow this gilt   of his grace one.   135
     Full wyde hafe I walked   amonges thies wyes one,
Bot sawe I never siche a syghte,   segge, with myn eghne;
For here es alle þe folke of Fraunce   ferdede besyde
Of Lorreyne, of Lumbardye,   and of Lawe Spayne;
Wyes of Westwale   þat in were duellen,   140
Of Ynglonde, of Yrlonde,   Estirlynges full many
Þat are stuffede in stele,   strokes to dele.
And 3ondere a baner of blake   þat one þe bent hoves
With thre bulles of ble white   brouden withinn,
And iche one hase of henppe   hynged a corde   145

---

108 Yes; lasts. 109 comes down. 110 prepared; got ready. 111 enclosed; low. 112 armour for neck and torso. 113 arm protection; linked. 114 protect. 115 tunic; close-fitting. 116 coat of arms. 117 made naturalistically. 118 Surrounded; soldier. 119 in years; sharpest. 120 man; knew. 121 quickly. 122 Proceeds. 123 To where; armies'; wait. 125 message; pleases. 126 man; on. 127 Once; move; nearer. 128 troop; realm; proudly. 129 Boldly; peace. 130 custom; be. 132 powerful; except; alone. 133 lose his. 135 offence; alone. 136 Very widely; people. 137 such; sir. 138 gathered; beside. 139 Those of. 140 People of Westphalia. 141 Easterlings. 142 equipped with; deliver. 143 on the battlefield waits. 144 colour; embroidered. 145 hemp.

Seled with a sade lede,   I say als me thynkes.
That hede es of holy kirke –   I hope he be there –
Alle ferse to the fighte   with the folke þat he ledis.
   Anoþer banere es upbrayde   with a bende of grene,
With thre hedis white-herede   with howes one lofte,   150
Croked full craftyly   and kembid in the nekke.
Thies are ledis of this londe   þat schold oure lawes 3eme,
That thynken to dele this daye   with dynttis full many.
I holde hym bot a fole þat fightis   whils flyttynge may helpe
When he hase founden his frende   þat fayled hym never.   155
   The thirde banere one bent   es of blee whitte
With sexe galegs, I see,   of sable withinn,
And iche one has a brown brase   with bokels twayne.
Thies are Sayn Franceys folke   þat sayen alle schall fey worthe.
They aren so ferse and so fresche   þay feghtyn bot seldom.   160
I wote wele for wynnynge   thay wentten fro home,
His purse weghethe full wele   that wanne thaym all hedire.
   The fourte banere one the bent   was brayde appon lofte
With bothe the brerdes of blake,   a balle in the myddes,
Reghte siche as the sonne es   in the someris tyde   165
When it hase moste of þe mayne   one Missomer even.
That was Domynyke this daye   with dynttis to dele;
With many a blesenande beryn   his banere es stuffede,
And 3ythen the pope es so priste   thies prechours to helpe,
And Fraunceys with his folke   es forced besyde,   170
And alle the ledis of the lande   ledith thurgh witt
There es no man appon molde   to machen þaym agayne,
Ne gete no grace appon grounde   undir God hymselven.
   And 3itt es the fyfte appon þe felde   þe faireste of þam alle:
A brighte banere of blee whitte   with three bore hedis.   175
Be any crafte þat I kan   Carmes thaym semyde
For þay are the ordire þat loven   oure lady to serve.
If I scholde say þe sothe   it semys no nothire
Bot þat the freris with othere folke   shall þefelde wynn.
   The sexte es of sendell   and so are þay alle,   180
Whitte als the whalles bone   whoso the sothe tellys,
With beltys of blake   bocled togedir,
The poyntes pared off rownde,   þe pendant awaye,
And alle the lethire appon lofte   þat one lowe hengeth
Schynethe alle for scharpynynge   of the schavynge iren.   185

---

146 heavy seal. **147** leader. **148** keen; leads. **149** displayed; diagonal stripe. **150** lawyer's wigs; high. **151** curled; combed. **152** men; care for. **153** fight; blows. **154** fool; debate. **156** battle-field; colour. **157** sandals. **158** strap. **159** be fated to die. **160** brave; bold; fight. **161** profit. **162** persuaded; here. **163** raised. **164** borders. **165** Just such; time. **166** its strength. **167** Saint Dominic; blows; fight. **168** splendid knight. **169** willing. **171** men; lead. **172** earth; against. **173** victory. **175** wild boars'. **176** know; Carmelites. **177** order; Virgin Mary. **178** nothing else. **180** silk. **182** fastened. **183** trimmed; gone. **184** leather. **185** razor.

The ordire of þe Austyns,   for oughte þat I wene,
For by the blussche of the belte   the banere I knewe.
And other synes I seghe   sett appon lofte:
Some of wittnesse of wolle   and some of wyne tounnes,
Some of merchandes merkes,   so many and so thikke   190
That I ne wote in my witt,   for alle this werlde riche,
Whatt segge under the sonne   can the sowme rekken.
And sekere one þat other syde   are sadde men of armes:
Bolde sqwyeres of blode,   bowmen many,
Þat if thay strike one stroke   stynt þay ne thynken   195
Till owthir here appon hethe   be hewen to dethe.
Forthi I bid ʒow bothe   that thaym hedir broghte
That ʒe wend with me   are any wrake falle
To oure comely kyng   that this kythe owethe;
And fro he wiete wittirly   where þe wronge ristyth   200
Thare nowthir wye be wrothe   to wirche als he doeth.'
    Off ayther rowte ther rode owte   a renke als me thoghte,
Knyghtis full comly   one coursers attyred,
And sayden: 'Sir, sandisman,   sele the betyde!
Wele knowe we the kyng,   he clothes us bothe,   205
And hase us fosterde and fedde   this fyve and twenty wyntere.
Now fare þou byfore   and we schall folowe aftire.'
And now are þaire brydells upbrayde   and bown one þaire wayes;
Thay lighten doun at þe launde   and leved thaire stedis,
Kayren up at the clyffe   and one knees fallyn,   210
The kynge henttis by þe handes   and hetys þam to ryse,
And sayde: 'Welcomes, heres, as hyne   of oure house bothen.'
The kynge waytted one wyde   and the wyne askes;
Beryns broghte it anone   in bolles of silvere.
Me thoghte I sowpped so sadly   it sowrede bothe myn eghne,   215
And he þat wilnes of this werke   to wete any forthire
Full freschely and faste   for here a fitt endes.

Bot than kerpede the kynge, sayd: 'Kythe what ʒe hatten,
And whi the hates aren so hote   ʒoure hertis bytwene;
If I schall deme ʒow this day   dothe me to here.'   220
'Now certys lorde,' sayde þat one,   'the sothe for to telle,
I hatt Wynnere, a wy   that alle this werlde helpis,

186 know. 187 gleam. 189 in witness; wool; casks. 190 merchants'. 191 don't know.
192 total count. 193 resolute; determined. 194 bold-hearted squires. 195 to cease.
196 army; cut. 197 Therefore; here. 198 go; before; misfortune. 199 country owns.
200 knows clearly; after; fault lies. 201 Needs. 202 From each troop; man. 203 war-horses.
204 messenger, well-being. 207 go. 208 pulled up; ready; journeys. 209 alighted; glade; left.
210 went; on. 211 clasps; orders. 212 sirs; servants. 213 around. 214 Men; bowls.
215 drank; deeply; stung. 216 desires; know; further. 217 Fill; quickly; soon. 218 spoke;
Reveal; are called. 219 enmities. 220 judge; let. 222 am called; man.

For I lordes cane lere   thurgh ledyng of witt.
Thoo þat spedfully will spare   and spende not to grete,
Lyve appon littill-whattes   I lufe hym the bettir.   225
Witt wiendes me with   and wysses me faire;
Aye when gadir my gudes   than glades myn hert.
Bot this felle false thefe   þat byfore ȝowe standes
Thynkes to strike or he styntt   and stroye me for ever.
Alle þat I wynn thurgh witt   he wastes thurgh pryde;   230
I gedir, I glene   and he lattys goo sone;
I pryke and I pryne   and he the purse opynes.
Why hase this cayteffe no care   how men corne sellen?
His londes liggen alle ley,   his lomes aren solde,
Downn bene his dowfehowses,   drye bene his poles.   235
The devyll wounder one the wele   he weldys at home,
Bot hungere and heghe howses   and howndes full kene.
Safe a sparthe and a spere   sparrede in ane hyrne,
A bronde at his bede-hede   biddes he no noþer,
Bot a cuttede capill   to cayre with to his frendes.   240
Then will he boste with his brande   and braundesche hym ofte –
This wikkede weryed thefe   that Wastoure men calles –
That if he life may longe   this lande will he stroye.
Forthi deme us this daye,   for Drightyns love in heven,
To fighte furrther with oure folke   to owthire fey worthe.'   245
    'Ȝee Wynnere,' quod Wastoure,   'thi wordes are hye,
Bot I schall tell the a tale   that tene schall the better.
When thou haste waltered and went   and wakede alle þe nyghte,
And iche a wy in this werlde   that wonnes the abowte,
And hase werpede thy wyde howses   full of wolle sakkes,   250
The bemys benden at the rofe,   siche bakone there hynges,
Stuffed are sterlynges   undere stelen bowndes.
What scholde worthe of that wele   if no waste come?
Some rote, some ruste,   some ratouns fede.
Let be thy cramynge of thi kystes,   for Cristis lufe of heven;   255
Late the peple and the pore   hafe parte of thi silvere,
For if thou wydwhare scholde walke   and waytten the sothe,
Thou scholdeste reme for rewthe   in siche ryfe bene the pore.
For and thou lengare thus lyfe,   leve thou no noþer,

---

223 can teach; instruction. 224 succesfully; save. 225 small amounts. 226 Knowledge comes;
guides. 227 Whenever; possessions. 228 wicked. 229 before he might cease. 230 skill/cun-
ning; ostentation. 231 scrape together; releases. 232 tie up; sew up. 233 rogue. 234 fallow;
tools. 235 dovecotes; pools. 236 marvels at; wealth; enjoys. 237 rented houses. 238 Except;
axe; hidden; corner. 239 sword; asks. 240 gelding; ride. 241 threaten; strut about.
243 destroy. 244 judge; Lord's. 245 forth; either; may die. 247 to annoy. 248 tossed and
turned. 249 lives near you. 250 filled. 251 beams; bacon. 252 silver pennies; hoops.
253 become; wealth; spending. 254 rats. 255 chests. 257 far and wide; consider. 258 weep;
pity; abundance. 259 longer; nothing.

Thou schall be hanged in helle   for that thou here spareste.   260
For siche a synn haste þou solde   thi soule into helle
And there es ever wellande woo,   worlde withowtten ende.'
    'Late be thi worde, Wastoure,'   quod Wynnere the riche,
'Thou melleste of a mater   tho madiste it thiselven.
With thi sturte and thy stryffe   thou stroyeste up my gudes: 265
In playinge and in wakynge   in wynttres nyghttis,
In owttrage, in unthrifte,   in angarte pryde.
There es no wele in this werlde   to wasschen thyn handes
That ne es gyffen and grounden   are þou it getyn have.
Thou ledis renkes in thy rowte   wele rychely attyrede;   270
Some hafe girdills of golde   þat more gude coste
Than alle þe faire fre londe   that ȝe byfore haden.
Ȝe folowe noghte ȝoure fadirs   þat fosterde ȝow alle
A kynde herveste to cache   and cornes to wynn
For þe colde wyntter and þe kene   with gleterand frostes   275
Sythen dropeles drye   in the dede monethe.
And thou wolle to the taverne   byfore þe tonne-hede,
Iche beryne redy with a bolle   to blerren thyn eghne;
Hete the whatte thou have schalte   and whatt thyn hert lykes,
Wyfe, wedowe or wenche   þat wonnes thereaboute.   280
Then es there bott "fille in" and "feche forthe" florence to schewe
"Wee hee" and "worthe up"   wordes ynewe;
Bot when this wele es awaye   the wyne moste be payede fore.
Than lympis ȝowe weddis to laye   or ȝoure londe selle,
For siche wikked werkes   wery the oure Lorde.   285
And forthi God laughte that he lovede   and levede þat oþer,
Iche freke one felde   ogh þe ferdere be to wirche.
Teche thy men for to tille   and tymen thyn feldes,
Rayse up thi renthowses,   ryme up thi ȝerdes,
Owthere hafe as þou haste done   and hope aftir werse;   290
Pat es firste þe faylynge of fode   and than the fire aftir
To brene the alle at a birre   for thi bale dedis.
The more colde es to come   als me a clerke tolde.'
    'Ȝee, Wynnere,' quod Wastoure,   'thi wordes are vayne,
With oure festes and oure fare   we feden the pore.   295
It es plesynge to the Prynce   þat Paradyse wroghte,
When Cristes peple hath parte   hym payes alle the better
Then here ben hodirde and hidde   and happede in cofers

---

262 boiling torment. **264** complain; grievance; caused. **265** violence; consume; produce.
267 extravagance; excessive. **268** wealth. **269** spent; before granted. **270** lead men; troop.
271 money. **272** fine. **273** taught. **274** gather. **275** intense; glittering. **276** After rainless
drought. **277** end of the wine barrel. **278** each servant; cup; dim. **279** Order. **280** dwells.
281 florins. **282** "get up". **284** it befalls to; mortgage. **286** accepted; left. **287** man; ought
to be the more frightened. **288** harrow. **289** houses for rent; clear. **290** Either; expect.
292 instantly; wicked. **294** empty. **296** created. **297** a share; it pleases. **298** heaped up; cov-
ered up.

That it no sonn may see   thurgh seven wyntter ones,
Owthir freres it feche   when thou fey worthes   300
To payntten with thaire pelers   or pergett with thaire walles.
Thi sone and thi sektours   ichone slees othere,
Maken dale aftir thi daye   for thou durste never,
Mawngery ne myndale   ne never myrthe lovediste.
A dale aftir thi daye   dose the no mare   305
Þan a lighte lanterne   late appone nyghte
When it es borne at thi bakke,   beryn, be my trouthe.
Now wolde God that it were,   als I wisse couthe,
That thou Wynnere, thou wriche,   and Wanhope thi brothir
And eke ymbryne dayes   and evenes of sayntes,   310
The Frydaye and his fere   one the ferrere syde
Were drownede in the depe see   there never droghte come,
And dedly synn for thayre dede   were endityde with twelve
And thies beryns one the bynches   with bonets one lofte
That bene knowen and kydde   for clerkes of the beste,   315
Als gude als Arestotle   or Austyn the wyse,
That alle schent were those schalkes   and Scharshull itwiste
Þat saide I prikkede with powere   his pese to distourbe.
Forthi, comely kynge,   that oure case heris,
Late us swythe with oure swerdes   swyngen togedirs,   320
For nowe I se it es full sothe   þat sayde es full ʒore:
"The richere of ranke wele   the rathere will drede;
The more havande þat he hathe   the more of hert feble".'
    Bot than this wrechede Wynnere   full wrothely he lukes,
Sayse: 'Þis es spedles speche   to speken thies wordes.   325
Loo, this wrechide Wastoure   that wydewhare es knawenn,
Ne es nothir kaysser ne kynge   ne knyghte þat the folowes,
Barone ne bachelere   ne beryn that thou loveste,
Bot foure felawes or fyve   that the fayth owthe.
And he schall dighte thaym to dyne   with dayntethes so many   330
Þat iche a wy in this werlde   may wepyn for sorowe.
The bores hede schall be broghte   with plontes appon lofte,
Buktayles full brode   in brothes there besyde,
Venyson with the frumentee   and fesanttes full riche,
Baken mete therby   one the burde sett,   335

---

299 sun; once. 300 or; are doomed to die. 301 pillars; plaster. 302 son; executors; destroys. 303 Give gifts; death; dared. 304 Feasts nor anniversaries. 305 donation. 306 lighted. 307 man. 308 as; devise. 309 wretch; Despair. 310 Ember Days; vigils. 311 neighbour; other side. 312 where; drought. 313 condemned. 314 judges' benches; caps. 315 recognized. 316 Saint Augustine. 317 shamed; men; together with. 318 rode out; peace. 319 Therefore; listens to. 320 Permit; to meet in battle. 321 long before. 322 abundant wealth. 323 possessions; faint-hearted. 325 unprofitable. 326 widely. 327 emperor; is loyal to. 328 knight. 329 owe allegiance to you. 330 summon. 331 each man. 332 vegetables. 333 bucks' hind parts. 334 wheat boiled with milk. 335 table.

Chewettes of choppede flesche,   charbinade fewlis,
And iche a segge þat I see   has sexe mens doke.
If this were nedles note   anothir comes aftir:
Roste with the riche sewes   and the ryalle spyces,
Kiddes cloven by þe rigge,   quarterd swannes,   340
Tartes of ten ynche   þat tenys myn hert
To see þe borde overbrade   with blasande disches
Als it were a rayled rode   with rynges and stones.
The thirde mese to me   were mervelle to rekken
For alle es Martynmesse mete   þat I with moste dele,   345
Noghte bot worttes with the flesche   withowt wilde fowle
Save ane hene to hym   that the howse owethe.
And he will hafe birdes bownn   one a broche riche:
Barnakes and buturs   and many billed snyppes,
Larkes and lyngwhittes   lapped in sogoure,   350
Wodcokkes and wodwales   full wellande hote,
Teeles and titmoyses   to take what hym lykes;
Caudils of connynges   and custadis swete,
Dariols and dische-metis   þat ful dere coste,
Mawmene þat men clepen   ȝour mawes to fill,   355
Iche a mese at a merke   bytwen twa men
Þat sothe bot brynneth for bale   ȝour bowells within.
Me tenyth at ȝour trompers,   þay tounen so heghe
Þat iche a gome in þe gate   goullyng may here;
Þen wil þay say to þamselfe   as þay samen ryden,   360
Ȝe hafe no myster of the helpe   of þe heven Kyng.
Þus are ȝe scorned by skyll   and schathed þeraftir
Þat rechen for a repaste   a rawnsom of silver.
Bot ones I herd in a haule   of a herdmans tong:
"Better were meles many   þan a mery nyghte".'   365
   And he þat wilnes of þis werke   for to wete forthe
Full freschely and faste   for here a fit endes.

'Ȝee, Wynnere,' quod Wastour,   'I wote wele myselven
What sall lympe of þe, lede,   within fewe ȝeris.
Thurgh þe poure plenté of corne   þat þe peple sowes   370
Þat God will graunte of his grace   to growe on þe erthe
Ay to appaire þe pris   and passe nott to hye,

336 Pies; grilled birds. 337 man; duck. 338 excessive affair. 339 soups; sumptuous. 340 split; spine. 341 it angers. 342 spread; piping hot. 343 decorated cross. 344 course. 345 concern myself with. 346 herbs. 347 owns. 348 ready; on a skewer. 349 Geese; bitterns; snipes. 350 linnets; syrup. 351 woodpeckers; simmering. 352 Teals; titmice. 353 Stews; rabbits; flans. 354 Pastries; pies. 355 Meat wine stew; stomachs. 356 course; costs a mark. 357 stings; pain. 358 It angers me; resound. 359 loud trumpeting. 360 together. 361 need; benefit. 362 reason; disgraced. 363 pay; significant amount. 364 hall; retainer's. 365 riotous. 366 desires; know further. 367 Pour. 369 become; a few. 370 you; a perfect plenty. 372 always; lower, it passes.

Schal make þe to waxe wod   for wanhope in erthe,
To hope aftir an harde ȝere   to honge þiselven.
Woldeste þou hafe lordis to lyfe   as laddes on fote,   375
Prelates als prestes   þat þe parischen ȝemes,
Prowde marchandes of pris   as pedders in towne?
Late lordes lyfe als þam liste,   laddes as þam falles:
Pay þe bacon and beefe,   þay botours and swannes;
Pay þe roughe of þe rye,   þay þe rede whete;   380
Pay þe grewell gray,   and þay þe gude sewes;
And þen may þe peple hafe parte   in povert þat standes,
Sum gud morsell of mete   to mend with þair chere.
If fewlis flye schold forthe   and fongen be never,
And wild bestis in þe wodde   wonne al þaire lyve,   385
And fisches flete in þe flode   and ichone ete oþer,
Ane henne at ane halpeny   by halfe ȝeris ende;
Schold not a ladde be in londe   a lorde for to serve.
Þis wate þou full wele   witterly þiselven:
Whoso wele schal wyn   a wastour moste he fynde,   390
For if it greves one gome   it gladdes anoþer.'
    Now quod Wynner to Wastour: 'Me wondirs in hert
Of thies poure penyles men   þat peloure will by,
Sadills of sendale   with sercles full riche.
Lesse ȝe wrethe ȝour wifes   þaire willes to folowe   395
Ȝe sellyn wodd affir wodde   in a wale tyme,
Bothe þe oke and þe assche   and alle þat þer growes;
Þe spyres and þe ȝonge sprynge   ȝe spare to ȝour children
And sayne God wil graunt it his grace   to grow at þe last
For to save to ȝour sones,   bot þe schame es ȝour ownn,   400
Nedeles save ȝe þe soyle   for sell it ȝe thynken.
Ȝour forfadirs were fayne   when any frende come
For to schake to þe schawe   and schewe hym þe estres
In iche holt þat þay had   ane hare for to fynde,
Bryng to the brod launde   bukkes ynewe   405
To lache and to late goo   to lightten þaire hertis.
Now es it sett and solde   my sorowe es þe more,
Wastes alle wilfully   ȝour wyfes to paye.
That are had lordes in londe   and ladyes riche
Now are þay nysottes of þe new gett   so nysely attyred   410

373 grow mad; despair. 374 want. 375 low-born men. 376 Bishops; care for. 377 merchants; pedlars. 378 Let; like; it happens. 379 bitterns. 380 fine. 381 soups. 382 a share; exists. 383 improve; happiness. 384 birds; trapped. 385 remain. 386 float. 387 would cost a half-penny. 388 There would not be. 389 clearly. 390 wealth. 391 man. 392 It amazes me. 393 furs; might buy. 394 Saddles; silk; rings. 395 Lest; anger. 396 wood; short. 398 seedlings; saplings. 399 declare. 401 in vain; earth; plan. 402 eager. 403 ride; woods; paths. 404 grove. 405 glade; bucks. 406 catch. 407 leased. 408 You waste. 409 Those that are held to be. 410 fools; immoderately.

With syde slabbande sleves   sleght to þe grounde
Ourlede all umbtourne   with ermyn aboute
Þat es as harde, as I hope,   to handil in þe derne
Als a cely symple wenche   þat never silke wroghte.
Bot whoso lukes on hir lyre,   oure Lady of heven,   415
How scho fled for ferd   ferre out of hir kythe
Appon ane amblande asse   withowtten more pride,
Safe a barne in hir barme   and a broken heltre
Þat Joseph held in hys hande   þat hend for to ȝeme.
All þofe scho walt al þis werlde,   hir wedes wer pore   420
For to gyf ensample of siche   for to schewe oþer
For to leve pompe and pride;   þat poverte ofte schewes.'
      Than þe Wastour wrothly   castes up his eghne
And said: 'Þou Wynnere, þou wriche,   me woundirs in hert
What hafe oure clothes coste þe,   caytef, to by   425
Þat þou schal birdes upbrayd   of þaire bright wedis,
Sythen þat we vouchesafe   þat þe silver payen?
It lyes wele for a lede   his lemman to fynde,
Aftir hir faire chere   to forthir hir herte;
Then will scho love hym lelely   as hir lyfe one,   430
Make hym bolde and bown   with brandes to smytte
To schonn schenchipe and schame   þer schalkes ere gadird.
And if my peple ben prode   me payes alle þe better
To see þam faire and free   tofore with myn eghne.
And ȝe negardes appon nyghte,   ȝe nappen so harde,   435
Routten at ȝour raxillyng,   raysen ȝour hurdes.
Ȝe beden wayte one þe wedir   þen wery ȝe þe while
Þat ȝe nade hightilde up ȝour houses   and ȝour hyne raysed.
Forthi, Wynnere, with wronge   þou wastes þi tyme
For gode day ne glade   getys þou never.   440
Þe devyll at þi dede-day   schal delyn þi gudis;
Þo þou woldest þat it were   wyn þay it never,
Þi skathill sectours   schal sever þam aboute
And þou hafe helle full hotte   for þat þou here saved,
Þou tast no tent one a tale   þat tolde was full ȝore.   445
I hold hym madde þat mournes   his make for to wyn,
Hent hir þat hir haf schall   and hold hir his while:

411 wide trailing; let down. 412 Trimmed; around. 413 difficult; dark. 414 innocent; embroidered. 415 hardship. 416 fear; far from; family. 417 ambling. 418 except for; child; halter. 419 noble one (Christ); protect. 420 Though; ruled; clothes. 421 such (humility); teach. 425 scoundrel; buy. 426 ladies; rebuke; clothes. 427 Since; allow; pleases you. 429 happy mood; to please. 430 faithfully. 431 ready; swords to strike. 432 avoid; disgrace; men. 433 magnificent. 434 them; noble. 435 misers; sleep. 436 Snore; stretching; buttocks. 437 give orders to wait; curse. 438 that you hadn't improved your buildings and organized your household. 439 error. 440 cheerful. 441 death-day; distribute. 442 wish; acquire. 443 wicked executors; disperse. 445 pay no heed to. 446 mad; is worried; mistress. 447 would embrace.

Take þe coppe as it comes,   þe case as it falles,
For whoso lyfe may lengeste   lympes to feche
Woodd þat he waste schall   to warmen his helys   450
Ferrere þan his fadir dide   by fyvetene myle.
Now kan I carpe no more,   bot Sir Kyng, by þi trouthe,
Deme us where we duell schall,   me thynke þe day hyes.
ȝit harde sore es myn hert   and harmes me more
Ever to see in my syghte   þat I in soule hate.'   455
    The kynge lovely lokes   on þe ledis twayne,
Says: 'Blynnes, beryns, of ȝour brethe   and of ȝoure brode worde
And I schal deme ȝow this day   where ȝe duelle schall,
Aythere lede in a lond   þer he es loved moste.
Wende, Wynnere, þi waye   over þe wale stremys,   460
Passe forthe by Paris   to þe Pope of Rome,
Þe cardynalls ken þe wele,   will kepe þe ful faire,
And make þi sydes in silken   schetys to lygge,
And fede þe and foster þe   and forthir thyn hert
As leefe to worthen wode   as þe to wrethe ones.   465
Bot loke, lede, be þi lyfe,   when I lettres sende
Þat þou hy þe to me home   on horse or one fote,
And when I knowe þou will come   he schall cayre uttire
And lenge with anoþer lede   til þou þi lefe take.
For þofe þou bide in þis burgh   to þi beryinge-daye   470
With hym happyns þe never   a fote forto holde.
And thou, Wastoure, I will   þat þou wonne
Þer moste waste es of wele   and wyng þer untill.
Chese þe forthe into þe chepe,   a chambre þou rere,
Loke þi wyndowe be wyde   and wayte þe aboute   475
Where any potent beryn   þurgh þe burgh passe.
Teche hym to þe taverne   till he tayte worthe,
Doo hym drynke al nyȝte   þat he dry be at morow;
Sythen ken hym to þe crete   to comforth his vaynes,
Brynge hym to Bred Strete,   bikken þi fynger,   480
Schew hym of fatt chepe   scholdirs ynewe,
"Hotte for þe hungry"   a hen oþer twayne.
Sett hym softe one a sege   and sythen send after;
Bryng out of þe burgh   þe best þou may fynde,
And luke thi knafe hafe a knoke   bot he þe clothe sprede.   485

---

448 chance when it comes. **449** live; it befalls. **450** Wood; heels. **451** Further; miles. **452** speak. **453** Judge; live; passes. **456** two men. **457** Cease; men; bold. **459** Each man; where. **460** Go; swift. **462** know; nobly. **463** your body; sheets. **464** encourage. **465** Eager; crazed; make angry. **466** ensure, man. **467** hurry. **468** ride further away. **469** stay; leave. **470** though; remain. **471** get a foothold. **472** wish; dwell. **473** wealth; hurry there. **474** Go; market; set up. **476** powerful man. **477** Show; he might be merry. **478** Make; thirsty. **479** introduce; sweet wine; spirit. **480** beckon. **481** sheep; many forelegs. **482** or two. **483** seat; then send for him. **485** servant; blow; unless.

Bot late hym paye or he passe   and pik hym so clene
Þat fynd a peny in his purse   and put owte his eghe.
When þat es dronken and don   duell þer no lenger,
Bot teche hym owt of the townn   to trotte aftir more.
Then passe to þe pultrie,   þe peple þe knowes,   490
And ken wele þi katour   to knawen þi fode,
The herouns, þe hastelete3,   þe henne wele serve
Þe pertrikes, þe plovers,   þe oþer pulled byrddes;
Þe albus, þis oþer foules,   þe egretes dere,
Þe more þou wastis þi wele   þe better þe Wynner lykes.   495
    And wayte to me, þou Wynnere,   if þou wilt wele chefe:
When I wende appon werre   my wyes to lede
For at þe proude pales   of Parys þe riche
I thynk to do it in ded   and dub þe to knyghte,
And giff giftes full grete   of golde and of silver   500
To ledis of my legyance   þat lufen me in hert.
And sythen kayre as I come   with knyghtes þat me foloen
To þe kirke of Colayne   þer þe kynges ligges . . . '

---

486 let; before; rob. **487** That you would find. **488** spent in drinking. **489** direct; run.
490 poultry-sellers'. **491** direct; caterer. **492** roasted meat. **493** partridges; plucked. **494** bull-
finches; egrets. **495** waste; wealth. **496** pay attention; prosper. **497** war; men. **498** palace.
501 men; allegiance. **502** ride; are loyal. **503** Cologne.

Index of Titles and First Lines